Perspectives
in
Communication
Policy
and Planning

COMMUNICATION
MONOGRAPHS   Number 3

September 1977

Perspectives in Communication Policy and Planning

Edited by

SYED A. RAHIM

JOHN MIDDLETON

EAST-WEST CENTER
EAST-WEST COMMUNICATION INSTITUTE
1777 EAST-WEST ROAD
HONOLULU,HAWAII 96848

Abstract

This volume provides perspectives (rather than make detailed analyses of particular problems), and thereby attempts to stimulate research; interest in the field of policy and planning of communication. The 14 papers are divided into three sections: Theoretical Issues, National Level Communication Policy and Planning, Institutional Level Communication Policy and Planning.

Printed in the United States of America.

Contents

Theoretical Issues

National Level Communication Policy and Planning

Institutional Level Communication Policy and Planning

Foreword

Research is undertaken for various reasons, ranging from a search for pragmatic solutions to specific problems to the pursuit of knowledge simply for the gratification of intellectual curiosity. Unfortunately, policy makers and administrators too frequently are frustrated, disappointed, or disillusioned with research. Perhaps it would be more accurate to say that they are frustrated by the failure or inability of researchers to explain the practical significance of their work. In short, there is a "communication gap" between researchers on the one hand and policy makers and administrators on the other.

Their frustration is intensified by a growing sense of urgency that sometimes borders on desperation as these policy makers and administrators seek to channel the forces of development into productive paths. The nature of these problems may or may not differ from one country to another. But in rich as well as poor nations, public officials are facing unprecedented problems and they feel communication media and processes should be able to contribute to solutions. Instead, they frequently find that the mass media are culprits that undercut rather than aid their work.

Like the other units of the East-West Center, the East-West Communication Institute is a complex organization. Our academic staff engages in the design and implementation of research as well as the education and training of students and professionals. We have done much work in the area of family planning communication and rural development communication programs. We are doing studies to trace the long-term changes that follow the introduction of new media in communities as well as shorter term studies focusing on specific aspects of communication content and the exchange of content between nations.

These and all our other activities have value in their own right as contributions to knowledge. But we see them as having a higher order of value. We intend that they will feed into our effort to develop a systematic approach to communication policy and planning, to bridge the communication gap between researchers and those on the front line of national and institutional planning and administration.

In this effort we will draw not only upon the resources of the work originating within the East-West Communication Institute but from other scholars as well. This volume is the first in what we hope will be a series of volumes to help bridge that gap.

JACK LYLE
Director, EWCI
September 1977

The Authors

Richard J. BARBER, Assistant to the Director of the Social Sciences and Linguistics Institute, University of Hawaii.

Luis Ramiro BELTRAN S., Information Science Representative in Latin America, International Development Research Center.

Rogelio CUYNO, Associate Project Leader, Action Research Project on Integrated Rural Development, University of the Philippines at Los Baños (UPLB).

Alan HANCOCK, Division of Development of Communication Systems, Unesco, Paris.

L. Stanley HARMS, Professor of Communication, University of Hawaii, Honolulu.

Eddie C.Y. KUO, lecturer, Department os Sociology, University of Singapore.

William H. MELODY, Professor of Communication, Simon Fraser University, Canada.

John MIDDLETON, Assistant Director, East-West Communication Institute.

Edwin B. PARKER, Professor of Communication, Stanford University.

Ithiel de Sola POOL, Professor of Political Science, M.I.T., Cambridge, U.S.A.

Robert RABINOVITCH, Director General of the Social Policy and Program Branch, Department of Communication, Government of Canada.

Syed A. RAHIM, Research Associate, East-West Communication Institute.

Rehman SOBHAN, Visiting Fellow, Queen Elizabeth House,
    Oxford, England.
Astrid SUSANTO, Acting Head of the Bureau for Information,
    Culture, Science and Technology, National Planning
    Agency, Indonesia.

THEORETICAL
ISSUES

This part includes four papers on theoretical concepts, frameworks, and methods. Each one of them looks at the problem area from a different perspective and notes the difficulties in establishing a theoretical basis for communication policy and planning research.

William Melody reviews the economic development theories and observes that in the neo-classical theories communication is viewed either as an external factor introduced for inducing development or as a routine domestic matter for additional investment. The development planners treat communication on an ad hoc basis as economic infrastructure, investment alternatives, new technology, information transfer, or networks. Both in theory and practice, development economics failed to integrate communication into the development processes and planning. But the theoretical framework for development economics is changing. The economists are becoming more concerned with the interrelationship between economic and other components of society. They are beginning to adopt a systems approach in analyzing development. They are viewing the development process as an integral part of the economy, not as an external factor. In this new view, communication is also treated as an endogenous factor, not an exogenous agent of change. This modification of approach should lead ultimately to a better theoretical framework and to a more coordinated and comprehensive communication planning.

Edwin Parker argues that *information* is an intrinsic factor of development in the highly industrialized as well as the developing countries. Therefore communication policy and planning is an essential part of development policy making and planning. A number of communication policy choices are available for developing countries. Parker discusses these choices under five categories: (1) the investment priorities for communication, (2) the geographic distribution of communication infrastructure, (3) the selection of technology, (4) the choice of institutions and organizational structures, and (5) the contents of communication.

L. S. Harms presents a new *paradigm* for communication policy and planning sciences, and discusses its three main concepts. These are (1) communication resources, (2) communication needs, and (3) right to communication. These three concepts in combination provide new perspectives for communication policy and planning research.

Finally, Ithiel de Sola Pool examines a number of conceptual issues in an international context. After discussing some problems relating to high technology, multinationals, sovereignty, and cultural autonomy, Pool concludes that the basic policy question in international communication for development is how to ensure inexpensive and free flow of information. Pool says that the communicators themselves will have to face this challenge of building a free and low-cost world communication system.

*INTRODUCTION: THE SCOPE OF COMMUNICATION
POLICY AND PLANNING RESEARCH*

Syed A. Rahim

AN EMERGING AREA OF RESEARCH

Communication policy and planning is an area of research in its early stage of development. A survey of papers published during the last ten years in seven well-known journals of communication* shows that the terms "policy," "planning," or "strategy" appear in the titles or subtitles of only 0.7 percent of the total articles. Most of these articles, 13 out of 17, have been published during the period 1970-76. The references used in these articles also show evidence of lack of research literature in communication policy and planning.

In a more systematic search of the social science literature on communication policy and planning, this author has recently compiled about 400 items in an annotated bibliography (Rahim, 1976). The entries in this bibliography cover a variety of problems and issues relating to telecommunication, mass communication, extension and other organized interpersonal communication, new communications technology, and application of communication in development. The entries also cover the problems in a variety of settings in more than 50

Journal of Communication, Gazette, Journalism Quarterly, Journal of Broadcasting, Public Opinion Quarterly, A-V Communication Review, Columbia Journalism Review, and *Human Communication Research.*

5

different countries and regions. But, in most of the bibliography items, the communication policy and planning problems
are either raised in a rather narrow context, or implied in the
discussion of other substantive problems. The communication
policy and planning questions are mostly raised either in the
context of adoption and use of new communication technologies or in making use of communication in development projects of agriculture, health, family planning, etc. There is very
little literature on the concepts, models, theories, and methods
of communication policy and planning.

RATIONALES FOR
POLICY RESEARCH

How do we define policy and planning research in communication? How is this kind of research related to the broader area of research in communication? How does it stand in
relation to the major issues and future directions in mass communications research?

Seeking precise answers to these questions is a part of
the overall research problem in our emerging area. At this
moment we cannot provide the answers but can briefly outline
some trends of thinking and research. Let us see how these
questions have been raised and discussed in the literature
reviewed by us.

Mass Communication Research Priorities

In writing about some priority directions for future
research in mass communication, P.W. Davidson and F.T.C. Yu
(1974) list five major problem areas: "What social and individual needs can the mass media help to satisfy? What is the preferred relationship, for each society, between mass communication and interpersonal channels? What type of media and content are best suited to what kinds of tasks? How can standards
of mass media performance be defined? How can the media
confer the greatest benefit at the lowest cost?" The important
thing about these questions is that they are concerned about

societal objectives and ways of realizing these objectives. The policy and planning dimensions of human communication problems are clearly emphasized, and the need for research on them is recognized. *We may add that the communication policy and planning processes in different societies and the factors influencing those processes are also important research problems. Both the substance of policies and the method of their formulation and implementation are legitimate concerns of policy and planning research.*

Another scholar of communication policy, Douglass Cater of the Aspen Institute, advocates communication policy research in a humanistic fashion so that we can avoid the Orwellian future of communications as instruments of mass enslavement by a controlling elite. To devote attention to "society's claim on communications for the achievement of the public good," research should be broadened to include multi-disciplinary study of media's social role, policy analysis, and designing of humanistic communications future (Cater, 1976).

Techno-economic Rationales

The rationales given for communication policy and planning research seem to be associated with two broad perspectives: (1) the techno-economic perspective and (2) the political economy perspective. In the first case, the focus of attention is on technology assessment, innovation, utilization, technical and economic efficiency, and cost-effectiveness. The broader sociopolitical factors including the public needs and participation, access, equity, power, monopoly, dependency, and imperialism are the focus of attention in the second case. The research of individual scholars and institutions discussed below contain elements of both the perspectives, but some of them clearly emphasize one view or the other.

The techno-economic rationale is most clearly presented by telecommunications systems engineers and economists. Their model of the *cybernetic society* leads to policy and planning for building technological and control systems. They have been conducting planning research for some years, and are currently focusing on the problems of technology assessment, modeling and simulation of large-scale systems, man-machine systems, computer telecommunication link-up, information economics, pricing of services, transportation-communications trade off, and new problems of the social and biological processes of control and communication (Institute of Electrical and Electronic Engineers, 1975).

Some social science researchers also find a strong rationale for policy and planning research in the technological and economics problems. In a recent article Ithiel de Sola Pool (1974) writes about research on alternative ways of structuring and organizing communication systems in societies. The need for communication policy research is growing because of the rapid innovation and growth in communications technology, social concerns about effects of communication, and the potential role of communication in the modernization of developing countries. Policy research is necessary in society's effort at building more efficient, open, and pluralistic systems of communication.

The implications of new communication technology is a special source of communication policy and planning research. E.B. Parker (1974) mentions four research tracks: social history of communication and cross-cultural comparison of diffusion of technology; technology assessment, socioeconomic consequences of technology adoption; techniques for increasing effectiveness of communication; and the economics of communication. Parker also says that the motivations behind policy research are often normative. The concern is what public policy should be if different effects of communication are envisaged.

Political Economy Rationales

The significance of policy research in communication is also explained in terms of public needs, participation, and changes in the power relations in society. The Harvard University's program on information technology and public policy explains this as follows:

> The public has a vital interest in the rapid and fundamental changes occurring in: How information systems perform; what controls information flow; and on what terms that information is made available to users to meet their needs for the knowledge and understanding required to participate fully in our society.
>
> Of central importance is the question of who holds how much power over whom. (Harvard University Program on Information Technologies and Public Policy, 1975, p. 3).

In another view, the need for communication policy and planning research arises due to concerns about inequality of access and utilization of information among different social classes and groups in society. A vicious circle persists in communication: the well-informed have more access to knowledge and information and seek more information; the ill-informed and socioeconomically depressed have less access and often do not regard information as particularly important. The pattern of distribution of information is dependent upon media policies, planning, and production levels, and these in turn are determined by a wide range of factors—material living conditions, socioeconomic structures, and ideological and cultural factors. A concern about this is reflected in the global tendency toward a holistic approach and policy orientation in mass communication research (Nordenstreng, 1976).

The need for communication policy and planning research is probably felt more acutely in countries concerned with rapid development of their communication system, and at the same time, deeply disturbed by "communication and cultural imperialism." A recent article by H.I. Schiller (1976) presents the problem of national communication policy as follows:

> The struggle to overcome domination—external, where the power resides outside the national community; internal, where the power is exercised by a domestic ruling stratum—is the central, if not always recognized, issue in contemporary communications policy making. . . .
>
> Technological innovation does not arise out of thin air. It is encouraged (or discouraged) by the prevailing social system and, moreover, is integrated into that system, usually to achieve the objectives of the dominant elements already commanding the social scene. . . .

What is evident now in the United States and in other countries in the midst of sweeping technological innovation in communications is *an intensification of the struggle for domination,* which is taking place on several levels. Foremost is the rivalry between the established owners of existing communication facilities and new investors in new technology. . . .

Another side of the conflict concerns the national and international communities. . . . It is, then, the largely but not entirely successful effort of the dominating stratum to introduce and regulate the new technology for its own objectives (profit making and system maintenance) that ingites and illuminates the discussion and debate in the society-at-large. Increased interest in national communications-cultural policy making is best understood from this perspective.

The existing pattern of unequal and unilateral information flows and the discoveries in communication technology are specifically identifiable factors that partly explain the increasing effort in many countries to formulate national communications policies. Less visible but not less significant is the result of a long-term historical process that is still unfolding.

In Schiller's view, information and communications are vital components of administration and influence the multinational corporations' hegemony over the world economy. The effects of communication go far beyond the commercial interests of the multinationals into the process of socialization and the style of life of the people of the dominated societies. National communication policies and the research supporting policy and planning are arenas of social struggle between the dominating and the dominated at the national as well as international levels. A basic responsibility of communication policy and planning research, as implied by Schiller, is to generate knowledge that will contribute toward resolving the struggle in favor of those who want to be liberated from domination.

INSTITUTIONAL INTEREST

Research institutions' interest in communication policy and planning has been growing in recent years. Our program at the East-West Communication Institute is one of the several indications of this fact.

At the international level, Unesco has been active in this area for a number of years. It has published a series of studies on national communication policies (Mahle and Richter, 1974; Arvamović, Marjanovic, and Ralic, 1975; Stapleton, 1974; Szecsko and Fodor, 1974). Recently, Unesco has taken some steps in promoting and supporting research on communication policy and planning. By organizing expert meetings, regional seminars, and intergovernmental meetings, Unesco has drawn attention and created interest among communication research-ers and decision makers. Besides Unesco, a number of other international agencies have also sponsored or conducted studies on communication policy and planning. The World Bank has conducted feasibility and pre-investment studies for its clients. The International Telecommunication Union (ITU) has pre-pared regional telecommunication plans and carried out studies on economics of communication (1972). The International Broadcast Institute, with the help of Ford Foundation, has sponsored studies on broadcasting and national development (Katz and Shinar, 1975a, 1975b, 1975c; Wedell and Pilsworth, 1974, 1975a, 1975b). The Organization for Economic Coop-eration and Development (OECD) has carried out studies on computer and telecommunications interaction policy (1973). Similar government and private sector interest in communica-tion policy and planning can be noted in India, Japan, Canada, Australia, the United Kingdom, Sweden, and Finland.

At the national government level, studies on long-term communication policy and planning have been conducted in Australia (National Telecommunications Planning Branch [NTP], 1975), Finland (Nordenstreng, 1974), Canada (Tele-commission Directing Committee, 1971; Pelletier, 1973), and other countries.

In the United States, a number of institutions have cur-rent research programs in communication policy and related problems (Rivers and Slatters, 1975). Among these institutions are: the Aspen Institute Program on Communications and Society; the Research Program on Communications Policy, Massachusetts Institute of Technology (MIT); Institute for Communication Research, Stanford University; the Program on

Information Technologies and Public Policy, Harvard University; Center for the Study of Communications Policy, Institute of Policy Sciences and Public Affairs, Duke University; Media Service Center, University of Cincinnati; Center for Communications Policy Research, the Annenberg School of Communication, University of Southern California; the Academy for Educational Development; and the Rand Corporation.

Within the U.S. government, much interest in communication policy and planning problems can be noted in the activities of the Federal Communications Commission, the Department of Commerce, the President's Office of Telecommunication Policy, and the National Aeronautics and Space Administration (NASA). The Bell Telephone system has also shown interest in this area.

RESEARCH APPROACHES

A general review of the current literature shows that there are a number of different approaches used or advocated by different institutions, scholars, or practitioners in dealing with the issues and problems of communication policy and planning. These approaches are often influenced by the broader assumptions, concepts, and theories of communication and its role in society.

Long-range Planning

In the research and planning activities currently pursued in Canada and Australia, the concern is about the long-range communication futures of society. In this type of planning the emphasis is on long-range communication needs, objectives, and policies—the main interest is on the exploration of alternative scenarios rather than specific targets (NTP, 1975). The context is the rapidly changing technology and the transition of industrial society into a post-industrial era in which a massive application of knowledge and information for adaption to a rapidly changing environment will be a major social concern. In that context, the policy goals are toward universal access to

communication and equitable distribution of communication
power in society (Telecommission Directing Committee, 1971).

Comprehensive Planning

Unesco's work on communication policy and planning
shows preference for a comprehensive approach. Communication policies are defined as sets of social norms "established to
guide the behavior of communication systems." The attention
is focused at the national level on a complex structure of a variety of interrelated components constituting the communication system. The components constituting the communication
system include telecommunication, mass media, print, book
publication, library and documentation centers, computers, and
satellites. A balanced growth and coordinated functioning of
the different components of the system are considered major
problems of policy and planning. The sequence of planning
process is identified as (1) assessing communication needs,
resources, priorities; (2) evaluating cost-benefit implications of
alternative approaches; (3) designing an overall program covering the entire area of communication; and (4) working out the
details of specific projects—objectives, strategies, budget, investment, training, scheduling, etc.—with the broader program
(Unesco, 1971; Sommerlad, 1975; Lee, 1976).

The Unesco approach advocates communication research by interdisciplinary teams working "together in subordi-
nation to a common plan and purpose aimed at improving our
complete awareness and fullest understanding of this vitally
important social and human phenomenon" (Lee, 1976). It emphasizes the need to examine communication in a broader socio-
political framework of the society and also in an international
structure where nations are related to and interdependent of
one another.

Development Support Communication

In contrast to this, another UN agency, the Development Support Communication Services (DSCS) of the United
Nations Development Programme (UNDP), approaches the

problem of communication planning from the point of view of supporting development projects from within. It begins with the assumption that communication planning, along with and complementary to planning of financial and material resources, is essential for effective and efficient implementation of development projects. The project and group level communication planning aims at diffusion and sharing of ideas and information among participants in development projects. This function cannot be accomplished by planning mass communication at the national level, hence the need for development support communication. Clearly, this approach emphasizes the supportive function of communication within specific projects of development in agriculture, health, population, education, and other sectors.

Technology Transfer and Assessment

Analyzing the technical potentials, social implications, and structural impact of new communication technology constitutes another approach to research in communication policy and planning. Technological innovations in communication are taking place at a much faster rate than their social application, thus widening the knowledge and social practice in communication. Large-scale and efficient use of satellite communication, cable television, telecom-computer link-up and many other innovations raise complex issues of technology assessment, environmental impact, organizational and institutional change, and economics of communication (Parker, 1974). The exponential acceleration of technological change is leading the industrial society toward a state of constant flux. "That makes the communications system itself an object of research. The important issues for scholars looking at the next decade are not only how people behave in the existing communications systems, but what the communication system itself will be" (Pool, 1974, p. 33).

Control and Regulation

With the rapid technological and institutional growth

of communication systems and their pervasive influence in society, the problems of control, regulation, and coordination of communication systems become very complex. New demands for communication policies, legislative measures aimed at more or less regulation of the media, and institutional arrangements for the implementation of policy and planning research examines and analyzes intricate legal problems; complex relationships between and among the government, private industry, and organized consumers; coordination of the communication sector with other sectors of economy; and international relations, agreements, and contracts in communication. This approach of research is dominant in the policy research projects at Harvard, MIT, Berkeley, Stanford, and the Aspen Institute.

Normative and Goal-oriented Approach

An innovative approach toward communication policy research has been used by the Finnish Broadcasting Company—Yleisradio (YLE). This approach is aimed at having an *information program policy* in which broadcasting plays an active participant role in the political and cultural life in the society. The principles of the informational program policy assert the importance of conveying socially relevant information of different political and ideological orientation to all classes and groups in society. The objective is "to cover the social reality in all its aspects, each under equal conditions, regardless of the priorities set up by the traditional hegemony," to create "intellectual activation of the audience, the broadening of the people's world view (Weltanschauung) . . . to offer the public a view which changes as the world changes, and as our knowledge of it increases, changes or becomes more perfect. . . . Different, even opposed views of life and the world can and should be presented in the programs, but the evaluation of these views is an individual affair which does not belong to broadcasting, but to each member of society" (Nordenstreng, 1974, p. 23, 25, 26).

In normal commercial or ideological communication, the messages tend to remain consistent with a particular political, religious, economic, or commercial idea, usually that of the dominant class and authority (hegemony). Informational communication is just the opposite—it ensures pluralism while maintaining objectivity and covering social reality. Under the principles of informational policy, the communication researcher is reoriented toward an analytical role. The research approach is more normative and goal oriented, rather than empirical and positivistic. The research becomes an integral part of long-range communication planning processes (*ibid.*).

Information Economics

A recent trend of research in information economics indicates a new sectoral approach of information/communication planning (Porat, 1976). In the highly industrialized economy information/communication is a major factor determining the structure and strength of the economy. It is important both in terms of employment and contribution to the gross national product. The structure of the economy can be seen as consisting of four sectors: (1) the information sector, (2) the private productive sector, (3) the public productive sector, and (4) the household sector. The information sector can be divided into a primary and a secondary sector. The primary information sector includes all industries manufacturing communication goods and providing communication services, distributing those goods and services, financial and educational institutions whose primary function is information, and all political and professional organizations including labor unions. The secondary information sector consists of the public and private bureaucracies.

On the basis of this structure an accounting system can be developed where information/communication will be a major element. The flow of information and its effects can be analyzed by using the methods of inputs-outputs analysis. The method can be very useful in policy formulation and planning the economy and the information sector of the economy.

An Integrated Approach

The different approaches of communication policy and planning research have emerged under different institutional contexts and needs. We expect that with further expansion and intensification of research and development of a stronger theoretical framework in this field, these approaches will converge toward a unified comprehensive methodology. Communication researchers will borrow ideas from other planning fields and will modify some of the well-known planning techniques for use in communication planning. Better measurements of communication will be developed and greater use of quantitative techniques will be made. At the same time, the techniques of qualitative and normative analysis will be improved and expanded. In our communication policy and planning project at the East-West Communication Institute, we are working toward these objectives.

MAJOR ISSUES AND PROBLEMS

In the twentieth century, the technological progress in communication message production, transmission, storage, and retrieval has been phenomenal. Western society is experiencing an exponential rate of growth in communication. The current tempo of technological progress and innovations suggests that another communication revolution (the last one was electronic communication) is around the corner.

Despite great technological progress, comprehensive application of technology for better communication in society has been far less significant. Historically, the social application and large-scale use of electronic technology lagged behind scientific inventions and discoveries, and the gap was widening over time. Today the most advanced communication techniques are developed and applied in the defense and space programs where much of the research and application is classified under security regulations. This knowledge and technology is not immediately available for large-scale public service application. If and when the technology is available, the existing institutional structure is often a serious constraint in its large-scale adoption.

In this context, a basic issue of communication policy analysis and planning is *the contradiction between normative and pragmatic aspects of communication.* The contradiction has been present all the time, but the rapid development of technology seems to have intensified the basic contradiction.

At the normative level, *freedom of communication* is a fundamental social value that sets the parameters of policy and planning in both the development and application of communication technology. Free and open development and application of communication technology in society is a highly desirable social goal. The society has a basic obligation to provide the best possible communication network for its individual members to communicate freely and openly with one another and with members of other societies. Such freedom is essential for maintaining and improving the quality of life at the individual and societal levels. From this point of view, public investment in (but not government control of) the communication infrastructure for making communication available to all at the lowest possible cost, is a major concern of communication policy and planning.

On the other hand, the hard realities of commercial and political interests, national security and integration, internal law and order, and international relations impose various overt and covert forms of manipulation, control, and restrictions over communication in society. These are the factors with which the decision makers are more concerned in their day-to-day operations. These pragmatic factors influence policy and planning decisions, particularly short-term decisions made to overcome immediate problems and crisis situations, more than the normative factors. Once these decisions are made, they tend to persist and influence long-term policy and planning. These factors influence the direction of scientific and technical research and innovations as well as the social application of communication technology. As more and more technology becomes available, the scope of manipulation and control enlarges. This increases the potential and actual intensity of conflict between the normative factors and the pragmatic factors.

Another basic problem of communication policy and planning is the contradiction between the technology and the organizations of communication handling technology. Brenda Maddox (1974) explains this point as follows:

> More and more communication is turning into a single com-
> modity—a medium for carrying messages. Television, telephone
> calls, telex, facsimiles of photographs, and data for computers all
> travel along together. . . . But the organization of communications
> is still handled as if various kinds of messages and different types
> of transmission were quite distinct from one another. . . . Within
> most countries, there is no coherent national policy on the use and
> development of communications. Instead, the various special inter-
> ests—the military, the broadcasters, the space researchers, the air-
> lines, and the telephone and telegraph authorities—concern them-
> selves with their own particular requirements, often unaware that
> their actions are in direct conflict with those of another agency of
> government or public life. The result is that the structure of com-
> munications is a hodge-podge nationally as well as internationally
> (p. 40).

This contradiction is partly the result of conflict between the normative and the pragmatic aspects of communication mentioned earlier. Partly it is the result of not seeing communications as a basic factor in the socioeconomic life of the
society and not formulating comprehensive policy and plans
for their development and social use. Particularly, the social
scientists have not paid attention to this vital area of communication policy, while communication engineers and technologists have gone ahead with their tasks of building and maintaining the society's communication infrastructure. Moreover,
commercial interests have taken advantage of the informative
and persuasive power of modern mass communication in selling
goods and services, and in the process, have acquired excessive
control of mass communication systems in certain societies.

There are other policy and planning issues that deserve
better attention from communication researchers. Ithiel de
Sola Pool mentions some of these issues (1974). Should broadcasting be a commercial enterprise or a government monopoly?
Where should the money come from for communication services, and how much control should the financiers have? How
should the costs of communication be accounted for and the
rates for services set? How much access should the public have
to government information? What kinds of censorship, restrictions in trade, and discrimination should a country tolerate to
maintain full control over its communication system? What
should be the role of communications in development?

DELIBERATIONS AT THE
EWCI CONFERENCE

At an international conference of the East-West Communication Institute (EWCI), held in Honolulu April 5-10, 1976, one of the major themes of discussion was the scope of communication policy and planning and the research needs and methodology in that area. The conference was attended by scholars and administrators from Asia, the United States, Canada, and Latin America.

In an opening statement on "the Western approach of communication planning," Wilbur Schramm pointed out the relevance of the systems approach in policy formulation and planning of communication. The systems approach is a powerful methodology widely used in the industrialized West. It is a useful planning tool and is becoming increasingly popular with the planners in different fields.

Schramm noted seven elements basic to the systems approach to planning: (1) it is logical and rational, (2) it is systematic (that is, interactive and comprehensive), (3) it has clearly defined behavioral objectives, (4) it is the result of as comprehensive an analysis as possible, (5) it contains a cost-benefit analysis, (6) it is a carefully designed method of change with the time and sequence of activities reflected in PERT charts and flow diagrams, etc., and (7) it is based on research at every stage of the planning process.

In reacting to Schramm's presentation, Rehman Sobhan noted that the Western approach to planning (including the systems approach) is grounded in certain Western ideas and values, particularly in neo-classical economic thought. The substance as well as the method of planning is obviously shaped by these social parameters in the highly industrialized Western societies (capitalist and socialist). The essential function of planning consists of working out a series of resource-optimizing solutions within the framework of objectives set by the social parameters. But, in the highly populated and resource-poor, import-dependent Asian developing countries, the social parameters are quite different. In these countries, capital intensive and high technology-oriented planning is not suitable. The methods suitable for capital intensive high technology planning are, therefore, not suitable for these countries. The main planning concern in these countries is with changing the social parameters and setting new goals and objectives, rather than finding solutions that optimize resource allocation. Obviously, the methodology for this kind of planning needs to be quite differentfrom the methodology of planning in the Western societies.

In discussing these contrasting views, the conference participants raised a number of crucial issues and problems. These were further elaborated during the presentation of case studies on national level and institutional level planning and subsequent discusssions of them. The conference participants realized that although the nature of planning and policy formulation may differ in the highly developed Western societies and the less developed Eastern societies, there are a number of common problems. Many of these problems have arisen because of the technological options available to both East and West in shaping the future of their communications structure and functions.

It was generally agreed that communication policy formulation and planning cannot be separated or examined in isolation from the political framework and the overall policy and planning for societal, national, and international development. In the final session of the conference, Frederick Yu proposed three fundamental concerns that need to be better recognized. These are (1) differing ideologies and views of man (individualist or collectivist), (2) different attitudes (and tolerance) toward control and manipulation, and (3) different levels of technological sophistication. Pool sketched a framework for policy and planning research in the development context consisting of systematic and interrelated categories. The categories include different communication subsystems: government, business corporations, intelligentsia, development workers and extension agents, the rural population, and foreign sources of information and technology.

ABOUT THIS VOLUME

We have compiled this volume by selecting a number of papers presented at the April 1976 conference at EWCI. This introduction was not a conference paper; it was prepared later to introduce the subject matter of this monograph.

The purpose of this volume is to provide perspectives rather than to make detailed analyses of particular problems.

It is divided into three parts: (1) Theoretical Issues, (2) National Level Communication Policy and Planning, and (3) Institutional Level Communication Policy and Planning. Each section presents different points of view arising out of different experiences and different ideological orientations. The reader will clearly feel the sensitive nature of the issues raised and discussed. There is no doubt that communication policy is a politically/ideologically sensitive area. Recently, it has become an important issue in the East-West, North-South dialogue and confrontation in international meetings and forums. One thing is evident in those dialogues and discussions: more facts and a systematic analysis of events and experience are needed. Communication policy and planning research is a felt need at the national and international level. We hope that this monograph will stimulate research interest and help investigators in their initial survey of the field.

Works Cited

ARVAMOVIC, M., MARJANOVIC, S., and RALIC, P. 1975. *Communication Policies in Yugoslavia.* Paris: Unesco Press.

CATER, D. 1976. "Communications Policy Research: The Need for New Definitions." In W. Rivers and W. Slater (eds.), *Aspen Handbook on the Media,* Palo Alto, California: Aspen Institute Program on Communications and Society, vii-x.

DAVIDSON, P.W. and YU, F.T.C. 1974. *Mass Communication Research: Major Issues and Future Directions.* New York: Praeger Publishers, 184-188.

HARVARD UNIVERSITY PROGRAM ON INFORMATION TECHNOLOGIES AND PUBLIC POLICY. 1975. "A Perspective on Information Resources." *Annual Report, 1974-75,* vol. 1. Cambridge: Harvard University.

INSTITUTE OF ELECTRICAL AND ELECTRONIC ENGINEERS. 1975. *Proceedings of 1975 Conference on Cybernetics and Society.* 1975. New York: IEEE Systems, Man and Cybernetics Society, the Institute of Electrical and Electronic Engineers, Inc.

INTERNATIONAL TELEGRAPH AND TELEPHONE CONSULTATIVE COM—MITTEE. 1972. *Economic Studies at the National Level in the Field of Telecommunications 1964-1972.* Geneva: ITU.

KATZ, E. and SHINAR, D. 1975a. *The Role of Broadcasting in National Development: Brazil Case Study.* Jerusalem: Hebrew University.
_____. 1975b. *The Role of Broadcasting in National Development: Peru Case Study.* Jerusalem: Hebrew University.
_____. 1975c. *The Role of Broadcasting in National Development: Thailand Case Study.* Jerusalem: Hebrew University.

LEE, J.A.R. 1976. *Towards Realistic Communication Policies: Recent Trends and Ideas Compiled and Analysed.* Paris: Unesco Press.

MADDOX, B. 1974. *Beyond Babel: New Directions in Communication.* Boston: Beacon Press, 40-42.

MAHLE, W.A. and RICHTER, R. 1974. *Communication Policies in the Federal Republic of Germany.* Paris: Unesco Press.

NATIONAL TELECOMMUNICATIONS PLANNING BRANCH. 1975. *Telecomm 2000.* Melbourne: Australian Government Printing Unit.
NORDENSTRENG, K., ed. 1974. *Informational Mass Communication: A Collection of Essays.* Helsinki: Tammi Publishers, 23-30.
NORDENSTRENG, K. 1976. "Recent Developments in European Communications Theory." In H.D. Fischer and J. C. Merrill (eds.), *International and Intercultural Communication.* New York: Hastings House Publishers, 457-466.

ORGANIZATION FOR ECONOMIC COOPERATION AND DEVELOPMENT. 1973. *Computer and Telecommunications.* OECD Informatics Studies, no. 3. Paris.

PARKER, E.B. "Implications of New Information Technology." In Davidson and Yu (eds.), 1974. *Mass Communication Research: Major Issues and Future Directions,* 171-182.
PELLETIER, G. 1973. *Proposals for a Communications Policy for Canada: A Position Paper on the Government of Canada.* Ottawa: Ministry of Communications.
POOL, I. Spring 1974. "The Rise of Communications Policy Research," *Journal of Communication.* 31-42.
PORAT, M. U. 1976. "The Information Economy." Ph. D. dissertation, Stanford University.

RAHIM, S.A. 1976. *Communication Policy and Planning for Development: An Annotated Bibliography.* Honolulu: East-West Communication Institute.
RIVERS, W. and SLATER, W. eds. 1975. *Aspen Handbook on the Media,* 1975-76 Edition. Palo Alto, California: Aspen Institute Program on Communications and Society.

SCHILLER, H.I. Winter 1975-76. "Communication and Cultural Domination," *International Journal of Politics,* 1-125.
SOMMERLAD, L. 1975. *National Communication Systems: Some Policy Issues and Options.* Paris: Unesco.
STAPLETON, J. 1974. *Communication Policies in Ireland.* Paris: Unesco Press.
SZECSKO, T. and FODOR, G. 1974. *Communication Policies in Hungary.* Paris: Unesco Press.

TELECOMMISSION DIRECTING COMMITTEE, MINISTRY OF INFORMATION, CANADA. 1971. *Instant World: A Report on Telecommunications in Canada.* Ottawa: Information Canada.

UNESCO. 1971. *Proposal for an International Program of Communication Research.* Paris: Unesco Press.

WEDELL, E.G.,O'BRIEN, R.C., and PILLSWORTH, M.J. 1975. *The Role of Broadcasting in National Development: Senegal Case Study.* Manchester: University of Manchester.
WEDELL, E.G. and PILLSWORTH, M.J. 1974. *The Role of Broadcasting in National Development: Algeria Case Study.* Manchester: University of Manchester.
_____. 1975a. *The Role of Broadcasting in National Development: Nigeria Case Study.* Manchester: University of Manchester.
_____. 1975b. *The Role of Broadcasting in National Development: Tanzania Case Study.* Manchester: University of Manchester.

THE ROLE OF COMMUNICATION IN DEVELOPMENT PLANNING

William H. Melody

INTRODUCTION

It is generally accepted that communication can, and in fact must, play a crucial role in the development of all nations. Communication is a necessary, but not a sufficient condition for development. This means that a lack of communication, or a failure of communication, *can* be a barrier to development. But it does not mean that the introduction of a new communication technology, an expansion of communication facilities, or even an increase in communication will necessarily *stimulate* development. The effects of an expansion of communication depend also upon the many other interrelated and interdependent factors that constitute the environment within which the expanded communication takes place. In certain circumstances, an expansion of particular kinds of communication may be detrimental to development.

Thus, the effects of communication depend upon the particular, and often unique, characteristics of the society within which communication takes place. The effects of changes in communication opportunities for any nation depend upon that nation's inherited structure of economic, social, and cultural institutions; the types of communication systems and networks that operate within that institutional structure; and the compatibility of specific proposed changes in communication with both the existing institutional structure and the overall development effort. Where the absence of a specific kind of communication is creating a blockage for the realization of development advances, the effective expansion of this specific kind of communication could yield enormous benefits. But where the constraining factors limiting development do not include a lack of effective communication, the contribution to development of any such expansion in communication may be minimal. And where the expansion of a specific kind of communication is inconsistent with a nation's overall development plans, or when it is not applied properly because the implementing institutions have misdirected incentives, or where it brings about unanticipated consequences that run counter to the development effort, then its effects will be deleterious.

At the present time, the discipline of communication is in a very frustrating position. Communication is indispensible to development, but little is known about how development plans or policies should recognize this indispensable characteristic. Communication is an essential part of the life support system of a nation and of society. To the extent that communication processes can be better understood and improved, all of society's interrelationships also should be improved. In fact, it is widely believed that most problems in society can be related to a failure of communication. Therefore, the solutions, or at least some part of them, for an infinite array of society's problems are believed to reside in communication.

There is evidence that indicates that new communication technology has enormous potential for providing communication opportunities that can overcome the pressing problems of the day and stimulate quantum jumps forward in development. But there are no guarantees. In the past, the application of new communication technology has almost never lived up to the expectations initially claimed for it. In most circumstances, existing communication systems and networks are not being used as effectively as they could or should be. Thus, communication is crucial and pervasive, the opportunities for applying improved communication to stimulate development appear substantial, but the road to such successful implementation is unmarked and sometimes treacherous.

Unfortunately, analysts, policy-makers, and development planners know very little about the effects of specific kinds of expanded communication on the development of any nation at any particular juncture in its evolution; and an expansion of particular kinds of communication facilities, services, or opportunities on the basis of faith alone is at best a risky policy. The fundamental problem is that the role of communication in development has not been made operational and integrated into development plans: The relationships between the communication sector and other sectors of society have not been developed; both the short-term and long-term contributions of communication systems and services have not been measured; alternative ways of integrating communication into the development plans of a nation have not been assessed; the past, present, and potential contribution of communication for development cannot be compared effectively to that of other sectors of society. Hence, it is not known how communication should be evaluated in the decisions of national government to allocate resources.

When viewed narrowly, the problem appears to be one that requires extensive communication research directed to the discovery and explanation of essential communication relationships, effects, and policy alternatives. But development is a much larger process than communication. The system that must be analyzed and understood is the system of development, of which communication represents one or more components or subsystems. If development planning is deficient, and the theories and models on which it is founded are weak or irrelevant, then it will be small consolation indeed to understand the role of communication in an inapplicable model of development. Therefore, in seeking solutions to the problems of communication in development, researchers must first look to the larger system that constitutes the development process, and then to the role of communication within that larger system.

Unfortunately, the development theories, plans, and policies as applied to developing countries have not established a record of enviable, or even satisfactory, performance. Based heavily on theories of economic growth derived from examining the economic conditions in advanced, industrial nations, development theories and models applied to the developing nations either have failed or have achieved marginal success in the crucible of reality. Now, traditional concepts and theories of development are being reassessed and the role of economic factors in development is being reexamined. This makes the task of studying the role of communication in development a difficult one, since the study of communication's role in past development planning models is the study of failures and, therefore, is of limited value. Moreover, the study of the role of communications in the new evolving developmental models is akin to trying to hit a moving target. But a moving target is more likely to be a relevant target, especially when it is recognized that the development models must be implemented in changing real-world circumstances.

An examination of the role of communication in the development theories, models, plans, and policies of advanced industrial nations indicates that communication planning has not been fully integrated into development plans in these nations either. Although the communication problems—especially as possible blockages to development—appear to be more evident and acute in developing countries, the situation is not significantly different in developed countries insofar as an understanding of the effects of communication upon development is concerned.

The remainder of this paper is addressed to the following: (1) a critique of traditional development theories and models and their utilization (or lack of it) of communication as a component in the development process; (2) the changing theoretical framework that offers promise for improving our understanding of both development processes and the role of communication in those processes; and (3) the characteristics of the newer concepts of development and suggestions relating to the role of communication in the development process, and how this role can be analyzed productively and incorporated fully into development planning.

TRADITIONAL DEVELOPMENT MODELS

The cornerstone, if not the entire edifice, of the various concepts of development has been economic development. The foundation of all development policies has been provided by economic theory and economic models derived from it. Unfortunately, neither of the two dominant paths of Western economic theory has proven very useful as the basis for explaining the process of long-run development.

The earlier, classical economists addressed themselves to the problems of long-run growth and development of economies. For Adam Smith, David Ricardo, and Karl Marx, the central subject of economics was the accumulation of the means of production and property. About a century ago, the theory of marginal utility emerged within a theoretical framework of static equilibrium and it redirected the path of economic theory and analysis. This branch of neo-classical economic analysis is thriving today as microeconomics. It is directed toward the examination of problems of static economic efficiency and the static allocation of a fixed supply of a nation's resources, assuming that the preferences of consumers as represented by aggregate demand is given. The neo-classical theory was developed in terms of the equilibrium position of an economy at an instant in time, and assumes perfect knowledge of all relevant information and a given state of technical knowledge. The passage of time and the introduction of change of any kind were treated as exogenous shocks to the system that jolted the economy from one equilibrium position to another. Economic growth and development were not considered as part of the theory. Rather, they were caused by factors that were external to the theoretical system. One could use this theoretical framework to compare different equilibrium positions and to explain the process of economic growth or development from one equilibrium position to another.

Nevertheless, the idea of static equilibrium analysis and the objective of obtaining an optimum allocation of a given fixed bundle of resources had great influence on the thinking of economists and policy-makers about the use of a nation's resources, the process of economic growth and development, and international trade. As a narrowly-specified, deductive system of analysis based on a priori premises, the theory was used and continues to be used today as a framework for deducing appropriate economic policy. The neo-classical theory provided the analytical framework for deducing Say's Law, which stated that there cannot be unemployment of resources—including labor—in an economy if the suppliers of the resources will accept the *prevailing market price* for the use of those resources. This conclusion provided the basis for policies of laissez-faire, the non-intervention by national governments into the workings of the economic system. The massive unemployment in the Great Depression of the 1930s demonstrated vividly and cruelly the inadequacies of the neo-classical theory in explaining economic reality. John Maynard Keynes demonstrated the deficiencies of the neo-classical theory and offered an alternative theoretical framework (Keynes, 1936).

The neo-classical static equilibrium theory also gave support to policies of laissez-faire in international trade; the rule of comparative advantage could be logically deduced by comparing equilibrium positions under assumptions of full employment within domestic economies, a balance of imports and exports for all countries, and a perfectly competitive market system. Since Keynes, it has been recognized that the theory cannot justify laissez-faire when the critical assumptions do not approximate reality. Nations may well find it in their economic interest to establish protectionist practices to promote industrialization, to defend particular industries or firms from the consequences of severe international competition, or to overcome a deficiency of effective demand in the domestic economy which is causing domestic unemployment. Clearly, the case for free trade cannot be applied to the developing countries. In some major respects, the very concept of national economic development conflicts with the notion of free trade.

Although the neo-classical theory did not address the dynamic problem of long-run development, it provided apparent theoretical support for two fundamental policy presumptions regarding development.

First, free trade was presumably in the interests of the trading nations, so there was no reason to restrict trade in the interest of national development. Second, economic growth and development came about as a result of external shocks to a situation in equilibrium. These policy presumptions set the stage for the view of economic development that has prevailed in most development theory. This view assumes that economic development will occur when externally supplied capital, technology, expertise, information, etc., are injected into a developing country, because these factors will bounce it to a new equilibrium position—presumably at a higher plane—that will be optimal under conditions of free trade. The neo-classical theory may be deficient, but it has provided the basis for much development theory and policy.

In his new theory, Keynes viewed the economic system as a going concern operating at a phase in its historical development. He did not view the economy in terms of timeless stationary states, but in terms of a past that cannot be changed and a future that is uncertain. He observed that in capitalistic economies (or sectors of economies) investment is undertaken by private business under conditions of uncertainty and that equilibrium can be achieved at output levels where resources are unemployed because of a deficiency of effective demand.

Therefore, laissez-faire did not necessarily result in full employment of resources. There was not only an opportunity but also a responsibility for national governments to intervene in the economy to establish policies that would stimulate a full employment of resources.

Although the Keynesian analysis moves away from static equilibrium, it is essentially a short-run theory in which investment plays a key role. The unemployment of resources that Keynes was examining included the underutilization of an industrial capacity that had already been created. He was concerned about economic depression in an advanced industrial economy, a depression that had resulted from a decline in effective demand. Because the analysis was established entirely in the context of an advanced industrial economy with highly developed financial institutions, Keynesian theory has very little to offer developing countries whose unemployment exists because the capacity and effective demand have *never* been great enough (Robinson, 1962). After the Keynesian revolution in economic theory, the problem of economic growth created by capital accumulation and technical progress was brought back to the attention of economists. Over the past 25 years, there has been a proliferation of models of economic growth. Most have been addressed to growth in developed countries and most have fallen back on an equilibrium framework of analysis to determine a "natural" rate of growth. None has proven very useful as a theoretical basis for devising economic development policies in developing countries. Unfortunately, there is no general theory of economic development for developing countries. Most of the current models still treat growth and development as if they were always stimulated most effectively by exogenous factors because development cannot be handled effectively within the models. Thus, despite the lack of a sound theoretical base, it is still believed that economic growth and development will be enhanced by injections of capital, technology, expertise, and information into the economies of the developing countries.

Until recently, development was defined in narrow economic terms. It required economic growth initially as a prerequisite to other kinds of growth. Social, cultural, and other societal amenities provided secondary objectives that might have to be sacrificed somewhat if they conflicted with economic growth. With the general failures of both the theories and the policies of development for developing countries, the concept of development is now being broadened in many economic models to include noneconomic factors. Economists' definitions of development are being broadened to encompass the advancement of the entire social system. This is undoubtedly an improvement in the concept of development, but it makes the task of creating a theoretical framework for development analysis even more difficult, and it reduces the relevance of currently available *economic* data as indicators of development. This step is, of course, necessary; however, it leaves a weak foundation upon which to examine the role of communication in development.

Consistent with the standard framework of traditional theories of economic development, communication is viewed either as a routine domestic investment opportunity or as an exogenous factor that is injected into a developing country for the purpose of inducing desirable change. Communication is analyzed in different ways depending upon the circumstances and objectives of development planners.

Communication As an Investment Alternative

Investment in communication facilities (hardware or software) can be evaluated in terms of standard economic criteria for allocating resources. Under this approach, investment possibilities in communication are not differentiated from investment possibilities in steel production, manufacturing, or the supply of other goods and services. If a communication investment opportunity ranks high relative to alternative investment opportunities in terms of its anticipated rate of return, benefit, or some other measure, the investment will be made. If it ranks low, investment will be deferred or rejected.

Communication investment opportunities frequently do not fare well under this approach because communication systems often tend to be capital intensive with long-term, rather than short-term benefits. Also, many benefits of communication are not recognized in market prices and their worth is not easily measured. This evaluation of communication as an investment alternative can be and is made both in allocating a nation's internal capital resources and in allocating exogenous inputs of capital into the economy of a developing nation.

Communication As an Economic Infrastructure

Recognizing that investments in communication systems can provide fundamental building blocks upon which a nation's economy is structured, and which will enable the entire economy to operate more efficiently, standard economic analysis can be extended to recognize a multiplier effect upon the benefit calculations of investments in communication. Although quantification of this multiplier effect is almost impossible except in the crudest terms, the recognition of it tends to raise the ranking of communication investment opportunities.

Communication As New Technology

Because communication technology has changed so rapidly in recent years in developed countries, technology itself becomes a truly exogenous factor that can be injected into developing countries. Whereas the exogenous input of capital to a developing country carries with it a wide range of options with regard to where and how it is expended, the exogenous input of technology reflects a much narrower range of options because the production technique and type of facility have been predetermined by economic conditions in the country where the technology was created—usually the developed economies.

Whether or not the injection of any given technology will benefit the economic development of a developing country depends upon the economic and social conditions in the developing country, the characteristics of the technology, and the alternatives available to that technology. Frequently, exogenously induced technology will provide a developing country with short-term benefits but long-term disadvantages because the technology constrains the development of domestic industries. In many circumstances, the acceptance of technology from developed countries will be a better alternative than rejection of the technology, but that technology may be a long way from being the most appropriate technology for developing countries. The dominant thrust of technological development in developed countries has been to substitute capital for labor. The economies of developing countries are operating under quite different economic conditions.

In recent years, it has begun to be recognized that if technological advances arising from research and development in developed countries are pushed a few extra steps and adapted and directed to the conditions of developing countries, substantial improvements in the applicability of the technology can be made. For example, the initial satellite systems required very expensive earth stations because the satellites had been developed as point-to-point transmitters of large quantities of traffic. Stimulated by the problems of serving remote areas in Alaska and northern Canada, further research was directed toward the establishment of satellite systems that would serve many sparsely settled outlying locations with much smaller amounts of traffic. This research has enormously reduced earth station costs and may well provide further reductions in the future. In addition, consideration is now being given to the development and application of intermediate technologies for developing countries (Schumacher, 1973). Intermediate technologies may not appear to be as immediately beneficial as more advanced technologies, but they may be more likely to stimulate long-term development within a developing country.

Communication technology can make a claim for special treatment because it provides part of the economic infrastructure of a developing nation, but it cannot claim to always be beneficial. Whether or not the adoption of any exogenous technology will be beneficial or detrimental to a developing nation depends upon the nation's economic and social structure as well as the effects of that technology upon the nation's long-term development.

One-way Communication and Information Transfer

In developing countries, communication is generally viewed as an exogenous factor that is applied to a given economic and social condition in an attempt to stimulate development. Communication from a central source provides a transfer of relevant information—for example, on agriculture or birth control—to the populace to enable them to develop economically and socially. This process of one-way communication attempts to provide for the diffusion of ideas, for education, and for the inculcation of those values believed necessary for development.

The record of success of this communication in developing countries has not been particularly good, but that must be attributed, at least in part, to the failures of economic development theory and policy. Here also, communication is heavily based upon an extrapolation of the experience of developed countries, which has not been demonstrated to be relevant to developing countries. When evaluating the benefits of communication programs, it is difficult or even impossible to provide even crude estimates. Thus, it is difficult to justify the expenditure of resources on communication programs in competition with alternative investment possibilities where benefits can be more directly quantified. These one-way communication programs are typically distributed throughout the different ministries of a country for planning purposes—for example, education and agriculture—and therefore lack full coordination and integration. As a result, communication programs tend to become expendable functions in other ministries and often become the initial victims of budget reductions. Clearly, there is a need in developing countries to coordinate the presently fragmented structure of communication programs so that the aggregate benefits of communications can be assessed and effective communication planning can take place. But there is also a need to determine whether the messages being sent are having their intended effect and whether that effect is conducive to development.

The Creation of Communication Networks

Communication networks link those people with interests in common. A network may be viewed as a community of interest. People will belong to many different communities-of-interest depending on their interests and their ability to have access to those networks. The networks may be local, regional, national, or international. As the communication networks of people extend beyond the family or local group, special communication facilities generally are required. One measure of development that has come to be recognized occasionally in recent years is access to and participation in communication networks. However, it is difficult to value such access and participation, especially when much of it takes the form of social communication that produces no obviously quantifiable economic gain.

In many developing countries, two-way telecommunication services have been established primarily as a service to business and government, which can afford to pay the necessary market prices for using a system justified on economic grounds.

Other uses are primarily for one-way communication and information transfer from a central source to outlying communities. In most places, the print media tends to be essentially of a one-way nature. But in many instances, people in outlying areas desire to communicate with other outlying communities, and such communication may provide a significant step for development of the social structure. Little is known about the characteristics of communication networks, access to them, and participation in them. Perhaps these characteristics will provide both a basis for designing effective communication policy and good indicators of development. This is an area that communication researchers should pursue so that future development planners will not ignore it.

The study of communication networks and their characteristics can shed considerable light on the debate surrounding the free flow of information concept, a debate reminiscent of the laissez-faire debate regarding free trade. The establishment of international communication and information networks will affect the conditions under which national, regional, and local networks operate. The very existence of one network will prompt people to make different choices regarding their communication and information opportunities than they otherwise would have. A national network may weaken a local network, but it does not necessarily have to, just as an international network may weaken a national network, but it does not necessarily have to. One could cite circumstances where the free flow of certain information and the creation of international communication networks would facilitate other national networks and permit increased economic efficiency. But one could also cite circumstances where the free flow of other information and the creation of other networks would destroy national and local networks and simply increase the problems of dependency facing a developing country. If development is to proceed along desired paths, a developing country is going to have to be able to choose which communication networks it should promote, which networks it should attempt to regulate, and which networks it should attempt to preclude at any particular stage in its development. This requires an understanding of communication and information network characteristics that goes well beyond what is known today.

TOWARD A CHANGING
THEORETICAL FRAMEWORK

It is apparent that substantial improvements in development theory are needed to expand our understanding of development processes. These improvements must treat growth and development as an integral part of the theory and not as an exogenous factor. The treatment of development as an exogenous factor in economic models has reflected the inability to incorporate development into the models. It was assumed to be autonomous because the models could not explain it. By making it exogenous, the models have "assumed away" the substance of the problem of development.

The treatment of communication as an exogenous factor in development models and in development planning has a similar effect. Because past analytical efforts have been unable to integrate communication into developmental processes and plans, it has been treated as an exogenous factor. This treatment has signaled that little is known about the implications of communication and that conventional analytical approaches cannot fully come to grips with it. An improved theoretical framework for analysis of economic development must incorporate growth and development processes into the theory. An improved theoretical framework for analysis of the role of communication in development must incorporate communication into the developmental processes.

The traditional theoretical framework in development research has been conditioned by the doctrines of reductionism and mechanism, for example, breaking a problem down into its ultimate indivisible parts and examining it analytically within a closed system in terms of cause and effect. The concept of static equilibrium is a perfect example. Within its theoretical framework, the world is viewed as deterministic and important factors tend to be excluded from the closed system by assumptions that often render the final analyses irrelevant to the very problems that the theory is attempting to solve.

In recent years, for many problems, the systems mode of analysis has provided an improved analytical framework. Under the systems mode of analysis, the doctrine of reductionism is replaced by the doctrine of expansionism—for example, the treatment of all objects, events, and factors as parts of larger units. A system is not an ultimate indivisible element but a whole unit that can be divided into parts. A system is more than the sum of its parts, and the characteristics of a system may be different than the characteristics of its parts. System performance depends upon how well the parts fit and work together, not on how well each part performs independently. In addition, system performance depends on how well the system relates to its environment, which is yet a larger system (Ackoff, 1974).

A systems approach to the analysis of development in developing countries and the role of communication in development can overcome the problems of closed theoretical systems that tend to banish the important variable to the category of exogenous factors. A systems approach to development is clearly more compatible with the treatment of development as a process rather than an exogenous factor that somehow influences the movement of an economy from one equilibrium position to the next. Under the systems approach, communications can be viewed as a system with many components. The communication system can be examined as one component in the larger system of national development. Moreover, national development can be viewed as a component in the larger system of the world economy. The development of a useful theory using the systems approach will not be easy. But it will recognize communication as an integral part of a nation's development system, and a nation's development system as conditioned by the international environment in which it must thrive.

CHANGING CONCEPTIONS OF DEVELOPMENT

The broader definitions of development that go beyond considerations of economic factors require that development be analyzed as a system. In essence, what has been discovered from experience is that characteristics of economic development as measured by aggregate economic indicators may be in conflict with broader conceptions of development based upon changes in the entire social system. Whereas the reductionist view of development has tended to seek specific individual measures of the performance of the components of development (for example, radios per person), the expansionist view will require the creation of new measures of performance for the broadly defined development system.

Under a system's approach, development can be examined as a dynamic process where cause and effect is not unidirectional and sequential, but circular, interdependent, and iterative. Time can be specifically recognized as an important variable in development models and cumulative effects can be considered. Analysis will be more readily able to examine the interrelations among components of a system and between a system and its environment.

A systems approach to analysis should lead ultimately to a modification of developmental planning processes in directions that will overcome the fragmented planning processes that currently characterize much communication planning and which tend to relegate communications to the role of a tool that can facilitate the implementation of the objectives of other disciplines. It will permit the incorporation of both economic production and distribution into the same development models, thus overcoming the bias against distribution that prevails in most traditional models because they "assume away" distributional considerations. This should bring the issue of equality to the center of analysis of development. The tendency of traditional models to separate artificially the issue of productivity from the issue of equality, and then to measure development in terms of incomes and wealth, has led not only to the unduly narrow conception of development, but also to the neglect of the problems of distribution. But productivity and distribution are clearly related. G. Myrdal (1974) has concluded that higher productivity and greater equality are more closely tied together in developing countries than in developed countries.

Under a systems view of development, the principal task for development analysts will be to discover the important interrelations among all major segments in the social system, to identify the direction of relationships, and to place relative weights on the strength of the various interrelationships. This obviously will require a monumental amount of research and analysis. Communication research and analysis must examine communication in two respects. First, it must focus attention on the system of communication and its relationship to its component parts. Second, it must examine communication as a component in the larger system of development and its relationship to other components in that system. A systems approach can be used to establish the structure of models that can encompass development as a process and communication as an integral component of that process. It is the task of theory to design appropriate and relevant model structures. It is the task of research to provide the substance for its implementation through development planning and policy formulation.

Works Cited

ACKOFF, R.L. 1974. *Redesigning the Future: A Systems Approach to Societal Problems.* New York: John Wiley & Sons.

KEYNES, J.M. 1936. *The General Theory of Employment, Interest and Money.* New York: Harcourt, Brace and Company.

MYRDAL, G. 1974. "What is Development?" *Journal of Economic Issues,* 8: 4.

ROBINSON, J. 1962. *Economic Philosophy.* Chicago: Aldine Publishing Company.

SCHUMACHER, E.F. 1973 *Small Is Beautiful.* New York: Harper and Row.

PLANNING COMMUNICATION TECHNOLOGIES AND INSTITUTIONS FOR DEVELOPMENT

Edwin B. Parker

Communication has been widely viewed as a major force for national development, at least in the years since the early pioneering work of Wilbur Schramm (1964). The early work on the relationship between communication and development focused on the messages in the mass media and how they could be utilized to create a sense of national identity, foster attitudes favorable to modernization, or fulfill the goals of particular campaigns such as family planning, disease prevention, or agricultural development projects. Other studies of communication and development focused on the potential effect of the content of general entertainment or news media for broadening horizons and inculcating modernizing attitudes (Lerner, 1958). While drawing on that rich tradition, this paper shifts the focus of attention to the technology of communication and to the institutional structures supporting or made possible by the communication technology. Rather than assuming that present technologies and institutions are immutable, we start with the assumption that technologies and institutions, as well as messages, can and should be planned to support the goals of national development. The following sections begin with a general discussion of the goals of national development, the role of information as a factor in development, and information policy choices open to developing countries. The discussion then turns to the specifics of communication in support of development, including communication technology, institutional structure, and choice of messages. A concluding section summarizes the policy and planning issues associated with national development support communication.

GOALS OF NATIONAL DEVELOPMENT

In order to have effective policies for communication in support of national development, it is important to have a clear picture of the national development goals that the communication policy is supporting. Although different nations have differing goals, we can begin with a general statement of goals that might apply in more or less modified form to most nations seeking rapid development.

Economic Development

Rapid economic development is often defined in terms of economic development or standard of living, with Gross National Product (GNP) or per capita GNP as the basic indicator of economic development. Although the improved quality of life that economic development brings is usually the major goal of development, economic indicators are imperfect measures of the quality of life for which they are surrogates. Human development is a better label for the implicit underlying goal of improved human happiness and quality of life. In any society of human beings, economic development is a means to the end of greater well-being for the members of the society. It would be a perversion and confusion of means and ends to use conventional measures of economic growth as the sole indicator of that greater well-being, especially if important human values are subordinated to the economics in the process. A major difficulty leading to this potential confusion is the fact that we lack satisfactory national measures of quality of life and human development; nations are compared with other nations or their own prior state on the basis of the sometimes misleading economic indicators. Denis Goulet, in his book, *The Cruel Choice,* speaks of bread, dignity, and freedom as the three goals of development, none of which should be subordinate to the others, important as bread (his shorthand for economic development) may be (1971).

Equitable Distribution

Even a very high rate of economic development, or perhaps *especially* a high rate of economic development as measured by conventional indicators, may lead to some sectors of the population being relatively or absolutely worse off than they were before. There is a suspicion that the economic development plans of some countries are designed not to create the maximum economic growth for the country as a whole, but to maximize the increases in the wealth of that sector of the society that is already relatively wealthy. Some people try to justify the widening economic disparities between rich and poor by claiming that it is an inevitable and necessary consequence of economic development. If this were true, then humane governments, remembering that the purpose of economic development is to improve the quality of life of their people, would place compensatory programs high on their list of development goals. The development goal could be stated as a reduction of economic disparities by improving the well-being of less privileged people through full employment, equitable distribution of services, and equitable access to resources necessary for economic advancement.

The claim that widening gaps between rich and poor are necessary may be false and self-serving, even when it is a well-intentioned honest belief. The goals of rapid economic development and equitable distribution may not in fact be in conflict. Edgar Owens and Robert Shaw (1974) argue persuasively that inequitable distribution (the "trickle down" theory) leads to inefficient development. The conflict between those arguing for a human development strategy and those arguing for a capital-intensive resource development strategy may be a conflict about who is to benefit most from development. Those arguing for a capital-intensive resource development strategy tend to suggest short time scales for measuring development. But sustained development over a long period may require investments in human and physical infrastructures that require a longer term before rapid self-sustaining growth is possible.

The natural resources of any country are fixed, even though they may not be fully known or fully exploited. What is variable is the human knowledge, labor, and initiative that is brought to bear on those resources. Investing in the human resources of the society in order to increase the level of knowledge, the productivity of the labor, and the incentives for initiative may lead to greater return on national investment than much direct investment in physical facilities. But the return on the investment may not show on the financial statement of the immediately following fiscal year. The economic payoff from improved health of babies or improved education for children may come in decades rather than years. Plans intended to maximize economic growth over a 20-year period are likely to include more such investment than plans designed only to maximize growth in short intervals. Private investment in the development of human resources is always less than needed to optimize the potential, even the most conservative economists admit (Friedman, 1962). The society has more to gain from informing and motivating the least well educated and cared for members of the society, because the gap between their actual and potential contributions is greatest. But these are precisely the people who are least able to invest in their own self-improvement. And, at least in societies that prohibit human slavery, it is difficult for individual members of the society to obtain a full return on any investment they make in the education of others. Because the society as a whole is better off when the brainpower and laborpower of all members of society are mobilized effectively, investment in the equitable distribution of services such as health and access to information may be the most promising investment a society can make, even when judged on narrow economic criteria.

National Cohesiveness

One of the prime goals of most developing nations is to create a sense of national identity within a society often composed of disparate ethnic, tribal, or linguistic segments. Although militant nationalism leading to hostility between nations can be deplored, few people question the value of integrating and interconnecting in cooperative fashion the diverse cultures and interests within a society. Nationalism is preferred to tribalism, even by idealists who hope for an end to competitive nationalism in a world in which the sense of family of humankind predominates. However, if that nationalism is based on coercion or exploitation of some groups by others, then it is doubtful whether the apparent "cohesion" is stable and certainly doubtful whether such "cohesion" contributes to development.

The economic historian and communications scholar,

Harold Innes, was one of the first and most persuasive in drawing attention to the role of communication in linking together a nation (1972). Maintaining political control over any geographic area required a communication technology permitting messages to be easily transmitted over the entire area. Just as communication through space was essential, so a satisfactory technology for communication through time (for example, writing on stone tablets) was essential for continuity of a nation over time. Innes also cites historical evidence to show that communication capability linking together the members of a society is essential to national survival. He points out that no national governmental structure can survive indefinitely without at least the acquiescence of the people who are governed by it. If the communication system of the society is monopolized by a minority class (even a powerful ruling minority) that does not have adequate communication linkages with the rest of the society, then, over time, that minority may grow sufficiently out of touch with the rest of the society that the nation cannot survive without major upheavals in governmental structure. On the other hand, with sufficiently good communication, a minority may prolong its influence through a strategy of gradual evolutionary change, expanding access to the system at a rate sufficient to forestall more violent upheavals.

A communication system linking together the members of a society and permitting continuity through both space and time does not guarantee national cohesiveness. Such a communication system is a necessary, though not sufficient condition. If the messages transmitted over the system lead to mutual adaptation and cooperation among the different regions, tribes, ethnic and linguistic groups, or classes, then a national identity results from the mutual accommodations. On the other hand, if the messages are part of a process by which one segment of a society is exploiting another, then improved communication may merely expose that pattern of exploitation and hasten a polarization that will destroy hopes for national cohesion.

It is misleading to think of messages as causes leading to the effect of national cohesion. National cohesion should be defined as a state in which the diverse elements of a society are interconnected so that they can and do communicate with one another. If one segment of a society maintains monopoly control over the messages of the communication system in an attempt to impose national cohesion on the rest, then the result may well be the opposite of that intention. Thus, the goal of national cohesion, by my definition, cannot be achieved as an effect of the messages in the communication system. The goals of national cohesion are synonymous with the goal of creating a communication system through which people in every segment of the society have bi-directional communication with other people in the society.

Human Development

Many people, including this writer, consider the goals of human dignity and human freedom of choice to be as important as economic development and national cohesion. Economic development is extremely important because it can enhance human development. Those who argue that economic development should be given precedence assume that the goal of economic development is contradicted or impeded by other values and point out, quite rightly, that starving people have no freedom or dignity. In fact there is no contradiction or conflict between economic development and enhancement of human freedom and dignity unless there is exploitation of some members of the society for the benefit of others. If the benefits of economic development are being equitably distributed, then the improved economic well-being contributes to human freedom and dignity. At the same time, when they know that they will share fairly in the benefits of economic development, people who have maintained their human dignity and free choice will be more strongly motivated to contribute to the economic development that benefits all. The conflict arises when some humans are being exploited for the benefit of others, in which case the conflict is not between economic development and human dignity. Rather, it is a conflict between one segment of the society getting more economic benefits and dignity, and another segment getting less of both.

INFORMATION AS A FACTOR IN DEVELOPMENT

In a fundamental sense there are only two factors of production. These are conventionally labeled as land and labor. Development strategies focused on land can be called resource development strategies, while those focused on labor can be called human development strategies. In this sense, land means all of the natural resources of a society. It includes the land, forests, water, climate, and existing stock of seeds and animals that form the resource base for its agriculture. It includes oil, coal, sunlight, or flows of water that can be used to create energy, and the ores and minerals that can be shaped into products desired by the society or exported in exchange for such products. The second factor of production is the human labor that must be applied to these natural resources to make them useful to meet human needs and desires. This factor includes human knowledge and brainpower as well as physical labor. As Buckminster Fuller (1970) has pointed out, the physical resources of a society are finite, but the human resources are potentially infinite because human brainpower can be used to discover, invent, or implement improved techniques for processing the available material resources. Some societies that lack an abundance of natural resources have been able to achieve economic growth through improving their techniques for acquiring and processing natural resources. Japan is the most frequently cited example of such a society.

For some purposes it is useful to discuss capital as an additional factor of production, even though it could be subsumed under the two-factor definition. Capital is that portion of natural resources and human labor that is not used to produce output for current consumption or trade, but is used instead to build tools or factories that then produce the goods and services of the society. Even a society that is not developing must allocate some portion of its land and labor to capital rather than consumption because the tools, buildings, and machines of the society, however primitive, need to be periodically replaced if the society is not to regress to a more primitive and less productive state with consequent decline in the products available for consumption.

Viewed from another perspective, the chief factor of production in modern time, in both developed and developing countries, is information. This factor is sometimes referred to as knowledge, education, or human capital. Much economic development depends on improvements of techniques, whether or not new technologies are involved. The level and kind of education or skill required in an advanced technological society are much different than those required in a poorer society. With adequate information, it is often possible to find substitute materials rather than to import scarce and expensive materials. If sufficient information is available, a society with much under-utilized and relatively unskilled labor can develop production techniques requiring less expensive imported equipment and taking advantage of the available labor. With sufficient information and a sufficient level of education or skill on the part of the labor force, it may be possible to import only the blueprints or the ideas for a new factory or industry without the expense and foreign exchange cost of importing the technology itself.

A highly developed telecommunications infrastructure will permit a society to have more efficient coordination in the production and distribution of its resources (whether in a capitalist or socialist economy) because it will be easier to make the appropriate quantity of needed goods and services available when and where they are most needed. A competitive economic system requires perfect information to reach the most efficient level of production, according to neo-classical capitalist economic theory. (How fairly the output is distributed is another question, however.) Planned economies must have accurate information to substitute for the flow of money that signals, to capitalist producers, how much of what goods should be produced. Effective use of a highly developed communication system will permit improved coordination in the distribution of goods and services as well as in their production. More equitable distribution, coupled with information about examples of more productive behavior, may change the incentive structure such that more members of the society become motivated to increase the productivity of the society.

A developing country with a sufficiently well educated labor force may be able to adapt better the ideas of more developed societies to their local culture and conditions. Some of the technology and some of the institutional structures of developed societies, as well as the ideas imbedded in them, may be quite harmful to the indigenous culture if they are imported. It often may be preferable to import and adapt the ideas to local culture and circumstance than to import all the trappings of another society. This is particularly true in the case where the technology and institutional arrangements may be harmful, even to the societies they are imported from (Schumacher, 1973).

In the most highly developed societies, a large investment in scientific research may be a major factor in stimulating economic productivity gains. In less developed societies, it may be more efficient to invest in scientific research at a level that facilitates the understanding, the importation, and the adaptation of ideas to local conditions. These examples of the role of information, broadly defined, should indicate how information itself may be the key factor of production. Economic theories devised to deal with a stable set of technologies and failing to assume changes in the information structure will be quite inappropriate to developing societies. In developing societies, the very nature of development requires that the level of knowledge itself be changing as well as the rate at which existing knowledge is applied to the enterprises of the society.

INFORMATION POLICY CHOICES FOR DEVELOPING COUNTRIES

There are four dimensions of development strategy on which developing countries can make significant information policy choices. In each of these dimensions the choice is not an either/or dichotomy, but a matter of how to strike a balance.

Information versus Capital Investment

Societies with insufficient financial capital resources for extensive resource development have no choice but to emphasize an information-based human development strategy if they wish to develop. Tanzania, Cuba, and China might be cited as examples where heavy emphasis is placed on education and mobilization of the human resources of the society. In cases where adequate capital is available (for example, through the export of oil), the constraint limiting development will be the level of education and the degree to which the laborpower and brainpower of the society can be mobilized. The construction of telecommunication systems that facilitate the education and mobilization of the human potential is thus an essential development requirement within capital-intensive resource development strategies.

Similarly, within information-intensive human development strategies, the prime task is, by definition, to discover and implement procedures that more effectively train and mobilize the human resources. Since there are always shortages of teachers

and fieldworkers to implement such information-intensive
strategies, and because there is great difficulty in coordinating
their work in areas lacking effective telecommunications facilities, even capital-poor societies need to examine carefully the
possibility that the capital resources they have might be best
allocated to the telecommunications infrastructure. Better
communication capability may be more important to an information-intensive development strategy than direct investment
in transportation, electrification, or irrigation facilities. This is
because, with effective communication, it may be easier to
mobilize the labor and create the incentives that lead to the implementation of other needed facilities.

Infrastructure versus Projects

The infrastructure of a society is that set of facilities that
does not directly produce the agricultural or industrial products,
but is essential for their efficient production and distribution.
For a country or region to develop there must be transportation
facilities (railroads, roads, air transport, etc.), electrical power,
water supplies, and communication facilities (telephone, telegraph, mass media, etc.). For example, in countries or regions
lacking adequate supply or distribution of water, then dams,
canals, and other facilities necessary to ensure the availability of
water for consumption, for agricultural irrigation, and for industrial use may need to be given high priority. Without these
basic infrastructure facilities, it is difficult to carry out many
desirable specific projects.

The development of a society can only occur as rapidly
as the availability of the infrastructure permits, and in only those
locations where the infrastructure exists. Successful mass media
campaigns require that media be available to the people the campaign is trying to reach. Industrial development is impossible
without development of the power, water, transportation, and
telecommunication infrastructure. Sometimes short-run success
can be accomplished by particular projects in locations with pre-
existing infrastructure, but sustained rapid growth will require
extensive infrastructure development. Much of the payoff from
the investment in infrastructure may not occur until specific
projects are implemented making use of that infrastructure. For
example, agricultural marketing cooperatives may depend on
better communication to determine demand and on better

transportation to be able to deliver produce to locations of greatest demand. Development strategies looking for immediate benefits may foster projects utilizing existing infrastructure, but this may hamper later development if project investment is at the expense of of infrastructure. Development of a telecommunications infrastructure permitting the flow of information throughout a society may be the single most powerful engine of sustained development.

National versus Regional Development

One of the major strengths of the United States and German economies, relative to the economies of nations such as France and the United Kingdom, is the strong regional character of the United States and Germany. Regional centers of business, government, and culture may permit a more rapid development than a single national center. Regional pride may foster regional development activities that would be less likely to occur if each region remote from the capital felt inferior, reflecting the reality of being dependent on distant decisions for development within their region. The move of the capital of Brazil to Brasilia was part of the strategy for developing the interior region of that country. Regional differences in geography, resources, and level of prior development may require somewhat differing development strategies that can only be implemented within a framework of more regional autonomy than is possible in a country with only one national center of business, government, and culture.

For a regional development strategy to succeed, it is necessary to have excellent communication and transportation facilities linking together the regional centers. Within each reg region, it si also necessary to have communication and transportation infrastructure developed in order to facilitate regional access to the services of the city serving as the regional center. A decision to stimulate regional development implies a commitment to develop the communication facilities essential for regional interconnection.

Urban versus Rural Development

The development experience in the last few decades has made it clear that an industrial development strategy does not automatically bring about improvement in agricultural productivity or rural incomes. When successful, industrial development strategies can lead to gross disparities between the quality of life in urban and rural areas with consequent migration from rural areas to urban slums. The resulting congestion strains the available urban services and threatens to reduce the quality of life in urban areas (Vakil, 1975). Compensatory programs to improve the quality of life in rural areas are required, not only out of considerations of social justice, but also to influence migration patterns.

Agricultural development may be a key factor in the plans of any country aspiring to rapid development. Even if exports of minerals and the development of manufacturing capability produced sufficient foreign exchange to permit imports of foodstuffs on a major scale, it could be a major policy mistake not to have local food sources to guarantee at least a minimal level of food supply for everyone in the country. At a period in history when worldwide food shortages are to be expected, a strong domestic agriculture may be a major national policy requirement, even if the country's land and water resources do not make it an ideal agricultural nation.

A large peasant or nomadic subculture living not far above the subsistence agriculture level of existence will be a major drag on the economic and social development of any country, making it much harder to reach national goals for a higher average quality of life. If rural life is improved only by compensatory programs without rural productivity gains, then the rural sector will be a drag on the rest of the economy. Only if the brainpower and laborpower of those living in rural areas are also mobilized for national development can rapid development be achieved.

Nations trying to maximize economic development on a year-to-year basis may be tempted to invest only in short-term, high-payoff urban industrial projects. The World Bank now officially recognizes that urban industrial development strategies are hard pressed to keep a growth rate sufficient to compensate for population growth and consequent declines in per capita productivity in many rural areas. The World Bank's officially stated development policy is to support projects that will aid the most disadvantaged 30 percent of the population—in other words, the rural poor (World Bank, 1974).

One reason sometimes cited for lack of investment in

rural areas is a supposed lack of profitable investment opportunities. This, in turn, follows from the poor state of development of infrastructure in most rural areas of developing countries. To break this vicious circle of rural poverty will require commitments to development of rural infrastructure, including the telecommunication infrastructure. The absence of rural infrastructure may have to be treated as a major investment opportunity rather than as an excuse for lack of investment. The relative underinvestment in rural areas that is typical of developing countries may also be the result of too few examples of successful rural development to be used as models to follow.

Recent changes in communication technology may now make it economical for many countries to plan a rural development strategy based on the implementation of a rural telecommunications infrastructure and the utilization of that technical capability for human development strategies (that is, education and facilitation of local initiative). For a detailed discussion of the potential role of telecommunications technology for rural development, see Heather Hudson and Edwin Parker (1975).

DEVELOPMENT SUPPORT COMMUNICATION GOALS

The specific goals for development support communication must, by definition, be in support of the development goals of the nation and consistent with the choices made by the developing nation on each of the strategy dimensions outlined in the preceding section. For example, if the country decides on a regional development strategy, then regional television and radio stations or networks would be required. Messages in support of regional development all emanating from a centralized national media channel would be ineffective because the nature of the source would inherently contradict the message. If the national policy is to encourage local initiative, then national or regional messages to that effect will be less effective than arrangements that permit local access to broadcasting facilities. As these examples indicate, both the goals of development support communication and the process by which they are reached must be consistent with the national development goals.

Since the goals of development support communication are dependent on the specific development plans they are supporting, it is easier to discuss such goals in a more specific context. At the International Conference on Communication Policies for Rapidly Developing Societies held at Mashhad, Iran, June 1975, Iranian development planners and international communication experts discussed these issues in the context of Iranian development. The working group assigned to consider development support communication reached a rough consensus concerning the goals of development support communication summarized in the following eight points:

1. Determine the needs of people and give political credibility to the expression of those needs. (Provide sufficient citizen access to the communication system to serve as effective feedback to the government concerning its development goals and plans.)
2. Provide horizontal and vertical communication linkages at all levels of society. (Much more than a one-way broadcast communication system with feedback channels is required. In addition, there must be communication channels through which people at all levels of society and in all regions and localities have the capability to communicate with one another to accomplish the coordination necessary for both resource development and human development.)
3. Provide local community support for cultural preservation. (Preservation of culture through events and entertainment on national radio and television would not be sufficient to preserve culture, which inheres in the activities of local people in their local communities. Local media and local support mechanisms are required in addition to the encouragement implicit in national recognition.)
4. Raise people's awareness of development projects and opportunities.
5. Help foster attitudes and motivation that contribute to development.
6. Provide relevant information, for example, job and vocational information, and consumer information.
7. Support economic development through industrial linkages, for example, the electronics industry, the computer industry, printing, and the performing arts.
8. Provide support for specific development projects and social services, including health care delivery, agricultural or vocational skills training, and public health, sanitation, or family planning projects.

Other lists, or variations on these themes could be easily elaborated. Different lists may be appropriate for countries with different development goals.. Communication strategies for meeting these or similar goals are discussed in the following three sections dealing with communication technology, institutional structure, and choice of messages.

COMMUNICATION TECHNOLOGY PLANNING

Perhaps the most serious mistake that can be made in a development support communication plan would be to make a prior assumption about the technology that should be used, based on what is commonly in use in other countries, especially developed industrial countries. The development goals of other nations may be different, the institutional structures may be different and inappropriate to the developing nation, and the capabilities for production of messages to be transmitted through the technology may be quite different.

In writing about the transition from agricultural to industrial societies prior to the invention of much of the information and communication technology of today, Marx argued that the technology and the physical resources of society (the underlying forces of production) at one time determine the institutional structure of the society at a later time (the social relations of social organization of production), and that the institutional structure at one time determines the laws, culture, and ideas of the society (the superstructure) at a later time. If there is any truth at all in these insights about technology in general, they seem to apply with even greater force to the communication technology of a society. The communication technology of a society determines who can speak to whom, over what distances, with what time delays, and with what possibilities for feedback or return communication. This is the heart of what is meant by social organization. It makes less sense to say that the social organization is caused by the pattern of communication interactions in the society than it does to define the social structure in terms of the patterns of communication (including order-giving). The culture of a society can be defined by the messages that are transmitted in these social patterns. The messages of a society are obviously shaped by the media they are transmitted through as well as being creations of the institutional structure of the society. Therefore, careful attention should be paid to the form of the communication technology installed in support of development. The existing social organization largely determines which kind of technology is implemented. For example, a one-way nation wide transmission system emanating from a single central source would force a centralized institutional structure, potentially subverting development goals of a country attempting to create a decentralized structure. Also, a technology requiring more costly message production than can be supported within a country, for example, color television, may create pressures to import programs from another society, leading to a cultural dependence on that other society rather than development of the national culture (Katz, 1973; Contreras et al., 1975; McAnany, 1975).

One ot the goals for national development support communication cited above was "support economic development through industrial linkages." One of the major goals for India's participation in the communication satellite experiment in 1975-76 was to stimulate development of India's electronics industry. Although primarily an educational television demonstration project, the national decision to develop and manufacture all ground stations within India had an additional beneficial effect in aiding development of India's embryonic electronics industry. Other countries may also wish to plan their communication technology in ways that foster national economic development, rather than by simply importing foreign technology. Importing the technology, rather than importing the ideas that make the technology possible, may create unwanted technical dependencies (even when sufficient foreign exchange is available).

Importing the ideas rather than the technology (or maximizing the import of technical ideas while minimizing the import of hardware) may have another beneficial effect that is harder to achieve with imported technology alone. The further benefit results from designing the technology to meet the local or national goals within the local or national environmental conditions. In the Western industrial world, communication technology has developed over a period of years. New developments had to be competitive with what came before. Technologies appropriate for adding small increments to what already exists are quite different from what would be utilized if entire systems were installed *de novo*. Many of the technical designs are appropriate to high density communication routes rather than low density routes. They may be designed for a different scale of production or for a different ratio of technology and labor than is appropriate for a different country. They may be designed to require a higher level of training among the maintenance staff than may be available in some countries. They may assume the availability of a reliable power supply that does not fluctuate outside narrow voltage limits, rather than be designed for stand-alone rechargeable batteries that could be used in communities without electricity or with unreliable supplies. They may be the products of an institutional structure that is designed to maximize profits (even though some social needs remain unmet or remote regions unserved), rather than to maximize the national development effects of the technology.

Communication technology is a rapidly cost-declining technology, thanks to the invention of computers, transistors, integrated circuits, and other technical advances. Given adequate knowledge and a willingness to change the assumptions that underlie other people's technology, it is quite possible for a developing country to implement communication technology that is much better suited to its needs and also costs less than apparently comparable technology installed in the so-called developed nations. Those nations wishing to achieve rapid development of rural areas should be particularly wary of Western technology designed primarily for urban environments (Hudson and Parker, 1975).

What kind of communication technology will best facilitate rapid development? The most significant communication technology for development, especially rural development, is the telephone, or possibly two-way radio. Two-way voice communication does not require literacy and can provide rapid coordination and feedback. It can be used in any language and does not require program production expenditures. It can facilitate trade, supervision of teachers, and other development workers, and the delivery of health care (Hudson and Parker, 1973).

Traditionally, telephones have been installed only in response to strong demand as an enterprise that is expected to be highly profitable in the short run. In 1975, the World Bank, despite its polices supporting loans for development of services for the rural poor, was still following the traditional practice of only granting loans for telephone development that can return a sizeable profit in a short time—in other words, for expansion of urban telephone service. It is to be hoped that the

World Bank will soon modify its actions in telecommunications to be consistent with its new development policies instead of maintaining conventional telecommunication policies. Traditionally, costs of extending telephone service to rural areas were very high. Recent advances in telecommunications technology, including mini-computers for reduced-cost switching, satellites for long distance circuits with costs independent of distance, and single channel per carrier equipment for low density routes, have changed the cost considerations in telephone planning. Until the 1970s telephone planning in all countries has been based on serving or interconnecting the most populous areas and then extending service incrementally beyond those areas. Prior to the recent planning by Iran, no country had taken the policy decision that all areas of a country are to be served, requiring the cost analysis of system alternatives to be based on complete coverage rather than on costs of reaching either the largest communities or those most easily reached (Lusignan et al., 1975).

Nations planning rapid development should not assume that telephone technology need be restricted to two-party conversations. For many development purposes, it may be highly useful to have conference circuit capability such that a group of teachers in a region can have a conference with a regional supervisor or a group of health workers can have a conference with a physician. Conference circuits are rare in highly developed Western countries for historical reasons that may not apply to developing countries. First, the old telephone technologies that are already in place make conference circuits difficult. This constraint need not apply to newly implemented systems. Second, given the manner in which they are implemented in European and North American telephone systems, conference calls are not as profitable for the telecommunications entity as a series of individual two-party calls would be. Much more attention is now being paid to the potential of teleconferencing techniques for reducing travel costs in developed countries. Developing countries can plan such capability at the outset of installation of new facilities without having the difficulty of attempting awkward modifications later.

In the United States, where most communities were already served by terrestrial telephone lines and microwave interconnection, it was found that the satellite was the most economical way to reach the approximately 100 communities in Alaska that in 1975 did not have telephones (Davis, 1975).

Decisions concerning which technology to use (or which mix of technologies) are quite dependent on the assumptions made at the outset. A policy to serve primarily the urban areas and to extend service to those nearby rural areas that can be cheaply served will result in technical choices different from those that would follow from a policy decision to serve close to 100 percent of the communities in a country. Similarly, a decision to provide telephones only to those areas that already have both roads and electricity will lead to different technical choices than a decision to use communication to lead rather than follow these other developments. Once a communication satellite for domestic telephone service is considered as an alternative under a policy goal of reaching the entire country, the conclusion for many countries is that satellite communication rather than terrestrial microwave is more economical for most locations within the country. This conclusion is based not on the million dollar Intelsat ground station technology, but on small satellite ground stations costing US$20,000 or less (Lusignan *et al.*, 1975).

As indicated above, however, these decisions ought not to be based on cost comparisons alone, but also on questions of potential international dependencies (for example, satellite launch capability, importation of technology, or regional sharing of satellite capacity), foreign exchange considerations, and plans for development of a local electronics industry. Technical choices that are correct for one country may be quite wrong for another country with a different set of policies and development goals.

The second most important technology to consider is radio broadcasting. Because it is cheaper to implement the one-way broadcast voice communication of radio than two-way telephone (or two-way radio) technology, radio may be the first communication technology to achieve 100 percent coverage in developing countries. On the other hand, the cost of adding radio technology to a telecommunications plan for two-way voice communication to all communities is very minimal. Radio has many technical advantages when compared to print media or to television. It can be programmed in local languages; it does not require literacy; it is highly portable (for example, farmers can take small transistor radios into their fields; and for a wide variety of subject matters, it has been demonstrated to be as effective a teaching medium as television at much lower cost (Schramm, 1973; McAnany *et al.*, 1975).

Planning for radio technology in support of national development goals should also include the technical capability for regional and local radio origination. Local radio capability, even at the most basic level of being able to plug a locally produced audio cassette into the local relay transmitter for a few minutes a day (or in case of a local emergency) is technically easy, very economical, and potentially a significant factor in meeting local development goals. For a more detailed discussion of the technical and economic considerations involved in radio planning, see Edwin Parker and Bruce Lusignan in Spain (1976).

The third communication technology necessary to support national development is printing. Printing of national and regional information and provision of textbooks and other printed materials in support of education should be high priority development goals. Literacy programs require print materials, not only for their training classes, but for new literates to practice and maintain their reading skills. Effective implementation of print technology requires more than provision of printing and publishing capabilities. Distribution networks and libraries must also be established to make print materials accessible to those who need it. In developed countries distribution depends on existing road, rail, and airline networks, and established postal services. Developing countries need to plan their print distribution networks in concert with the development of these other facilities. In cases where electronic communication networks are being established for telephone and radio, careful consideration should be given to the electronic distribution of print materials (for example, through facsimile or telecopier techniques), especially for locations without rapid and reliable transportation networks. Library and distribution services established for print media could also be used for storage and distribution of audio recordings, films, and other audio, video, or electronic information.

The glamorous and prestigious communication technology for a developing country is television, especially color television. The potential of television for bringing a shared national culture to all of the people of a nation is considerable. The potential of television for augmenting and extending education services is great. The costs are also great, especially for production of programs for television. The availability of television technology without adequate budgets for program production may lead to a higher rate of importing television programs from outside the nation than is desirable to further the cause of national development. Providing television, especially entertainment television, to only the urban population might be considered more in the nature of an urban luxury consumption item than part of communication for national development. On the other hand, television can be used effectively in support of development goals, especially if used for vocational skills training, literacy training, or other educational services to the least well educated segments of the population in rural as well as urban areas. If television is already available in urban areas of the country, technical planning to make that service available to the entire country may be an important development goal. The costs of such extension may be relatively small if they are part of a technical plan for extension of telephone and radio services, even though the costs may be very high if the technical system is designed as a special purpose facility solely for television.

The role of communication technology in development is not restricted to those countries usually labeled as developing countries. The so-called developed countries are themselves continuing to develop, sometimes with rates of development that widen the gap between developed and developing countries. The primary communication technology that is now playing a major role in the further economic development of advanced countries is computer technology. The place of computer technology in stimulating the development of technologically advanced countries was discussed extensively at a meeting of the Organization for Economic Cooperation and Development (OECD) in Paris in February 1975 (Parker, 1975). Nations attempting rapid development to close the gap between themselves and more advanced countries should also examine the potential of computer systems for their societies, at least to the extent of planning their telecommunications development in ways that will facilitate the later addition of computer networks and computer services.

INSTITUTIONAL STRUCTURE

There are three levels at which institutional structure is relevant to a discussion of communication and development. The first is the institutional structure in the larger society that is made possible by improved communication capability. In *Development*

Reconsidered, Edgar Owens and Robert Shaw (1974) argue that district-level organization in which local villages are connected to one another and to the district market town may be the most significant organization for development. That argument assumes that districts are also interconnected in regions. Without reliable telephone communication, effective district and regional organization with extensive participation may be difficult or impossible to maintain. The most significant contribution of communication to development may be the development of institutions appropriate for local, district, and regional development that were more difficult to organize prior to the introduction of communication capability.

The second level of institutional structure concerns the institution or institutions controlling the communication technology (for example, the telecommunications authority or national broadcasting authority). The institutional form controls the choice of technology, how it is distributed throughout the society, and who gets access to the facilities to transmit their messages. These are more important communication and development questions than many questions of communication content because decisions concerning distribution of and access to facilities severely limit the range of content choices that are possible. These problems are discussed in more detail elsewhere, in the specific context of planning radio services for development (Parker and Lusignan in Spain, 1976).

The third level of institutional structure, to be discussed in more detail here, concerns how to organize the flow of information for development. Since the intent, by definition, is to provide communication in support of development goals, a strong case can be made for including development support communication as a functional task within the organizations assigned the major responsibilities for development, such as departments of health, agriculture, industry, and so on. Because of the central role of communication in development, it will be important for each agency involved in development to have at least a small communication support group directly under its own control. Such a group or groups should perform or arrange for the performance of four tasks:

1. Producing messages in whichever media are appropriate
2. Arranging for the transmission of those messages to the locations where they are needed (or arranging

for those in need of the information to have adequate access to it)

3. Arranging the necessary utilization support or coordination with the ultimate receivers of the information so that the development task is effectively carried out

4. Bringing feedback and evaluation information from the recipients and intermediaries back to the attention of the managers of the development activity so that not only the communication support activities but the development program itself can be modified to ensure that it effectively meets the development goals.

Not all of these activities should be necessarily wholly carried out within each development agency. There are certain to be economies of scale and shortages of trained personnel that will require the sharing of physical communication facilities and experienced people among several development agencies. In addition, in countries committed to development, there is a need for national communication organization, or organizations, such as national broadcasting entity, that is independent of all other agencies. Without that independent communication entity that can report to the people on the activities of all the other agencies, there would be insufficient public attention to ensure that the other agencies were effectively carrying out their missions. Whether or not the national broadcasting entity owns and operates its own transmission channels, there is also a need for a telecommunications entity to provide common carrier communication channels that can be used for communication between any individuals and organizations within the society. That telecommunications entity should have the responsibility for facilitating the flow of communication within the society and therefore should have no structural incentives to censor or inhibit the flow of messages.

The organizational problem for the development agencies is to provide appropriate liaison with communication agencies, with the agencies that have the necessary message production skills and facilities (for example, television production capability), with the local organizations the development program is intended to serve, and with organizations that can provide objective feedback and evaluation information. In some cases it will be necessary for the development agency to have the capability to perform these functions within its own organization. In other cases it will be appropriate to perform the necessary functions through procurement of services from other organizations.

From the perspective of agencies assigned to provide development support communication, these same four tasks need to be considered. The organizational problem is two-fold. One is how to organize internally in order to carry out each of the four tasks. The other is how to provide the appropriate liaison mechanisms with the several development programs they are supporting. For programs to be effective, there must be communication linkages within and between the organizations involved at all levels. Good vertical command and feedback linkages within each organization plus coordination at the top of the two organizational hierarchies will not be sufficient. There must be horizontal linkages between program production staff in the communication organization and subject experts in the development agency. There must be horizontal linkages between regional and local field staffs of both organizations.

There is no simple prescription that can be given for devising workable organizational structures. It is seldom possible to implement an ideal structure *de novo*. Almost always it is necessary to work within a pre-existing institutional structure, making whatever adaptations, innovations, and reorganizations are possible. Previously existing institutions usually have a good deal of inertia, making change difficult. The specific national goals, the national geography, the existing technology, and the talents of the people involved all need to be taken into account.

Four general principles that should be taken into account in organizational planning are flexibility, decentralization, redundancy, and accountability. Flexibility is important, because rapid development means rapid change. With changing conditions, including changes in the underlying technology (for example, a shift to increased dependency on communication satellites with reduced dependency on terrestrial microwaves), different organizational structures will be appropriate. An organizational structure that is appropriate for one set of conditions may be quite inappropriate for another. Ability to modify the institutional structure itself in response to changed conditions should be a prime consideration.

Decentralization, and the delegation of responsibility and authority that goes with it, is particularly important in a rapidly developing country. The more that decisions have to be made centrally, the slower the pace of development will progress. Decentralization is effective if local initiative can be channeled into activities that support national development, rather than into destructive competition that threatens national cohesion or merely attempts to redistribute resources without increasing the total to be distributed. The organization responsible for development communications must take the lead in such decentralization, because it is highly visible and can be a model for other organizations.

Redundancy in the institutional structure may be the least understood principle. In attempting to create flexible, decentralized institutions that provide reliable, efficient services, it should be remembered that the components of organizations (the humans and groups of humans) are unreliable. It is quite possible, in theory and in practice, to devise reliable systems out of unreliable components, provided there is sufficient redundancy in the structure. If one subunit of an organization suffers from bureaucratic inertia and fails to adapt rapidly, there must be another unit that can be assigned the task at hand. The existence of an alternative unit that can perform similar functions is the best way to ensure that the first unit does not develop the complacency and inertia that is often associated with monopoly power. Redundancy may seem a remote goal for developing countries that are striving hard to create the first organizational unit to accomplish some task. It may also seem inefficient. But redundancy in organizations should be neither a remote goal nor a current inefficiency. Organizing the available production staff into two or more independent production teams should lead to more initiative and a higher level of total output than a single production team (Niskanen, 1971).

It may be more important to have redundant organizational components at lower and middle levels of an organization than to have completely parallel large organizations. For example, two independent national broadcasting organizations may each become somewhat inflexible and unresponsive to change if their internal structures are insufficiently flexible and redundant. It may prove more effective to have a single organization with flexibility and redundancy within its structure. With redundancy and decentralization at lower levels it is possible to restructure large organizations by reorganizing components. For example, and educational television unit could belong in a broadcasting organization or an educational organization (or both organizations could have educational television units) depending on which larger organization had the necessary flexibility and vitality at any given time.

It may appear obvious to say that institutions should be held accountable for the performance of their assigned tasks. Such accountability requires that the goals assigned to the organization be well specified, that there be appropriate measurement criteria by which success can be judged, and that the rewards coming to the organization and its members be related to how well the goals are met. For the organization as a whole to accomplish its task, the component organizations should be held accountable for their subtasks. This requires devising performance indicators and delegation of authority and responsibility so that the unit and its members can in fact be held accountable for their performance. A development organization, especially one as visible as a communication organization, needs to follow development principles in its process so that it can serve as a model for development in other areas. Therefore, the goals of widespread stimulation of initiative and acceptance of responsibility should be demonstrated within the development organizations themselves, as well as being a social goal for the effect of their activities on the larger society.

The application of these four principles to institutional structures established for development support communication may have different results in different environments. The particular development support communication function that may present the greatest organizational difficulties is the program of utilization and coordination in the field. The ultimate success or failure of a development program depends on what happens at the farms, villages, towns, and industrial locations where development is desired. Communication campaigns that do not have local coordination and feedback are virtually certain to fail. Local on-site fieldwork is needed to ensure that the messages get to the right people in an appropriate context at the right time. Local on-site fieldwork is also needed to provide to the message producers and development planners the feedback without which the development program cannot be sufficiently responsive to local needs and conditions in order to have much hope of success.

Fieldworkers, especially in remote locations, may have development tasks that cut across more than one development organization. Provision for adequate sanitary water supplies, irrigation for agriculture, and disposal of wastes that might be health hazards for humans and needed fertilizer for plants, are all interconnected, even though different branches of government may be involved. The education and communication requirements to permit a local community to carry out such a project on a local basis will need interagency coordination at the local level.

One possible organizational solution would be to have a development communication center within each district. That center could be given the responsibility of procuring and providing all of the printed, audio, or video information needed for that district in support of local development activities. There would be considerable merit in having such a unit be directly responsible to the district government rather than to a national agency so that local coordination is facilitated without interagency jealousies at a national level getting in the way. To be effective, the local utilization unit must have reliable communication links with regional and national communication support offices so that they can procure (or arrange to have produced) the materials they need. They could be local distribution centers for print materials (combining a library, bookstore, and newsstand function) as well as local audio and video centers making television, radio, video tapes, films, audio recordings, and other materials available in support of education, literacy training, health, agriculture, and development-related activities.

Whatever organizational form is adopted, it will be important to stay flexible, keeping open options for change based on the performance experience. It is usually wise to start with pilot projects and experimental programs in some regions or topic areas before committing national programs. The experience obtained in smaller programs may be essential to modify plans for larger programs to increase their probability of success.

In development activities, the most important point of institutional structure is not the internal structure of the development organizations and their relationships. The part of the institutional structure to be most concerned about is the relationship with the people who are to be developed. The goal should be to maximize the participation by the intended beneficiaries of the development activity. Doing things for people or to people may leave them passive and dependent (or, worse, resistant), with development proceeding slowly because it is wholly dependent on the activities of the development agencies. Doing things with people should be preferred to doing things to or for them. In that way, the people contribute their own energy and initiative, and learn that their own efforts can improve the quality of their lives. That learning process, which can only happen through participation, may be more important than the specific benefits of the specific project because it can start a "chain reaction" without which rapid development is unlikely to occur.

The main point of contact between a communication organization and the people it is attempting to serve may be through field utilization centers or units, as discussed above. Acceptance of direction from a local advisory board or community government may be necessary to generate sufficient local participation. For such an organization to be effective, the regional and national offices of the development support communication organization must be in a position to accept, respond to, and generally assist local initiatives. It would be preferable if the local workers were hired and directed by the local governmental unit (although possibly with funds provided by the communication agency) so that they can effectively communicate the needs and wishes of their communities and districts to more senior people in the communication agency. If they were direct employees of the communication agency, their incentives are likely to be for career advancement in the agency (which implies pleasing supervisors), rather than for development of the community, which may mean that supervisors in the communication agency may need to be told things they would rather not hear. The arrangements for obtaining community participation will obviously have to depend on the specific circumstances, so it is difficult to make detailed statements. Nevertheless, the importance of such participation, particularly in communication activities that provide visible models, cannot be overemphasized.

CHOICE OF MESSAGES

As the preceding sections have indicated, much of the content of communication will be determined by the technology and by the institutional structure that is implemented. The significant contribution of communication to development may be in linking the society together so that the entire nation is bound together in a shared interconnected system of communication. If the appropriate linkages are there so that people come to feel that they are part of a larger whole in which they participate, then the content of the messages becomes less important.

The structure of who can communicate with whom is more important than the message content (which is produced in accordance with that structure). In general, the greater the level of participation in the communication system, the faster the pace of development is likely to be.

We can divide concerns about the content of communication for development into three general categories: (1) the content of the national mass media—the cultural, entertainment, and news programming, (2) the content of media used for formal education, and (3) other communication directly in support of development. This section will be restricted to a few remarks about the residual category of development support communication other than the national mass media and formal educational media.

Development support communication is sometimes thought of as nonformal education, or as information and persuasion in support of a development campaign, for example, a family planning campaign, a campaign to change agricultural practices, or a campaign to improve sanitation and public health. This view of development support communication has the disadvantage of looking at the communication process primarily from the perspective of the sender or producer of the messages. It is implicitly, if not explicitly, manipulative and control oriented in its focus on how the communication process can be used to manipulate the receivers of communication to behave the way the senders want them to behave. It may not be conducive to the dialogue and collective decision-making processes that are likely to be required to mobilize the people of an entire nation to develop rapidly. This is not to say that nonformal education and information and persuasion campaigns are not extremely important. Rather, it suggests, as has been argued by Kaarle Nordenstreng (1974), that providing the information, context, and perspective within which people can make decisions and choices may be an even greater contribution to development. In Denis Goulet's terms, it contributes to freedom and dignity, but it is also likely to speed the process of economic development because of more effective mobilization of people to improve their own lives and their own communities (1971).

It might be more helpful to think of the ultimate goal of development support communication as providing the means for people to have on-demand access to the information they need to develop themselves. This implies that the messages are produced in ways that fit and are understandable within the context and viewpoints of the receivers. It means that receivers have a choice of information content so that they can receive family planning information when they are interested in that and agricultural information when that is their focus of attention. Stimulating information seeking and providing opportunities through which people can obtain the information they seek is consistent with the development philosophy of fostering participation and local initiative. Local or district development support communication offices or facilities (or communication components of district development offices) should have the tasks of responding to the expressed and felt needs of the people of their district and of obtaining from regional and national offices and kinds of information materials required to meet those needs. In some cases they may be able to participate in the local production of materials, such as local radio broadcasts or local bulletin boards and wall newspapers.

To help people obtain the information they need and to facilitate self-expression, there must be good technical channels of communication, so that requests can be passed on to information sources and that answers or appropriate materials received quickly. There must also be an organizational structure that encourages local offices to initiate communication instead of passively waiting for messages from central authority. This support function is different from a national broadcast media function, even though it could be conducted by an organization that also had broadcast responsibility, because it depends on the local distribution of stored media (books, newspapers, audio records or cassettes, pictures, video cassettes or films, etc.). Local distribution of appropriate materials at convenient times may require access to local broadcasting facilities—for example, occasionally substituting local audio cassette input for the national radio braodcast fed to a local radio repeater station. Even when a wide variety of materials is not available, providing local choice among even a small number of alternatives may lead to a more active commitment to development by those who learn to make those choices, and who perceive that they have some measure of power to develop themselves.

POLICY AND PLANNING ISSUES

It might be helpful to outline the major issues to

be faced in planning development support communication. 1. The first issue is the emphasis to be placed on information and communication relative to other development strategies. A commitment to human development, either as the major development strategy or as a way of providing the organized and motivated labor force needed to implement other development strategies, will require allocation of a significant portion of available development resources to communication.

2. The second issue concerns the geographic distribution of the technical communications infrastructure. Are information services to be made available only to urban areas or only to those areas that have previously developed transportation facilities and electricity? Or are information services to be extended to all areas, in advance of transportation and electrification if they cannot be supplied concurrently? It was argued that a commitment to complete coverage of the nation with communication facilities was desirable both on grounds of social equity and as an efficient strategy of development.

3. The third issue is the kind of technology to be adopted. The choices depend in part on policy decisions relating to geographic distribution of development. They also can influence these decisions because new technologies, including communication satellites, now make widespread distribution economically feasible in a way not previously possible. Technology decisions should also take into account trends in technological development, the costs of various technologies, the relationships with indigenous industrial development, international dependencies and balance of trade considerations, and a balance between technological possibilities and message production capabilities.

4. The fourth issue concerns the kind of institutional structure that should be established to carry out development support communication activities. Planning is required for message production, message distribution, utilization support, and feedback and evaluation. Such organizational planning should take into account requirements for flexibility, decentralization, redundancy, and accountability. It was also argued that institutions should arrange for maximum participation by the people whom the development activities are intended to serve.

5. The fifth issue concerns the choice of messages. National broadcasting policies and educational media policies were not discussed here. For other development support

communication activities it was argued that responsiveness to expressed audience needs and provision of access to a choice of materials should be given a central place in message planning.

Works Cited

CONTRERAS, E., LARSON, J., MAYO, J. and SPAIN, P. 1975. "The Effects of Cross-Cultural Broadcasting." Stanford: Stanford University, Institute for Communication Research.

DAVIS, R.T. September 1975. "Dissatisfied with Phone Service, Alaska Buys Its Own Satellite Earth Terminals," *Microwaves*, 12-14.

FRIEDMAN, M. 1962. *Capitalism and Freedom.* Chicago: University of Chicago Press.
FULLER, B. 1970. *Operating Manual for Spaceship Earth.* New York: Simon and Schuster.

GOULET, D. 1971. *The Cruel Choice.* New York: Atheneum.

HUDSON, H. and PARKER, E. 1973. "Medical Communication in Alaska by Satellite," *New England Journal of Medicine, 289,* 1351-1356.
_____. 1975. "Telecommunications Planning for Rural Development," *IEEE Transactions on Communication, 23:* 10,1177-1185.

INNES, H. 1972. *Empire and Communication.* Toronto: University of Toronto Press.

KATZ, E. 1973. "Television as a Horseless Carriage." In George Gerbner (ed.), *Communications Technology and Social Policy.* New York: Interscience Publication.

LERNER, D. 1958. *The Passing of Traditional Society.* Glencoe, Illinois: The Free Press.
LUSIGNAN, B. B., *et al.* 1975. *A Baseline System Configuration for Video Distribution and Telephony.* Vol. 3, First Year Report on Contract NIRT I, Assistance in Telecommunications Planning. Stanford, California: Communication Satellite Planning Center, Stanford University.

McANANY, E. September/October 1975. "Television: Mass Communication and Elite Controls," *Society,* 41-46.

McANANY, E., JAMISON, D. and SPAIN, P., eds. 1975. "Radio's Role in Nonformal Education: An Overview." Paper prepared for volume *Radio's Educational Role in Development* for the World Bank.

NISKANEN, W.A. 1971. *Bureaucracy and Representative Government.* Chicago: Aldine-Atherton.

NORDENSTRENG, K. 1974. *Informational Mass Communication.* Helsinki: Tammi Publishers.

OWENS, E. and SHAW, R. 1974. *Development Reconsidered: Bridging the Gap Between Government and People.* Lexington, Massachusetts: Lexington Books.

PARKER, E. B. with the assistance of PORAT, M.U. 1975. *Social Implications of Computer/Telecommunications Systems.* Report no. 16. Stanford: Stanford University, Center for Interdisciplinary Research, Program in Information Technology and Telecommunications.

PARKER, E.B. and LUSIGNAN, B. 1976. "Technical and Economic Considerations in Planning Radio Services." In P. Spain, *et al.* (eds.), *Radio for Education and Development: Case Studies and Syntheses.*

SCHRAMM, W. 1964. *Mass Media and National Development.* Stanford: Stanford University Press.
_____. 1973. "Big Media, Little Media," report to Agency for International Development. Stanford: Institute for Communication Research, Stanford University.

SCHUMACHER, E.F. 1973. *Small Is Beautiful.* New York: Harper & Row.

VAKIL, F. 1975. "A Macro-Econometric Projection for Iran." Prepared for the NIRT Symposim, Tehran, Iran.

WORLD BANK. 1974. *Education, Sector Working Paper.* Washington, D.C.: World Bank Headquarters.

TOWARD A SHARED PARADIGM FOR COMMUNICATION: AN EMERGING FOUNDATION FOR THE NEW COMMUNICATION POLICY AND COMMUNICATION PLANNING SCIENCES

L. S. Harms

INTRODUCTION

Early in 1972, at the close of a small conference on world communication held at the East-West Center, Daniel Lerner remarked:

> For most of the forty years we have been doing communication research, we have operated within a paradigm devised by Harold Lasswell which ran: 'Who says What to Whom through What Channel with What Effects.' . . . Right from the very beginning of this conference, that paradigm was put aside and dimension by dimension a new one began to emerge.

Among the dimensions identified by Lerner were participation, two-way interaction, and "talk back." He went on to say that "two-way interaction and feedback are essential concepts in our thinking about communication and its future." He concluded his remarks with the statement, "I view this to have been a landmark conference" (Lerner, in Richstad and Harms, 1973, pp. 86-87).

A few months later, speaking at EWC on the future of world communication, Lasswell outlined two future-oriented paradigms. The first of these he called *oligarchic* and it restates the earlier formulation widely attributed to him. The second paradigm he called *participatory* and he sketched it in this way:

> The demand for selective development increases the pressure for investment in intermediate, resource-parimonious technology that minimally disrupts the distribution of population and intensifies

78

> demand for the pluralization of values. Excessive concern with
> wealth and power gives way to a quality and style of life that cul-
> minates in expressive acts that are parsimonious in material
> requirements. Levels of frustration are held in check; oligarchies
> are deprived of support; the decision process is responsive to
> persuasive alignments of skill and other pluralistic groups; mass
> media provide attention opportunities that generate and re-edit
> common maps of man's past, present and future and strengthen
> a universal and differentiated sense of identity and common
> interest.

Lasswell went on to say that the "two contrasting scenarios of
the future are suggestive of the importance of continuing feedback of knowledge to those who are concerned as scientists or
executives with communication." He also proposed that a
"continuing seminar" be developed as an "institution of attention control" for the study of possible communication futures.
Lasswell did not, however, predict which of these two paradigms would become the dominant one (Lasswell, 1972, p. 24).

These related statements, the one by Lerner and the
other by Lasswell, establish a useful landmark or baseline for
the examination of selected post-1970 developments in the
field of communication. Of particular concern will be a shift
from an "oligarchic" to a "participatory" paradigm with attention to the implications of that shift for the communication
policy and communication planning sciences.

As T.S. Kuhn (1970) documents, paradigm shifts are
expected occurrences within any field. In the communication
field, however, the paradigm shift is accompanied by large
changes in technology, by global interdependence, and by cultural diversity. Thus, the current communication revolution is
occurring at two levels: the visible technology-interdependence-
culture level and the invisible paradigm shift level. But in this
two-level aspect, the current communication revolution appears
to be unique and unprecedented.

In the post-1970 international conference dialogue on
the role of communication in the local communities and in the
world community, three fundamental concepts move into a
paradigmatic relationship. These are: resources, needs, and
rights. But the concepts are also of wider interest as the examples below illustrate.

In a recent conference report on the "Planetary Bargain," H. Cleveland makes the following introductory observation, one that begins with a *resources* orientation.

> Barring some cataclysm, the centerpiece of world politics in the
> next few years will be the development of and distribution of
> resources to meet human needs. What human beings need is of
> course extremely relative—related to culture, to expectations, to
> time of life. . . . The fairness revolution is already well underway
> (Cleveland in McHale and McHale, 1975, p. iii).

Another recent conference report on *Human Futures* published by the IRADES group of Rome begins with the statement that research and discussion "on alternatives for the world should focus on the principal issue—Human Needs." Subsequently, the matter of developing resources to serve *needs* is discussed and, at times, the resource/needs problem is set within a human rights framework. As if often the case in futures study, the conference report devotes considerable space to communication (IRADES, 1974, p. 1).

The statement below takes its orientation from the *rights* concept, and is one of the first references to a right to communicate:

> If it be accepted that there is a 'right to communicate' all
> Canadians are entitled to it. New systems, new services that are
> coming into use today, and others that can be foreseen in the
> next decade or two, can be harnessed, given the will and the purpose to provide new opportunities, new alternatives, and new
> and more and more satisfying ways of life. . . . (Information
> Canada, 1971, p. 229).

The whole of *Instant World* can be read as a first attempt to view the interrelated resources, needs and rights concepts from policy and planning perspectives. Significantly, that book is a product of multicultural dialogue.

In September 1975, during the IBI (International Broadcast Institute) conference in Cologne, Germany, a multicultural, multinational group of about 30 professionals met on four successive days to discuss the question of a right to communicate. That group generated and agreed on the statement that is repeated below:

> Everyone has the right to communicate. It [Communication]
> is a basic human need and is the foundation of all social organization. It [the right to communicate] belongs to individuals
> and communities, between and among each other. This right
> has been long recognized internationally and the exercise of it
> needs constantly to evolve and expand. Taking account of

changes in society and developments in technology, adequate
resources—human, economic and technological—should be made
available to all mankind for fulfillment of the need for interactive
participatory communication and implementation of that right
(Harms, Richstad, and Kie, 1977, p. 130).

The subparts of the IBI statement deal first with the fundamental question of human rights, as expressed in the phrase "Everyone has the right to communicate." It moves next to establish a linkage between that right and communication needs, both personal and social. Finally, it states that if everyone has the right to communicate, it follows that resources for satisfying those communication needs should be developed and made available for all mankind. It is worth noting that the group intended only to *describe* the right to communicate—the needs and resources elements emerged out of the dialogue itself.

Discussion which begins with one of these concepts, or even with a part of one of them as experience begins to show, often expands to encompass the other two. The order may be: resource-needs-rights, or rights-needs-resources, or the other possible combinations. Taken together, these concepts form the core of the alternate, participatory paradigm.

In large part, the content of this paper is an outgrowth of the dialogue experienced at a number of communication conferences, mostly international ones. To fill in some gaps and round out the corners, a few perspective papers written in different parts of the world have also been reviewed. From these threads and themes, I have attempted to sketch a scenario for participatory communication or, more exactly, to outline one plausible shared paradigm for the field of communication. It is my hope that the new paradigm will also provide a solid foundation for communication policy science and for communication planning science.

PARADIGM: THE INVISIBLE REVOLUTION

Within a field, a paradigm provides the foundation framework both for the development of theories and the conduct of research, and for the organization of a body of application and practice. A *shared* paradigm provides the basic pattern that unifies the activity of scholars and practitioners and gives direction to that activity. It permits and legitimatizes the conduct of "normal science" and normal practice (Kuhn, 1970).

Until about 1970, the paradigm for normal science and practice in the field of communication has been the "oligarchic" one generally attributed to Lasswell:

"Who says What to Whom through What channel with What Effects."

Its general model is sketched below:

Communication is viewed as fundamentally one-way and linear, source and receiver are separated, messages are prepared and transmitted. Theoretic models set forth by a Claude Shannon or a David Berlo elaborate on the general model as do bodies of practice in radio and TV broadcasting and, for that matter, in the classroom lecture method. For the most part, the reports of research and descriptions of practice contained in the *Handbook of Communication* (Pool and Schramm, 1973) fall within this paradigm.

Although the fact has not been widely noted, and I think it is a particularly important fact, Lasswell was among the first to discuss an alternate paradigm for the field of communication. As a first approximation, its suggested verbal form is:

"Everyone has the Right to communication Resources required to serve communication Needs."

Its general model now appears to be something like the one below:

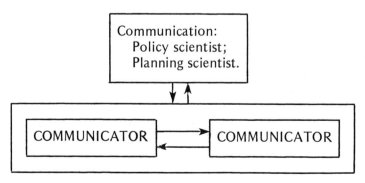

Communication is viewed as *fundamentally two-way* or multi-way rather than one-way, interactive, and participatory rather than linear, involving communicators rather than sources and receivers, purposeful, generating messages as well as transmitting them, and so on.

It would be premature to suggest that the dimensions of the alternate paradigm are well understood. They do not yet appear to be so.

Communication Resources

A recent *Intermedia* headline reads: "Communication as a Resource" (*Intermedia*, 1975, p. 1). Below are brief excerpts from that editorial:

> We are witnessing—and participating in—a new phase in the discussion about communications and media. . . . Underlying much of the current discussion is an emerging concept of communication as a resource—although different in kind to energy and materials resources. When communication is seen in its double aspect of process and product, whether judged abundant or scarce, there is a need for new approaches to be firmly related to resource and economic policies. . . .

Communication resources can be developed to serve human communication needs *directly* rather than indirectly through development support communication, or communication in service of national or economic development.

What is a resource? Most simply, a resource is something useful. Resources are the "materials" required and used to satisfy, meet, or serve needs.

Communication resources, quite probably, on close and detailed examination, will be shown to be unlike other resources, particularly the natural resources, in important ways. Nevertheless, it is useful to note that the resource concept is frequently used in many areas, particularly so in recent years. Food, energy, and other resources become issues for public discussion in many parts of the world. Communication resources may become community-level discussion topics as well.

Even though communication resources may be unique in important ways, a look at energy resources may remind us of some of the dimensions and characteristics of a resource. First of all, the concept of a resource seems to come into focus at a certain level of development and organization. Preagricultural man, for instance, would likely have had very little use for a concept of energy as a resource. In the agricultural era, enumeration of the separate energy sources was simple, and they could still be dealt with independently. In the industrial era, energy became a central concern, new sources of energy came into use, and others that required planning and coordinated effort such as atomic energy became of interest, and "energy resources" became of general concern. In the post-industrial era, at a time when shortages are feared and alternate sources of energy are being sought, the concept of energy resources is an essential one. It permits questions to be asked that would otherwise be very difficult to pose. More generally, at some level of complexity, perhaps at a time where enumeration of the separate elements becomes cumbersome or where planning is required, a new phase of development prepared for a reconceptualization of the many separate elements into a unifying entity, a resource.

The new "phase" in the communication field seems to begin around 1970. To the usual list of telephone and telegraph and radio and television, it became necessary to add cable and satellite and computer and dozens of other items. Curiously, the data presented in the recent Unesco *World Communications* handbook reveal the earlier perspective by the emphasis on the one-way mass media of radio, television, etc. and the omission of telephone and postal service (Unesco, 1975). As the separate media and technologies become more interconnectable, it becomes useful to look at them in relationship with each other, to see communication as a resource.

What elements are to be included as part of a communication resource? Obviously telecommunication technologies (the term media may no longer be useful) are included as would be the "human resource," the skilled communicator. In that face-to-face communication depends on passenger transport, to what extent do transportation networks form part of a communication resource? Or telephone networks? And postal service?

At this moment, the elements of a communication resource have not yet been organized into an easy to comprehend and useful format. While it seems evident that communication resources are likely to differ in important ways from energy, for example, it is not yet clear what the nature of these differences will be. Some large part of a communication resource seems to be "artificial" as contrasted to natural. It depends on organizations and institutions of many kinds.

But even at this preliminary stage, some observations are possible. For instance, there is a very large gap in a communication resource between two-way telephone and one-way television broadcasting even though many communities rely heavily on small group discussion and decision making in the conduct of daily affairs—a fact which probably has a major bearing on the demand for passenger transportation. Within the resource framework, one may wonder why television developed on the radio broadcasting model as contrasted with the telephone model—which it might have done if the computer and broadband cable capacity available today has been available at an earlier time.

As we consider communication to be a socio-technical resource, systematic procedures will be required for coordinating educational and training programs for human communicators. At present, very little effort is devoted to the design of programs of anticipatory communication skill building—programs designed to prepare communicators for the probable requirements in different future decades.

The question of availability of communication resources quickly leads to what are prior questions. Are communication resources inherently scarce? Or might they under some conditions become abundant? The answers depend on the nature of communication resources.

One suggestion for a starting point comes from John and M.C. McHale (1975, pp. 63-67). He points out that some elements of a communication resource, especially informational elements, differ from most natural resource elements in that they are not depleted through use. In fact, under some conditions, information use, or exchange, or sharing can be expected to increase information. The sharing and use of scientific findings, for example, do not deplete the store of scientific information.

A further suggestion comes from what is sometimes called the telecommunication-transportation-tradeoff problem. If passenger transportation networks are considered part of the communication resource, the question arises as to what extent capacity on a telecommunication network can be substituted for transportation. The problem usually studied is whether broadband cable can be utilized to reduce commuter traffic, or whether office workers can remain at home and "telecommunicate" to work. The goal is to trade a less costly resource element for a more costly one while maintaining or improving the social benefit (Kollen, 1974).

As the concept of communication as a resource develops and becomes familiar, as a minimum, the elements that are augmented rather than depleted through use should be known; techniques for trading high cost for low cost elements should be expected; and a better match between human skill building and other resource elements can be anticipated. However, if communication resources are to become abundant and known to be so, abundance must be measured in terms of human communication needs. Communication resources must be understood within the total communication environment.

Communication Needs

There is not yet a widely accepted description or definition of what constitutes a need. The term need is used in different ways even within the field of communication. The concept is an important but illusive one (André-Clément and Schwartz, 1974).

A first distinction must be made in the communication field between "user requirements" and the term used here—communication needs. In general, the user requirement orientation leads to questions posed within the framework of an existing communication service. The familiar "needs ascertainment studies" are more properly called user requirement surveys. Such surveys seek to discover what "other kinds of programs" a viewer would like to have on television or a listener would like to have on radio. The permissible questions are quite limited; the kinds of answers that can be acted on are also quite limited. "Educational needs assessment" studies have a similar purpose within existing educational structures or institutions.

The work of the psychologist Abraham Maslow constitutes an often cited general body of writing on general human needs (1970). He claims that each human is a "biological system encountering ever occurring needs." Maslow makes the further assumption that human needs can be divided into two types—basic and created.

Maslow identified and orders basic needs as:

- physiological—air, water, food, shelter, sleep, sex;

- safety and security needs;
- love and belongingness needs;
- esteem (from self and others) needs;
- growth needs such as aliveness, order, and meaningfulness.

The created needs are said to include "desires and wishes."

There is no equivalent body of work in the field of communication. The emphasis on communication needs, as distinguished from user requirements, has increased with the growth of interest in comprehensive communication planning. For instance, at the Unesco seminar on communication planning held in Kuala Lumpur in 1974, the importance of communication needs specification was stressed as was the relationship of these needs to various cultural objectives and social structures (Unesco, 1974). Similar statements can be found in other Unesco documents, in the Australian Telecommunication plan, and elsewhere.

A program of research and discussion on communication needs can be expected to yield:

- a set of criteria for defining a communication need— How do you know one when you find it?
- a list of defined communication needs—How many a are there? How are they unique?
- a procedure for organizing defined communication needs—Are some communication needs more important than others? How much so?
- a procedure for translating communication needs into operational and technical requirements—How can operational capabilities and facilities be acquired and made available?
- a procedure for estimating the quality and quantity of the communication resources necessary to satisfy the communication needs of a community—What is required in a community, between communities, and internationally?
- a procedure for monitoring communication need satisfaction in a community—How do we know communication needs are being met?

From the above perspective and based on a preliminary review of some of the published research "around and about" communication needs, there appear to be three general communication need areas under which specific needs can be organized as they are identified:

- *information needs,* including easily accessible information from a suitably diverse set of sources;
- *association needs,* encompassing participation, interactive participatory interpersonal relationships, and preservation of cultural heritage;
- *personal needs,* including silence, solitude, privacy, time for thinking and reflection, and self communication.

After setting aside the broadcast related "user requirement" studies, there remain relatively few studies that examine communication needs in a systematic way. One important study was completed by Elihu Katz and his colleagues (1973).

At least three research techniques have been employed:

- interviews and questionnaire surveys
- technology demonstration
- content analysis

The Katz study and work by Brenda Dervin (forthcoming) and others use a variety of interview and survey techniques. PEACESAT provides an example of using a technology to demonstrate what need communicators do have for a particular technology dependent "service," what use patterns prevail, what modifications are requested, etc. (Bystrom, 1974). The content analysis approach has been employed in a wide range of printed materials in search for indicators of need (Childers, 1975).

Fortunately, the usefulness of a well-grounded understanding of communication needs becomes widely appreciated as attention centers on "communication as a resource."

Right to Communicate

A human right is universal and belongs to everyone. In this sense, humankind has the right to communicate. In general, a human right proclaims an ideal, provides a standard for achievement, declares what ought to become, and serves as a long-range goal.

But, as is often noted, between the fundamental claim and the realities of the environment in which any human or group of humans live, there often are wide disparities.

The major elaborations of human rights are found in the various instruments on the subject developed within the United Nations. The most often cited of these instruments is the Universal Declaration of Human Rights. Article 19 of that Declaration contains the key phrase: "Everyone has the right ... to seek, receive, and impart information." The current receive-impart imbalance in information indicates that the ideal has not been achieved for everyone, even though the belief grows that it ought to be, and that the communication resources ought to be developed to make balance possible.

In a now classic paper, Jean d'Arcy (1969) predicted:

> The time will come when the Universal Declaration of Human Rights will have to encompass a more extensive right than man's right to information, first laid down [in 1948] in Article 19. This is the right of man to communicate.

Several years later, Lakshmana Rao (1975) asked:

> What has happened since 1948 that has brought about almost a total turnaround in our approach to the grandiose intentions in the field of flow in information? What is it that has gradually but perhaps inescapably led us to question all over again premises upon which the whole edifice has been built? What is it that the same UN agency which had successfully established agreements to facilitate the flow of information around the world, today finds it necessary to go through the whole exercise again and initiate studies to look into more or less the same question all over again under a different phrase: 'The Right to Communicate'?

Rao's question has been posed elsewhere as well.

The right to communicate phrase serves as the name for the current human rights effort in the field of communication. At a number of recent international conferences, that right has been the subject of intense discussion.

Tentatively, the concept can be organized into four levels:

- Universal Right to Communicate. The broad, long-range perspective for dialogue on the fundamental moral, ethical, and value questions in communication Also, serves as a framework for comparative analysis of specific communication rights.

- Specific Communication Rights. Includes a variety of rights with diverse histories such as a right to inform, a right to be informed, a right to listen, a right to speak, a right to privacy, etc. At present, the preliminary list of communication rights has some 50 items which can probably be consolidated to a dozen or less.
- Communication Issues. The value, moral, and ethical concerns in the right to communicate domain are often under discussion in one community or another. Such discussion often centers on two or more rights such as a right to inform and a right to be informed, or on a right to be informed and a right to privacy.
- Communication Environment. The value concerns of importance in a community may be discussed informally at a "pre-issue" level and may persist as part of a discontent that from time to time gets shaped into a communication issue.

Some work is underway at each of these levels in various parts of the world (Unesco, 1976). Almost the entire body of work on this concept has been undertaken since 1970.

The right to communicate concept begins to provide a framework and a means for clarifying values, especially in multicultural and multinational conferences. However, it also stands in a fundamental relationship to the concepts of resources and needs.

Some Related Observations

The movement, as I see it, is toward a shared paradigm, one that will legitimatize and normalize a broad range of scholarly and practical concerns. But the paradigm does not appear at this time to be in a stable form. For instance, it is not yet clear how the concept of "participation" will be developed. It could be relegated to part of the title, that is, the "participatory paradigm," but the concept seems too dynamic for a mere titular role. More likely, the concept will have implications for the basic structures of communication in society. Most important, the new paradigm seems to be developing rapidly, and transforming into a perspective inclusive and appropriate enough to be shared by a critical number of the professionals in the field.

COMMUNICATION: THE VISIBLE REVOLUTION

The term revolution is so often applied to cosmetic changes in communication that it becomes easy to overlook the fundamental and non-cumulative changes that do occur from time to time. At least four large, irreversible, wide scale communication revolutions in human communication history require acknowledgment.

Probably the first communication revolution occurred some 500,000 years ago when *interpersonal communication* became possible. Little is known in an exact way about its origins. In that almost all children everywhere in the world are skilled interpersonal communicators by age five in their home communities and local cultures, this revolution appears to be universal, or very nearly so.

The second revolution began about 5,000 years ago as writing and reading became possible—in a word, *literacy.* For a long period, literacy was the guarded province of a professional elite much as television program production is today, and the de-professionalization of literacy has been a slow process. Strangely enough, literacy skills are still learned only "at school," at a considerable cost, if they are learned at all. The literacy revolution is far from being universal and may never become so unless it becomes better fitted to human capabilities. Of the 4,000,000,000 persons on the planet, about half are over 17, and about half of those, or some 1,000,000,000 can write and read. Perhaps icons will help.

A third revolution gained momentum half a century ago—perhaps *mobility* is the best name for it—and it began to reach certain limits around 1970 as world communication networks began to function. About half a century separates the beginnings of broadcast radio and the SITE (Satellite Instructional Television Experiment) project in India, or local telephone service and International Direct Distance Dialing on the telecommunication side, or local scheduled train service and worldwide air travel on the transportation "communication" side. This revolution though widespread remains incomplete and the skills and technologies on which it so heavily depends are unequally distributed across the planet just as are the skills and tools and products of literacy.

At this time, the fourth revolution seems more subtle in

its dimensions than the earlier ones. There is still no widely used name for this post-1970 non-cumulative change even though I prefer the term Robert Theobald uses: *communication era* (Theobald and Scott, 1972). Like the revolution in interpersonal communication, the roots of the present revolution remain entwined in interaction and in the relationships between communication and cutlure in the small, local community. Like the literacy revolution, there is an element of informational interdependence linked to formal skills. Like the mobility revolution, the big, new technologies are prominent.

Together, culture, interdependence, and technology constitute the core of the current revolution, one where participation and privacy, interdependence-and-sanctuary, big-technology-and-small-technology, and other tensional pairs push and pull the structure of communication into novel and not fully anticipated configurations.

The outcome of the present revolution is difficult to forecast because of concurrent change on two levels. The paradigm shift is at a deep level and seems likely to affect notions of the appropriate role for communication in society as well as the study and practice of communication. The communication level is being influenced by developments in culture-interdependence-technology. And, of course, there appear to be multiple interactions.

One useful strategy amidst these uncertainties is to identify a number of general problem areas and, then, within these problem areas, to seek out and work on what hold promise of being strategic sub-problems. Five general problem areas that seem likely to be of enduring interest in the two-level post-1970 revolution are set forth below.

- Communication Resources in Relation to Needs.
  As it becomes possible to plan communication resource development, it also becomes possible to shape resource development in terms of human communication needs. However, clarification of communication needs is still at a very preliminary stage.
- Information Flow in Society.
  The current concern with information imbalance point to a small segment of a very large problem area on the distribution of available information

across society. Specific aspects of the general problem exist in the reporting of world news, availability of scientific information, etc.

- Communication Networking in the Communication Environment.

  A substantial body of knowledge and experience exists in the technical area in telecommunication and transportation networks. Equally, there is a general body of work on social networks and informal communication networks.

- Communication Skill Development.

  Educational institutions use knowledge developed in the past for instructional purposes in preparing students for the present. Given the rapid rate of change in the communication field, it now becomes important to use knowledge gained in the present to prepare for anticipated futures. Instruction must become anticipatory to a much greater extent than it has been in the past.

- Communication in the Public Interest.

  While market, government, and military interests are often aggregated and effectively organized, the "public interest" in communication usually is not. Clarification of communication public interest questions, particularly in relation to leader-follower relationships and the design of alternative futures, is of great importance.

At the early stages of the current revolution, comprehensive approaches to a number of problem areas will be required. Fortunately, there are two new "problem oriented" approaches.

TWO NEW SCIENCES: COMMUNICATION POLICY AND COMMUNICATION PLANNING

The preceding sections provide the foundation required for the emergence of two new communication sciences: communication policy science and communication planning science. While these two sciences are related, their histories, processes, and practices are sufficiently different to warrant being treated as separate sciences.

In the first section of this paper, some of the conditions surrounding a paradigm shift were sketched out. The second section discussed the nature of paradigms along with the three concepts of resources, needs, and rights which are of central importance. A review of communication revolutions followed and concluded with an identification of five broad problem areas: resources in relation to needs; information flow in society; communication networking; skill development; and, communication in the public interest.

A review of the literature on the sciences of policy and of planning reveal both to be "problem-oriented," that is to begin with "real" rather than "theoretical" problems. In both cases a three part organization is evident: general approaches, specific science, and studies. Hence, the discussion of the sciences follows that general pattern.

Communication Policy Science

The *policy sciences approach* has been set forth by Harold Lasswell in two key papers and elaborated by a number of other writers. In 1951, Lasswell stated:

> A policy orientation has been developing that cuts across existing specializations. The orientation is two fold. In part it is directed toward the policy process, and in part to the intelligence needs of policy. The first task which is the development of a science of policy forming and execution uses the methods of social and psychological inquiry. The second task, which is the improving of concrete content of the information and the interpretation available to policy-makers, typically goes outside the boundaries of social science and psychology (Lasswell, in Lerner and Lasswell, 1951, p. 3).

As recently as late 1973, a conference paper carried the title "The Rise of Communication Policy Research" (Pool, 1974). Even though ITU (International Telecommunication Union) has been engaged in policy-making for more than a century, the post-1970 activity in this area has been out of the ordinary, unprecedented. The reasons for its "rise" are multiple:

> The ways in which communication is used, the networks through which it flows, the structures of the media system, the regulatory framework for the system, and the decisions of people who operate it, are all the outcome of communication policies. Policies

are the principles, rules and guidelines on which the system is
built and may be specifically formulated or remain largely
implicit (Sommerlad, 1975, p. 7).

Communication policy is fast becoming an important "policy science."

From the perspective of the paradigm, a major task of communication policy is to "arrange the conditions" so that communication resources can be developed to serve human communication needs and to do so in a way that is in harmony with the cultural values inherent in the right to communicate. Such a task may be undertaken at global, national, and local levels.

The "rise" of communication policy science is evident in a number of contexts. For example, the theme for the 1975 IBI Conference was: *The Global Context of the Formation of Domestic Communication Policies* (IBI, 1975). Unesco has published in recent months two extensive papers on communication policy (Lee, 1976). Research programs are underway at RAND, MIT, EWCI, and elsewhere.

Some of the writing in communication policy science suggests that the right to communicate may become a policy issues (Richstad, 1977).

Communication Planning Science

While the parallel between the unfolding of policy sciences and planning sciences is quite strong, there are some important differences. For instance, no one seems to have outlined the planning sciences approach as Lasswell did for the policy sciences. Thus, the roots of the planning sciences appear quite diffuse.

While aspects of planning can probably be traced to antiquity, the modern "rethinking" of planning activity and its subsequent movement from art to science has largely come about in the last decade. One student states that planning science is:

The process by which a scientific and technical knowledge is
joined to organized *action*. Planning forms a critical sub-
process of *societal guidance* (Friedman, 1973, p. 19).

Again, as in the case of communication policy science, the

growth of a body of communication planning science is largely a post-1970 phenomena.

From the perspective of the paradigm, a major task of communication planning science will be to plan the communication resources required to serve human communication needs with due attention to the values of a right to communicate.

Communication planning science lacks cohesion at this time. Some parts of the science exist as telecommunication planning, other parts as community planning, etc. Major work is underway or scheduled at Unesco and EWCI, for example, and that work can be expected to help pull the parts of a planning science into a coherent whole.

IN SUMMARY

The purpose of this paper has been to set forth—in a tentative and preliminary way—a broad outline of some of the theoretic issues under discussion at a number of international communication conferences.

Some Unique Things

A two-level communication revolution seems to be a development that warrants being called unique. One level embodies an alternate paradigm for the field and includes the key concepts of resources, needs, and rights. From this perspective, we can see that:

- communication as a resource can become abundant if important elements do indeed increase through use, low cost elements can be traded on a substantial scale for high cost ones, communication skill building can become anticipatory, and if
- communication needs become known with sufficient precision to permit the "tuning" of communication resource development to those needs, and if need satisfaction does indeed improve the quality of life and enhance the humanness of being in local and world communities, and if
- the right to communicate does provide a framework

for the examination of cultural values and long-range goals and if

these three concepts (and perhaps others) fit together into an alternate and new paradigm for the field of communication of which the statement below is a first verbal approximation:

"Humankind has the Right to the communication Resources required to serve communication Needs."

And if that paradigm or, more likely, improvements of it, attracts adherents who are also interested in the second level new sciences of communication policy and communication planning (and resource management and perhaps others), and if the sciences in contact with the paradigm generate theories, methodologies, and a body of research, and if out of this knowledge base new applications, practices, and careers follow, and if this reorganization of the field of communication enables the solving of important old problems such as the one called "information imbalance" and the formulation of important new possibilities such as the conditions that can lead to resource abundance or a fair world policy, then . . .

Advanced Study

Then, if and as the paradigm becomes the one *shared* by a considerable percentage of the active professionals in the field, the focus of the field will shift, and the new paradigm will in time become the normal one.

Given the early stage of the paradigm and of the new sciences, the goals for a program of advanced study in this area would have to be formulated with care, as would the goals for any program in any field undergoing a major change. Indeed, an important concern is the anticipated rate of change in the future and the nature of the mechanisms to be built into a program to accommodate those changes. One important task would be the synthesis and reorganization of information. Equally, such a program would emphasize problem-oriented or action research, fieldwork, and internships.

Assuming such a program of advanced study is university based, the role of the university will need to be seen not as the transmitting agent for a body of well-tested knowledge from the past, but rather as an organizing and activating agent for a rapidly growing body of knowledge within a field of endeavor that itself will be changing substantially within the career life of those professionals involved in it.

Professional Careers

Then, career preparation would require grounding in the knowledge base consolidated within the framework of the new paradigm and a concentration on one of the new sciences both as a general science and as a communication science. Estimates of the number of career professionals needed have not yet been made, but given the growing awareness of the role of communication in society, it seems reasonable to expect a substantial number of new careers outside the university context as policy-makers and planners. However, such professionals should expect to an unusual degree to participate in the identification of the work to be done.

Prospective

Then, the way in which the new sciences connect to the knowledge base embodied in the paradigm, draw from it, contribute to it will be important. Of equal importance will be the linkages that develop between the two sciences and new theories of communication, research methodology, and research in the field.

Both communication policy and communication planning appear to have grown out of problems under discussion in international conferences. Lasswell has noted that quite a number of the new policy sciences appear to have grown up independently of the knowledge base provided by the policy sciences approach. A similar observation could be made about communication planning.

Thus, "getting the communication act together" appears to require a better information flow between the paradigm and policy and planning sciences levels, and a richer integration of current knowledge from the broad policy and planning approaches into specific communication policy and communication planning research and studies. Fortunately, a good bit of the basic work has been done, as an examination of recent reports from international communication conferences will reveal, especially those from the Communication Sector at Unesco.

Works Cited

ANDRE-CLEMENT, P. and SCHWARTZ, N. 1974. "The Concept of Needs: A Survey of Illusions," *Futures,* 6:16-25.

BYSTROM, J. 1974. "The Application of International Interactive Service Support Communications." Paper presented to the Royal Society of London.

CHILDERS, T. 1975. *The Information Poor in America.* New Jersey: Scarecrow Press.
CLEVELAND, H. in J. McHale and M.C. McHale. 1975. *Human Requirements, Supply Levels and Outer Bounds.* Princeton: Aspen Program in International Affairs.

d'Arcy, J. 1969. "Direct Broadcast Satellites and the Right to Communicate," *EBU Review,* 118, 14-18. Reprinted in L.S. Harms, J. Richstad, and K.A. Kie (eds.) 1977. *Right to Communicate: Collected Papers.* Honolulu: Social Sciences and Linguistics Institute.
DERVIN, B. In press. "Strategies for Dealing with the Information Needs of Urban Residents: Information or Communication," *Journal of Broadcasting.*

FRIEDMAN, J. 1973. *Retracking America: A Theory of Transactive Planning.* Garden City: Doubleday.

THE GLOBAL CONTEXT FOR THE FORMULATION OF DOMESTIC COMMU-NICATION POLICY. 1975. London: International Broadcast Institute.

Information Canada. 1971. *Instant World.* Ottawa: Information Canada.
INTERMEDIA. 1975. 3, 1.
IRADES. 1974. *Human Futures: Needs, Technologies, Societies.* London: IPC Science and Technology Press.

KATZ, E. *et al.* 1973. "On the Use of Mass Media for Important Things," *American Sociological Review,* 38, 164-181.
KOLLEN, J. 1974. "New Perspectives on the Travel/Communication Tradeoff," *Bell Canada,* 39.
KUHN, T.S. 1970. *The Structure of Scientific Revolutions.* Chicago: University of Chicago Press.

LASSWELL, H. 1972. "Futures of World Communication," EWCI paper 4. Honolulu: East-West Communication Institute, 24.
_____ "The Policy Orientation," 1951, in D. Lerner and H. Lasswell (eds.) *The Policy Sciences*, Stanford: Stanford University Press, 3-15. H. Lasswell. 1970. "The Emerging Conception of Policy Sciences," *Policy Sciences*, 1:3-14.
LEE, J.A.R. 1976. *Toward Realistic Communication Policies: Recent Trends and Ideas Compiled and Analyzed.* Paris: Unesco Press.
LERNER, D. in J. RICHSTAD and L.S. HARMS, eds. 1973. *World Communication.* Honolulu: East-West Communication Institute.

MASLOW, A. 1970. *Motivation and Personality.* New York: Harper and Row.
McHALE, J. and McHALE, M.C. 1975. *Human Requirements, Supply Levels and Outer Bounds.* Princeton: Aspen Program in International Affairs.

POOL, I. 1974. "The Rise of Communication Policy Research," *Journal of Communication*, 24:2, 31-42.
POOL, I. and SCHRAMM, W., eds. 1973. *Handbook of Communication.* Chicago: Rand McNally.

RAO, Y.V.L. 1975. "Information Imbalance in Asia," *Media Asia*, 2, 78-81. Reprinted in L.S. HARMS, J. RICHSTAD, and K.A. KIE, eds. 1977. *Right to Communicate: Collected Papers.* Honolulu: Social Sciences and Linguistics Institute.
RICHSTAD, J. 1977. *International Communication Policy Perspectives.* Honolulu: East-West Communication Institute.

SOMMERLAD, L. 1975. *National Communication Systems: Some Policy Issues and Options.* Paris: Unesco Press.

THEOBALD, R. and SCOTT, J.M. 1972. *TEG's 1994.* Chicago: Swallow Press.

UNESCO. August 1976. "Report on Means of Enabling Active Participation in the Communication Process and Analysis of the Right to Communicate." Report 19C/93.
UNESCO. 1974. "The Training of Communication Planners." Unesco Regional Seminar, Kuala Lumpur, Malaysia.

WORLD COMMUNICATIONS. 1975. Paris: Unesco Press.

THE INFLUENCE OF INTERNATIONAL COMMUNICATION ON DEVELOPMENT

Ithiel de Sola Pool

One of the vexations of underdevelopment is that it is all of a piece. It would be distressing enough if the only problem in developing countries were that people were poor. But along with that, life is short, medical care is inadequate, most people are lacking in education, security is poor, governments are corrupt and inefficient, progressive political movements are not well organized, and technological competence and entrepreneurial motivation are scarce. All the problems come together. Progress cannot be made on one front at a time; it requires what Mao called a "great leap" and what Walter Rostow called a "takeoff" on all fronts at once.

It has not always been recognized that the evils of underdevelopment form such an interlocked package. In the eighteenth century, there was in Europe a romantic notion of the noble savage. He may have been poor and lacking in science and culture, but he was somehow purer, more upstanding, and more understanding than his civilized successors. That romantic illusion is fairly well dead today except in the form of an occasional self-justification by the less successful governments in poor lands boasting of some intangible merit as a way of diverting attention from stagnation. In fact, all the evidence supports the more common sense notion that where people are richer, they are happier; where they have more access to the world's culture and knowledge, they make more and faster progress in both wealth and welfare (Inkels, 1974; Lerner, 1958).

Honesty in facing those facts is important, yet one is reluctant to assert them. Pride is an important condition of progress. Bald honest assertion of how bad, corrupt, and incompetent things may be in a poor country slides over easily into self-destructive negativism. Myths and illusions do play a role in human progress. Max Weber analyzed how, at an earlier stage in European development, the confidence of the Calvinists that they were the elect contributed to their effectiveness as entrepreneurs. So too in the developing countries today, ideologies about cultural uniqueness and special national merits play a curious double role. Often, and to a large extent, they are reactionary myths that serve to obstruct progress, but also often they are part of an ethos of pride and self-confidence that serves in fact to promote effective action and therefore advances change and progress. Under some circumstances, national traditionalism may, in Marx's phrase, contain the seeds of its own destruction by fostering a vigorous drive for development and progress.

The situation, in short, is not one to make simplifiers happy. We can start right out by dismissing all the usual clichés about the protection of national cultures, and equally dismiss their contraries. To achieve what makes people happy and what they choose for themselves when they have a chance—not necessarily what their governments or ideologists tell them they ought to want—developing countries need a complex mixture of things. They need a positive feeling about the greatness of their culture and their past. They also need to have new ideas translated into styles that they are comfortable with; even in successfully modernized countries like Japan, the cultural envelope may remain very distinctive indeed. But, on the other hand, they need and want enormously rapid change; the change must be much more rapid than anything experienced by the countries that modernized in the eighteenth and nineteenth centuries. If it is not, they will never catch up. They need to imitate on a grand scale, for that is the way most cultural change takes place. Any country doomed to invent everything for itself would be stagnant indeed.*

American culture contains a few local inventions such as the telephone and jazz, though even those could be traced back

---

*The relevant literature on this point is the anthropological corpus on invention versus diffusion. It records the fact that culture is overwhelmingly a product of diffusion.

to European and African origins. But 90 or 95 percent of American cutlure is nothing but a structured adaption of things of foreign origin. In that respect the United States is not unique; as a new society it may have a larger proportion of recent adoptions than, say, the culture of France, but even France is a conglomeration of foreign things. The vines on which the wine grows originally came from California, the towers of Neuilly and Montparnasse were invented in Chicago, and the cars on the street had their prototypes in Detroit. About half the electorate vote for parties whose ideas came from the German Marx, or the Russian Lenin. Their religion came from the Middle East. The list could go on for pages since progress is largely imitation.

The imitation that every country engages in is selective. It copies the things that meet its needs. The selection applies to both material things and ideas. In addition to technology, developing countries want to assimilate scientific thinking, secularism (sometimes), and democracy. They integrate the ideas and objects that they adopt into structures of their own.

The choice of what to adopt and of how to adapt it is not necessarily that of the government. There is no more congruence in the developing countries between what people want and what their governments think they ought to want than there is in the developed countries; indeed, the congruence is less because, in general, the governments in the developing countries are less democratic and less competent than they are where education, wealth, and participation have advanced farther.

SOURCES OF INFORMATION FOR THE DEVELOPING COUNTRIES

The information that the developing countries need in order to progress comes in a multitude of ways. Students go abroad for education. Colonists and missionaries earlier, and technical assistance personnel and businessmen now, settle for years or even decades at a time and introduce new ideas and practices. Trading minorities such as Lebanese or Chinese move in and around, and so do refugees. Foreign mass media messages arrive in books, movies, international broadcasts, and wire service reports. These are rediffused by the domestic media. There are government information programs and educational efforts.   ′

Some of the communication is commercially motivated,

either to sell products or to sell the media themselves. Some of it is ideologically motivated, produced, and disseminated by political movements or religious groups. Some of it is human-istically motivated as with the educators and foundations. Some of it is generated and passed along for reasons of fun and recreation. All forms of diffusion are important, and all contain a mixture of what is useful and what is not.

Among the various kinds of information, one that we should pay particular attention to is technical information that professional persons look up in reference sources as they work at productive and scientific operations. The importance of such information and the size of the archives needed for such pur-poses is growing rapidly.

The developing countries of the world require large injections of information in the form of technology transfer if they are to have economic growth and development. However, the means for acquiring it are largely beyond their reach. Today a chasm separates the research facilities available in developed countries—the Library of Congress, the Weidner and New York Public Libraries, the British Museum, the Moscow State Library—from the extremely limited research facilities in developing coun-tries. There is no conceivable way in which newly developing nations can each create conventional libraries of that sort for themselves in less than half a century.

With the development of data-base publishing to cope with the flood of new information, the position of the develop-ing countries will worsen. They will not usually have access to such computerized information resources. Given their poverty, they cannot be expected to make much use of modern informa-tion retrieval systems or computer communication unless pres-ent rates for them fall by at least an order of magnitude.

Such a fall in the rate for long-haul computer telecom-munication is not out of the question. It seems likely that an international data communications network using packet-switch-ing technology could make access to data bases available from anywhere in the world at a communication cost of less than a nickel per 100 words. With such a network, the information gap would be rapidly narrowed. A researcher in a university or planning office in a developing country without adequate refer-ence sources of its own could retrieve a fact from whatever data base he or she wished anywhere in the world for little more than the cost of a domestic telephone call, something he or she could afford.

In short, as advanced countries increasingly transfer their reference materials from hard copy libraries to computerized retrieval systems, the developing countries will either fall further behind in information capacity, or will begin to catch up depending upon whether or not they are linked to these new information stores by telecommunications.

Thus it would seem clear that international telecommunications is of great importance to the developing world. It can bring deficient information facilities at a leap up to the best, or its lack can lead to slipping further and further behind. The modern world's technical and scientific culture is a global one. A country that cuts itself off from the flow of knowledge in that global enterprise will pay a very heavy price to do so.

Yet in the developing countries, and even more outside among "experts" on them, one hears objections raised to a free flow of international telecommunications, though the developing countries are the ones that would gain from it. Three objections are often raised. First, it is objected that high technology is not appropriate to developing countries; they must learn to walk before they learn to run. Second, it is sometimes objected that the free flow of telecommunications will give foreigners, particularly multinational corporations, the opportunity to evade the sovereignty of their hosts by operating on data in sanctuaries abroad. Third, international communications raise fear of cultural intrusion and dependency.

In the remainder of this paper we shall deal with those issues.

HIGH TECHNOLOGY IN THE DEVELOPING LANDS

Often, it is unthinkingly assumed that the path of development of the developing nations must be the same as that followed by the now developed ones, but with a lag of some decades. That is only one possible path and in some respects an unlikely one. Those who come second on any course of development are likely to skip certain stages that the pioneers had to go through, for the successors can anticipate where the path is going and skip over stages. In Asia and Latin America, where

modernization came at an earlier date than in Africa, the establishment of newspapers played a major role in the instigation of
change and in the growth of national political movements.
Then in the 1950s and 1960s radio became the dominant
medium of mass communication there. Africa, where the hold
of colonialism broke only in the 1950s and 1960s never experienced the growth of an important press; it went straight to a
radio-based communication system. Thus even the process of
straight imitation does not lead to a duplication of earlier
sequences in development by those who come later.

Furthermore, it would be a mistake for poor countries
to simply imitate the media institutions and practices of the
wealthier ones. In the United States and Europe, television was
introduced as a household good; in India, it is properly being
introduced as a village facility. In the West, broadcasting is
done almost entirely over the air; in China, it is done mostly via
wired loudspeakers. Given the fact that wired loudspeakers do
not incur the monthly cost for batteries, a wired system is an
appropriate choice. The communications needs of the developing countries are different from those of the developed ones,
and will continue to differ in the future.

A four-media communication system seems likely to be
appropriate and therefore to develop in poor countries with
large terrain and scattered villages. The four media that seem
most important are radio, satellite television, satellite telephone,
and computer store and forward message delivery.

The use of radio is familiar by now. The transistor
receiver is found everywhere. It is the means by which news
spreads, by which the government can reach the people, by
which mass education and nation-building can be done. Television adds something to the effectiveness of educational broadcasting and to the quality of village life. However, it is too
expensive to be owned by many individuals. Its appropriate use
is as a community facility. Where territories are small and
densely populated, terrestrial transmission to the village set is
economic, but where the territory is large and dispersed, the
appropriate means of dissemination is that pioneered by the
Canadians with their programs to the Arctic, and by the Indians
in the SITE program: high-powered satellite to low-cost ground
stations. Telephony to remote locations can be delivered in the
same way. Satellites permit the national dissemination of village

phones without waiting for the spread of the terrestrial cable or microwave network.

Finally, developing countries can benefit greatly by attaching to their telephone systems a large number of text terminals with store and forward switches. Traffic carried on such a modern kind of teletype system has many advantages for developing countries. For one thing, telephone service is likely to be very bad in them, with gross insufficiency of circuits; a store and forward system levels the load, holding traffic until circuits are available at off hours. Also many more messages can travel in a given bandwidth as data than as voice. A single satellite voice circuit can probably handle all the national text traffic for a typical developing country (Pool and Corte, 1976).

An important aspect of all four of those media is that they are not confined by the boundaries of nations. Radio was the first medium to be indifferent to national boundaries. In virtually every country, broadcasts in the prevalent languages come not only from within the nation, but also pouring across the border. Satellite distribution systems that use low-cost ground stations are international in slightly different ways. The footprint of a satellite beam is typically much larger than most countries and always has boundaries that do not correspond to those of nations. Satellites, therefore, invariably have the capability of being used for international communication. More important, they are very economical for the purpose. The cost of satellite transmissions, within a single beam, are virtually identical in cost regardless of the distance covered. With a transmission 22,300 miles up and 22,300 miles down, it makes no difference whether the points linked are 500 or 5,000 miles apart. Thus international communication can be as cheap as domestic communication. Finally, the cost and the capacity of a satellite are beyond the resources and needs of most developing countries; satellites must be shared. Three television channels and 800 long distance telephone channels (including one for text transmission) might use one-third of the capacity of a typical satellite. At minimum, regional cooperation, if not global, is called for.

The picture that we have just outlined of appropriate future communication systems in developing countries may seem unrealistic to many readers. It is often assumed that if a developing country cannot make its ordinary telephone system work satisfactorily, then it certainly cannot use sophisticated new technology such as computer networks or satellites. That is a fallacious conclusion. One can imagine someone saying, just before the transistor radio revolution hit the poorer countries, that if those countries could not maintain a conventional press or wide dissemination of ordinary tube radios, how would they handle the new advanced technology of the transistor. As that example makes clear, while there are some advances in technology that make operation and maintenance harder, some make them easier. One has to examine the particularities of any technology before one can assess its appropriateness to the developing countries.

Satellites are particularly appropriate to meeting the needs of large, sparsely settled developing countries. The gradual building up of a landline network that reaches everywhere is a slow and expensive process. A satellite immediately radiates to any point in the footprint; wherever population is present one can place a ground station and immediately receive.

Computer communication using store and forward message switching is also a technology well suited to the need of the developing countries. It bypasses, rather than being dependent on, the ordinary phone system. With the ordinary voice telephone call, both parties have to be on the spot at the same time, which can be very frustrating if it takes a couple of hours to complete the circuit. With a store and forward system, as we have already noted, the message sits in the computer until the circuit is available. Furthermore, whatever sophisticated data processing operations are required by the information system itself or by users of it can be done by remote access to locations where the prerequisites in hardware and skilled maintenance staff exist.

The main problem at the grass roots is the servicing of terminals. Where hard copy printout is not required, rather reliable and easily maintained electronic display terminals without moving parts can be produced for use in isolated locations. Where hard copy printout is required, simple teletype terminals will be the order of the day for some time to come; those will convey orders to more sophisticated equipment located where it can be serviced. All that local lines must provide is the capability of carrying low grade code such as those currently delivering telex or telegrams. That kind of computer communication is well within the state of the art for the developing countries.

A combination of satellite linkage of isolated locations and computer-switched message traffic would have great benefits for use by governments, businesses, technical assistance agents, and agricultural and developmental programs in developing lands. Consider how useful it would be if a field agent in a technical assistance program could, whenever he or she wishes, consult an adviser in the capital or at a research center abroad at a cost of a few pennies and with either on-line responses or an answer a few hours later. Consider the advantage to some-one in a district town in Asia repairing a European-made machine if he or she could "talk" back and forth on a teletype, reporting the troubles, trying what he/she was told to try, and reporting back immediately on what happened. Consider the benefit to a nurse in a remote clinic if she could type in symptoms while the patient waited and get advice on treatment. These interactions serve in the same way that telephone does in the United States where it is cheap and works well. Developing countries cannot hope to have that kind of telephone service at prices they can afford within the next couple of decades, but low bandwidth text and data communication can make the same kind of interaction available at minimal costs on both a national and international basis. That will come about, however, only if a deliberate effort is made to develop this advanced technology for the specific needs of poor countries, and not by waiting to follow the course taken by the advanced countries.

SOVEREIGNTY, MULTINATIONALS, AND DATA SANCTUARIES

A second fear is that international communication networks can defeat the sovereign policies of weak nations by permitting data sanctuaries abroad. Clearly, there are such things as sanctuaries; people do move activities of a controversial nature to where they are not threatened. People go from countries where they could be endangered to countries where they are safe. Political exiles from dictatorships publish their journals in democracies where they are tolerated. Women go to have abortions where it is legal. Rich people put their money in countries where it is not taxed or in Swiss bank accounts where it is not reported. One can conceive of motives for keeping data in one country rather than another. Indeed, there is a recent example—

the data tape from an interview study of drug abuse in the United States was shipped to Canada for storage so that it could not be subpoenaed by U.S. law enforcement authorities.

But does any of this represent a serious threat to national sovereignty? Few of us would want a world where people could not escape the more erratic whims and impositions of governments by moving to another jurisdiction. This could only be viewed as a problem if the mobility were on such a scale that it threatened the very ability of a government to govern.

The bugaboo most often raised is that large multinational corporations might keep data about a country's market or on operations in it, in a different country to prevent the government of the first country from effectively regulating the company. It would be naive not to surmise that occasionally a company may spirit out an embarrassing piece of paper to another jurisdiction, just as it may sometimes burn one. But the notion that data can systematically be denied to the host country by a multinational to the point where the sovereignty of the host is threatened would seem quite topsy-turvy. A multinational does business in a host country by the permission and at the sufferance of the host. Nothing stops any government from laying down any levy it wants to on data that must be reported, nor is it stopped from requiring whatever documentation of the sources of the data that it wants. The multinational has little choice but to comply if it wishes to stay and do business. It makes little difference in which jurisdiction the data is located; it must be produced. The presence of international computer communication would help rather than hinder the government in compelling the production of data that it wants. Procrastination or obfuscation by a company would become harder if instantaneous addressing of enquiries to any office in the world were available, and replies could be sent with equal expedition.*

---

*Indeed, the only kind of data sanctuary that I can think of which might present real problems to any firmly resolved government is a sanctuary against the type of privacy laws that many governments are now adopting. Restricting the kind of credit rating information a credit bureau might keep could result in its escape to another jurisdiction where it could keep the data it wanted. In the instances we cited earlier, the government required of some private organization that wished to continue to function in the country that it present certain data that it had. That kind of requirement a government can probably enfore. In the instance of privacy legislation the government is saying to the private organization you may not keep certain information, even stored elsewhere where it is legal. That is a harder requirement to enforce. But that limitation on the effectiveness of government regulation is hardly a threat to national sovereignty and in any case not a special problem for the developing countries.

Another bugaboo occasionally cited is the misuse of earth resource data. In recent UN debates the specter has been raised that a few countries have the capability of observing by satellite the resources of other lands and then using that information to bid for development concessions or in bargaining on the world food market. While the advantages to be won would usually fall far short of destroying sovereignty, there are clear possibilities of taking advantage of such knowledge. To avoid such abuses, the United States adopted a policy of total public access to all ERTS (Earth Resources Technology Satellite) data. Under present circumstances, then, the problem is not that some special interest may obtain data that others cannot have; it is that while the data may be available to all, poor countries may lack the communications and information processing facilities to acquire and make use of all the data that they have the right to. Improved international data networks can help solve that problem (Corte and Warren, 1976).

It is ironic that while the governments of developing countries often worry about possible injury to them arising from the free flow of communication, the main barrier to free international flow that exists today tends to be one that protects the developed countries and hurts the developing ones. Copyright is that barrier. Whatever its merits in encouraging authorship and publication, one effect of copyright is to limit the access developing countries have to important bodies of information. Since virtually all copyrighted imports by developing countries come from developed ones, copyright payments represent a levy from the poor countries to the rich ones. Indeed, it is a testimony to the power of basic notions of fairness and law that so many developing countries have adhered to the international copyright convention. It is not in their self-interest to do so. They would benefit by rejecting that barrier to the free flow of information.

CULTURAL AUTONOMY

A third concern of developing countries about international communication is that the one-sided flow of information from the most advanced countries into the less advanced ones will undermine the cultural values of the latter. Cultural imperialism, it is asserted, will impose an alien commercial culture on the whole world.

This concern applies particularly to the mass media. The creation of mass media was one of the great sociotechnical inventions of the past two centuries. By delivering identical messages to hundreds of thousands or even to millions of people, it became possible to provide extraordinarily attractive material at pennies per exposure. Slick magazines with colored pictures, thick newspapers with detailed up-to-the-minute news and features from all over the world, top musical performances on radio, and exciting drama in movies and on television gave the person on the street daily exposure to a level of entertainment available in the past only to a privileged elite, and even for them only at occasional events. I am not evaluating the cultural level of the mass media, only their attractiveness to their audience.

The attraction of soap operas, Westerns, pop groups, and other diversions that the mass media have to offer is not limited to any one culture. These products have a universal human appeal, so a world trade in them has developed. The countries that had the lead in producing pop culture, most notably the United States, became exporters of such culture to the world. While that lead is temporary and fragile, as witness the multinationalization of the movie industry and the growth of slick magazines in Europe, still it lasts long enough to cause intense distress to those who see in foreign material a threat to indigenous cultures that they prize. The normative issue of what to do about cultural intrusion by foreign mass media material is a thorny one. It pits traditional cultural values squarely against the liberal principle of freedom of information.

The problem of cultural intrusion that has been bothersome in relation to the mass media arises also, put to a lesser degree, for the new technologies of point-to-point and computer telecommunications. There is some concern about international data flows. That concern is a carry over from concern about cultural intrusion by foreign mass media. The situation for point-to-point communication is, however, fundamentally different. A mass media item comes in canned fixed form, produced in one country and then often distributed elsewhere without reference to the cultural values or local needs of the receiver.

A data retrieval or person-to-person message is, however, an interactive, two-way process. In a telephone conversation, both parties want it; both provide input; each adapts to the other. It is cultural interaction, not cultural imperialism.

Interactive computer enquiries are somewhat like phone calls in that respect. Inputs to information bases are considerably more symmetrical than are mass media flows. Research units, governments, and observers from all over contribute to the world's knowledge. Yet there remains substantial imbalance in the location of input. Output, however, is controlled by the enquirer. An information retrieval request is initiated by the receiver; he or she asks for the information that he/she needs, not what some broadcaster chooses to tell him or her.

Yet even if imbalances in the flow of communication between the developed and developing world are smaller in the case of point-to-point communication than they are in the case of the mass media, still they exist. The question of importance is whether that is a self-perpetuating situation or a self-correcting one. The evidence is quite strong that it is not a self-perpetuating situation.

First, let us look at some analogous historical situations. Karl Deutsch has analyzed international and domestic mail flows, scientific journals, and scientific citations (Deutsch, 1956). What he found surprised him. He found that the proportion of foreign material declined with the maturation of the system. Originally, development would take place in one or a few locations. In the rest of the world in consequence there would be much interaction with those centers. Gradually, however, local businesses, or research centers, or journals were founded and people interacted more with others who were conveniently close to them. Contrary to the standard cliché about the world growing smaller, international interaction as a proportion of all interaction declined with time in maturing fields. Every one of us can give apparent counter-examples from our own experience of rapid growth of international contacts, but ask yourself if they are not in innovative stages of a process.

There are, however, also other counter-examples—cases where foreign dependence acquires a self-perpetuating character. That tends to be the case in highly capitalized activities, not in the kind of intellectual activity that Deutsch was talking about. If an oil field is developed in country A, its customers in other countries become significantly dependent on it. If superpower B sells jet fighters to a developing country, the latter becomes significantly dependent on B for training and parts. If a foreign investor opens an industrial plant in country C, there will be a continuing relationship over many years to follow.

In short, one must distinguish the developmental patterns that follow on different kinds of international relationships. Examples of quite different international patterns are offered by agriculture, extractive investments, industry, and intellectual activities. Foreign investments in agriculture whether by settlers or by creation of a plantation system have profound social effects usually ending up in more or less violent intergroup conflicts because so many thousands or millions of ordinary people are directly affected in their whole way of life. Investments in extractive industries are usually seen by the local people as particularly exploitative because few local facilities are built up, and so the end of the process is often expropriation or nationalization. Investment in heavy manufacturing has quite different effects. It is much more favorable to development, but also has the partially self-perpetuating character noted above. The intrusion of service and intellectual activities has a quite different effect because they are labor intensive and the initial foreign practitioners have no way of keeping their monopoly.

The development of movies illustrates the point. Once upon a time in the 1920s and 1930s, Hollywood had a franchise on the world cinema market. Hollywood pictures were made for the American audience, but they had a universal human appeal. As a result local entrepreneurs set up movie houses everywhere—luxurious palaces in some rich cities or benches in a shed in some developing villages. The films were mostly made in Hollywood, but that did not last long. In India, in Japan, in Turkey, in Mexico, local actors discovered that they could make movies too. They were not paid like the Hollywood stars or union cameramen. Production, being labor intensive, turned out to be cheap, if not slick. What is more, the local audience liked the local product; it was better attuned to their taste. So the original inflow of Hollywood films, by leading to the opening of movie houses, laid the foundations for a local industry. Far from Hollywood's activities being self-perpetuating, they turned out to be self-eroding. Today most American movie makers find that they must go into coproductions with foreign makers if they are to succeed at all.

To a large extent, that is the pattern that one can expect from international communication. If technicians in a developing country are trained to operate on a modern computer from a remote terminal, gradually, but fairly rapidly, programmers will be trained and analysts will learn to use the computer. Soon they will be doing their own input and developing their own data bases. In short, the main barrier to entering the game is trained humans and access to a machine. Remote access provides both at an early stage. Once the skilled personnel exists, minis and then larger computers will soon follow. International telecomputing accelerates, not slows down, the development of computing in the developing countries.

The same considerations apply to print media. The spread of literature from abroad is the preconditionsfor the development of a literate, sophisticated set of literati and a reading public. Once that comes into existence, domestically produced journals begin to appear and quickly become more interesting and successful among the local audience than anything brought in from abroad.

The same conclusions hold for broadcasting too. Domestic radio starts very quickly because voice transmission does not require either sophisticated equipment or very highly trained personnel. Television has a longer period of gestation, since television production is expensive and difficult. No small country, whether industrialized or pre-industrialized, can produce enough video material to keep the channels filled 16 hours a day, 365 days a year with programming of reasonable quality. That is a strain on the creative and productive resources of even a large and rich country. Thus a country going into television broadcasting needs, if it is to succeed, some low-cost source of secondhand programs. These permit it to fill the airwaves cheaply while its own creative organizations struggle to begin to stockpile some backlog of indigenous program materials. Thus every new television system falls back on cheap foreign materials for a while.

Gradually, as the system matures, the proportion of such imports will go down. How far down they go and how fast depends upon the size and wealth of the country and the method of funding of the television system. Hopefully, imports will not decline to the point where television ceases to reflect the world's cosmopolitan culture. American television would be a lot worse than it is without the occasional imports from the BBC or the occasional European movie classic. In general, the quality of a cultural medium can remain high only by openness to using the best material from wherever it comes. Nonetheless, there will always be a bias, both among the audience and among the producers, in favor of those things that are indigenous. Television can be counted on to use as much of that material as there is available. The problem is only how to foster the creative industry that makes such material available. Certainly one of the conditions for that is that there be a lively television system in operation. Use of foreign materials is therefore more likely to end up being a help than a hindrance to the growth of the indigenous industry.

SOME CONCLUSIONS

For a telecommunications system to serve the developing countries effectively as a bearer of technical knowledge, it must have certain characteristics. It must be cheap. It must also be reliable, relatively rugged, and not require highly sophisticated maintenance and operating personnel. It must operate even in the absence of an elaborate infrastructure of stable electric current, national microwave or cable networks, and smoothly functioning telephone service. Finally, it must link a developing country at its will to any possible sources of data, not just to ones in a favored metropole on which it is dependent.

These are not insoluble requirements. The first step was taken when widely dispersed cheap transistor radios gave rural populations the opportunity to hear not only their national voice, but also world news and information from abroad. The second step, now under way, is the linking of all population centers for both television and point-to-point traffic by means of high-powered satellites with low-cost ground stations. The third step, now feasible but not yet being undertaken, is the dissemination of computer terminals for text and data to all locations to provide the functional equivalent of telephone communication at a much lower price and on a global basis. This last step also integrates developing areas into the most advanced information systems in the world.

That combination of technologies meets the requirements of ruggedness, maintainability, and low cost. It also meets the political requirement of creating worldwide communication at the will of the user. Unlike cable and telephone networks and airline routes that fan out from the old colonial metropole to its former colonies and dependencies, the radio and satellite systems described above allow any-point to any-point communication, and free the user to seek advice or information wherever he or she wishes. Developing countries should insist on the freest possible access by telecommunications to the best available information resources from anywhere in the world. It is in their interest to oppose security restrictions, and commercial restrictions on the transfer of technical information all check the progress of developing countries. Rapid transfer of technology is facilitated by the maximum possible flow of travel, messages, literature, and on-line interaction across the world's borders.

Dependence occurs whenever advanced countries possess know-how and techniques that developing countries are not able to acquire for themselves at will. Independence is therefore promoted by unrestricted free flow of information between countries so that the developing country can acquire for itself whatever intellectual and cultural products it desires at the lowest possible price. The freer the flow of information, the wider the developing country's range of choice and the sooner it can acquire for itself the ability to produce the same sort of information or programming at home.

Protectionism in the intellectual and cultural field is, therefore, even more damaging to the country that practices it than it is in the field of material trade. In both fields a country pays a significant price for not doing those things in which it has a comparative advantage, but rather trying to do things at which it is inefficient. In physical trade, however, there may be certain self-perpetuating aspects to relying on imports. In things of the mind, however, the process of using a medium is also the process of learning to be its master. Protectionism in trade may facilitate learning to carry on an industry oneself; protectionism in regard to things of the mind, however, inhibits learning.

The conclusions being presented here are rarely accepted by governments, including the governments of developing countries. It should be no surprise that governments have an inherent bias toward controls, restrictions, and provincialism. The business of government, after all, is to govern; it is a rare government that is able to recognize when it is hurting its own people by its regulatory actions. It is a sad but undeniable fact that the largest part of all the oppression, brutality, and sadism in the world is done by governments. And the governments of the developing countries suffer from underdevelopment too; on the average they are among the less enlightened in the world. That few developing nations have encouraged, or even allowed, a free flow of information is, therefore, no test of its value for them.

On the value of the free flow of information to development, the judgment of international organizations is likely to be no better than that of the governments that compose them and instruct their representatives to them. International organizations are likely to misinterpret the needs of the developing countries, perceiving them through the distorting vision of government officials. It is true that over a quarter of a century ago the United Nations in Article 19 of the Universal Declaration of Human Rights proclaimed:

> Everyone has the right to freedom of opinion and expression; this right includes freedom to hold opinions without interference and to seek, receive and impart information and ideas through any media and regardless of frontiers.

The UN is unlikely to adopt such an insightful statement again in the near future.

While governments and international organizations are not prone to favor the interests of the developing countries in stimulating a free flow of international information, there is fortunately a coincidence between the true interests of development and the ideological and moral predispositions of at least one important group in society. Scholars, scientists, practitioners of the intellectual arts tend to be among the strongest advocates of free flow. To liberal intellectuals, the right to communicate is sacred; the doctrine of the free flow of information is a principle not to be compromised. There are, of course, always among intellectuals some who are apologists of tyranny; there are always intellectuals on all sides of all questions. Nonetheless, the important point is that, just as governments whose business is to govern have a bias in favor of regulating, so communicators whose business is to communicate have a bias in favor of communicating freely.

The best hope, therefore, that progress will be made toward creating the global system of low-cost and unfettered communication that the developing countries require to progress comes from the ambitions and desires of the communicators themselves. Fortunately, journalists wish to report what is happening in the world; radio and TV producers want to provide exciting and meaningful programs to large audiences; technologists wish to create global and efficient communications systems. As long as their professional ambition is fired by a perception of what an expanding communication system can mean to the people of the world, there is room for hope.

Works Cited

CORTE, A. and WARREN, C. 1976. "Policy Issues and Data Communications for NASA Earth Observation Missions Until 1985." Cambridge: M.I.T. Research Program on Communications Policy.

DEUTSCH, K. 1956. "Shifts in the Balance of Communication Flow," *Public Opinion Quarterly, 20:* 1, 143-160.

INKELES, A. 1974. *Becoming Modern.* Cambridge: Harvard University Press.

LERNER, D. 1958. *The Passing of Traditional Society.* Glencoe, Illinois: The Free Press.

POOL, I. and CORTE, A.B. 1976. "Implications of Low-Cost International Non-Voice Communications," Cambridge: M.I.T. Research Program on Communications Policy, 91.

NATIONAL LEVEL COMMUNICATION POLICY AND PLANNING

This part of our monograph includes five case studies. Three of these examine communication policy and planning issues and problems at the national level in Indonesia, Bangladesh, and Canada. One of them examines national experiences in Latin American countries, and another paper looks into communication planning in the state of Hawaii, in the United States. Altogether these papers provide a sketch of the current status of communication policy and planning in some developed and developing countries.

Rehman Sobhan writes from his personal experience as one of the architects of the first five-year plan of Bangladesh. He spells out the social context and the contradictions in the development policies and strategies, and examines the communication policy problems and needs in that light. His analysis of the situation in Bangladesh brings out some of the inherent problems of policy-making when the objective is to use communication as an external agent of development. He notes that the success of communication strategies alone might create more frustration among the people, because in the long run communication could not compensate for failures in development.

The paper on Indonesia describes some specific problems that communication planners in developing countries face in their work. Astrid S. Susanto points out the hard realities of financial, manpower, and resource constraints. She says that the communication planners should be able to accept these limiting conditions and make the best out of the existing situation. It is also important to make plans at various levels—national, regional, and rural.

123

In Luis Ramiro Beltrañ's paper, we find an assessment of the initial steps toward communication policy-making and planning in the Latin American region of the developing world. After reviewing the concept of national communication policies and its operationalization, Beltrán takes a closer look at the policy-making processes in Peru, Venezuela, and Brazil. He notes that although these countries in political ideology, each recognizes the importance of communication policies as essential components of national development programs. Beltrán concludes his paper by reviewing the supportive and opposing trends of activities for national communication policies in the international arena.

The last two papers in this part of the monograph are on communication policy and planning in developed economies. Recently, the federal government in Canada began working toward long-range communication policies and planning. The broad objectives of a national communication policy in Canada are to develop and safeguard the Canadian national identity and unity and at the same time to maintain the diversity of values and cultures of different communities. In a recent position paper, the Canadian Ministry of Communication outlined a number of proposals: (1) developing a mechanism for constitution and policy coordination between the federal, provincial, and private agencies; (2) formulating ways of utilizing technological innovations for all Canadians; (3) devising and consolidating laws relating to telecommunications and broadcasting; and (4) constituting a single federal agency for the regulation of telecommunication carriers and broadcasting operations subject to federal authority.

Robert Rabinovitch's paper on communication policy and planning in Canada gives us some idea of the complexity of issues and problems. Although the communication infrastructure in Canada has reached a mature stage, its ability to deliver social services seems to be limited. Rabinovitch believes that communications could be an effective and low-cost way of delivering social services. But there are institutional constraints in achieving this. The traditional approach of expanding hardware seems to have created many problems. There is a need now to devise innovative policies and plans. The planners in the Department of Communications in Canada have begun working in that direction.

Communication policy and planning at the level of state

government is the subject of Richard J. Barber's paper. In the United States, there are several agencies in the executive, legislative, and judicial branches of the federal government that carry out communication policy-making and regulatory functions. But planning is not a significant activity of those organizations. What is the situation at the state level? Barber gives us some idea in his study of Hawaii. The state of Hawaii has a fairly extensive set of development plans, but communication is not treated as a significant resource in those plans. The main reason for this is that communication is basically a private sector activity. Barber does not see any indication of significant change in the situation. But he suggests that because of the rapid changes in communication technology, long-range communication planning might prove beneficial for Hawaii.

THE ROLE OF COMMUNICATION POLICY IN DEVELOPMENT PLANNING IN BANGLADESH

Rehman Sobhan

COMMUNICATION POLICY AND THE POLITICAL PROCESS

Within the policy-making process the problem of communication has to relate to the need for communication between the rulers and the ruled. This relationship is a two-way process. The policy-makers, planners, and administrators need to inform themselves of the concerns and wants of the people. These aspirations as they manifest themselves within the peasant at the plough, the worker on the factory floor, clerk at his/her desk, or teacher in the classroom are in most cases unstructured and crudely formulated in their minds. The needs and aspirations of the people have to be identified, collated, aggregated, and conceptualized by policy-makers to serve as inputs into the policy-making process. Channels of communication have to be permanently open to secure feedback from the people on impact, so that policies can be reexamined, modified, or even withdrawn if popular reactions are unfavorable.

Correspondingly, policies made by the rulers have in turn to be communicated back to the people. It is presumed that rulers need to keep the people informed about what is being done. This is needed to project the image of the government as one of service and concern for the welfare of the governed. It also has a functional component where in fact popular support and participation are required in the implementation of particular policies.

This rather idealized conception of communication policy is centered on the notion that in the ultimate analysis communication

127

takes place between individuals and their social aggregates in the form of groups or classes. The media of mass communication is an instrument of communication that cannot transcend the basic nature of interpersonal communication or the essential message that has to be communicated. It is only when these central themes of communication policy have been sorted out that the instruments or modalities of communication acquire any relevance.

It is the central theme of this paper that in Bangladesh any understanding of the process of communication between the rulers and the ruled must be founded on an understanding of the political process. The political media contain within it the dialectic of the development process. This dialectic is a function of the historical background to the nationalist movement and the contradictory social forces that emerged out of the struggle for Bengali nationalism. The search for a successful communication policy in Bangladesh thus lies in the ability of policy-makers to communicate with the masses as represented by the village poor, the factory workers, and the urban poor who make up the overwhelming majority of the populace. This communication can only emerge when the contradictions within the development process are resolved in a policy explicitly directed to the involvement of the masses in the process and benefits of development. Failure to do so leads to blockages in the channels of communication, because communication process and messages then project images that are contrary to the perceptions and experiences of the masses.

The Significance of
Political Communication in Bangladesh

In Bangladesh, it is argued that the political media are central to communication policy both as to its implications for development policy and as an instrument of communication. The nature and timing of the message and the credibility of the communicator are thus critical ingredients of policy. Central to this process is the ability to win the confidence of the people in support of the development goals of the regime. This can only be meaningfully achieved by involving the people in the identification of development goals, seeing that they consciously participate in the realization of these goals and that they directly benefit from the fruits of policy. The nationalist movement brought abou their participation in the political process and aroused their expectations for a better life. But in the post-liberation period the politi process worked to alienate them rather than involve them in the tasks of nation-building. Given the unifying effect of a single national language, Bengali, understood by the whole population, and the sense of national consciousness created in the minds of the whole nation by the liberation struggle, this process of alienation was a serious loss of capital accumulated for building a communication policy.

The problems of communication arose because the political goals of nation-building tended to be far more contradictory than the single-minded direction of the nationalist movement. At that stage where the goals were limited, the contents of the message could be simplified and projected in meaningful terms to the people. The depredations of the Pakistan army made the dialectic of the liberation struggle tangible to the experience and fears of the most remote village household.

Contradictions in the Political Process

The more complex political tasks of the post-liberation period thus reaffirmed the importance of political communication and required more careful formulation of the goals of policy. Unfortunately, the goals of development could never be clearly formulated because of the inherent contradictions within the nationalist movement itself. The multiclass character of the movement meant that conflicting interests and expectations had to be reconciled by the leadership. These basic contradictions between the objective conditions as represented by the mass base of the movement and the need to satisfy the expectations of the masses were never satisfactorily reconciled with the more limited sectional interests of the leadership and party cadres. They felt that victory must compensate them for their own years of persecution and privation spent in the political wilderness. As a result, no clear-cut set of objectives could emerge to rally the masses or even satisfactorily mobilize the support of various elite groups.

Credibility and Communication

Even if the goals had been more consciously determined, it would have been a problem to make political leaders transcend the rhetorical style of address and get down to the more laborious and tedious task of educating the people. This would have involved first educating the leaders and party workers in the goals and tasks of development. They in turn would have had to live and work in the villages, securing the confidence of the masses and understanding their problems and concerns.

The failure to evolve a clear-cut set of objectives and a policy to communicate them to the masses led to the projection of a purely negative message—the exploitation of the Bengalis by their former rulers and the destruction visited on them by the Pakistani army. This was meaningful in the early phase as a prelude to harnessing their energies to the tasks of building a new society. To the extent that people were to be reminded of past depredations to invoke sacrifices for the days ahead, this technique was relevant. But an essential element of this approach is that sacrifices must be shared. Only when the masses see that their leaders are undergoing corresponding hardships, will they accept the credibility of this approach. Even then it has to be brought home that these sacrifices are related to future benefits to them and their families. For the very poor, these tasks have to be compensated by tangible material and psychological gains, however modest they may be.

In this milieu communication technology in Bangladesh may have a role to play in disaggregating the tasks of development into meaningful components to be articulated by political workers. Whether it is extension work for use of improved seeds or household hygiene programs, there is no better instrument than the dedicated political cadre to take development messages to the people. It is he who can convince the people of the meaning of development. But to do this he has to use his political capital with the people to define the objectives in simple terms related to their daily lives and problems and to articulate the costs and benefits of the innovations in terms that are comprehensible to unlettered villagers. In return he has to communicate the people's concerns to the policy-makers. Illiteracy is not a basic problem here, because the villager perceives his own problems and interests better than any extension agent. But the solutions have to be made tangible and comprehensible to him within his own value system, at the first instance, by people who have his confidence and political support.

In the context of Bangladesh, however, the political workers who could have played a seminal role in mobilizing support of the masses in fact found that they really had no coherent message to project. In the absence of any clear guidance, they exercised the traditional prerogative of bourgeois politics by using their access to the sources of patronage to compensate themselves, their families, and supporters and to build their political support base. In these circumstances, the masses saw the benefits of subsidized inputs and high prices go generally to the surplus farmer and specifically to those with access to the patronage system. When this was related in their perception to the public exhortations of itinerant politicians about sacrifice and hard work, it was understandable why the masses saw the goals of development as deceptive and without relevant content.

The Significance of the Masses

The national leadership conspicuously failed to resolve this contradiction. In this situation it was always constrained by the contradictions inherent in its power base and the path to power in formulating development strategy in the post-liberation period. In societies where liberation has come as a gift from the parting colonial rulers to their chosen successors within the nationalist movement, the masses tend at this stage to be irrelevant and sectional interests can be uncompromisingly served. However, where the nationalist movement had invoked mass support, the new leadership is put into a more critical dilemma. In Bangladesh where the masses not only fought for, but also massively suffered for, the liberation of their country, their involvement in the political process constituted a powerful element in the objective conditions facing the national leadership at liberation. At this stage, the leadership had the potential for transcending their immediate social base and going directly to the masses to mobilize them behind the tasks of development. They could have taken them into confidence about the Herculean tasks ahead and the sacrifices and labors demanded of them in the process. In return, the leadership would have had to involve the masses in defining the goals of development and to restructure rural society to secure for the masses the just fruits of their labor. Furthermore, they would have had to choose a development strategy and a technology involving the direct participation of the masses. The liberation struggle had substantially eroded the power and authority of the rural bourgeoisie while the embryonic urban bourgeoisie were in no way able to fill the vacuum created by the departing Pakistani entrepreneurs who dominated the urban economy of Bangladesh. The people's participation and commitment to the liberation struggle had made them fully receptive to fulfill this historic responsibility in nation-building.

As it emerged, however, the regime remained a captive to all the contradictions that were carried within the nationalist movement and that had been subsumed in the liberation struggle. It thus failed to get through to the masses with a clear message as to the goals of development and their role in the development process. At the same time, it built up no solid base of support within the elite groups by proclaiming a strategy and using a rhetorical style which could conclusively secure their support. In these circumstances the political media progressively ceased to be an effective means of communication, because the goals of development could never be made clear. Instead it degenerated into a purely rhetorical instrument, which ultimately became counter-productive to the interests of the regime by highlighting the contradictions between rhetoric and reality. As the party workers at the base became more alienated from the masses, the channels of communication to the policy-makers also were blocked and thus the growing gap between the self-image of the leadership and the perception of the masses widened.

THE ROLE OF GOVERNMENT IN COMMUNICATION POLICY

While the political process remains central to the role of policy-making, the inherent contradictions within the regime were directly manifested in the general and specific tasks faced by agencies of government in planning and its communication to the people. The remainder of this paper is intended to demonstrate how these contradictions constrained the planning process and inhibited efforts to communicate the plan to the people as an instrument of development policy. The absence of any direction in development policy led to the failure to resolve anything resembling a coherent communication policy. In specific sectors, however, there was a definite attempt to communicate development policies to the people. This is examined in the context of areas where communication was a functional ingredient in the sector plan. Finally the infrastructure of communication and the use of mass media are examined for their capacity to involve the masses in development.

The Ministry of Information

As the designated agency for formulating communication policy, the Ministry of Information emerged as the principal casualt of the contradictions afflicting the regime. The job of the ministry was to project the intentions and image of the government before the people. Unlike political cadres who function as a two-way channel of communication, the government information agencies can only function as image-builders for the regime. Within this role they can be essentially passive and simply communicate relevant materials made available from the development agencies to the public through the media. In contrast, they may claim a more creative role that evaluates development policies and determines what needs to be projected. Where no ideology exists, the information agency may even synthesize one by seeking to conceptualize the eclectic offerings of diverse policy-makers.

The creative approach to communication policy was conspicuously demonstrated during the Ayub Raj in Pakistan, particularly, under the regime of Altaf Gauhar, then central Information Secretary. The virtuoso efforts in communication policy constituted a significant element in the vitality of the Raj and eventually in its downfall.

In Bangladesh the role of the Ministry of Information has been decidedly passive. Within three years after liberation, the ministry had three different ministers. One of these phases saw the prime minister take over the portfolio though the minister of state for information functioned as *de facto* minister. The various minister's objective function tended to be to use the media for self-promotion or for publicizing political associates or factions identified with the minister. This personalized approach led to overpublicity of the statements and movements of ministers rather than to project policies and activities of the regime. The ministry thus failed completely to develop as a fountainhead for communication policy.

The Ministry of Information's lack of personality was seen in the contradictory approach toward the media under its control. The ministry presided over the radio and television media in Bangladesh, which were state monopolies. These functioned as semi-autonomous agencies with directors general as chief executives. The Television Authority had at one stage been an autonomous corporation but this autonomy was abridged and it was brought on par with radio. However, even in this state it tended to be relatively freer to shape policy than radio. The personality of the chief executive and the minister and the basic chemistry in their relations determined the degree of autonomy exercised by the media agencies. Under these circumstances, the ministry performed largely administrative functions of a negative character, dispensing patronage through jobs, promotions, and transfers, but hardly communicating any coherent guidelines to the agencies under its control. Whatever feeble policy impulses emerged in this area came from the initiative of the agencies.

Apart from the electronic media, the ministry had its own departments under its direct control. One department handled press publicity and relations with the news media. But external publicity was transferred to the Foreign Ministry following considerable internecine warfare. Government publicity through the printed word and through films is handled by a separate department in the ministry. These departments are staffed by cadre officers of the information services of the central and provincial administration in preliberation Pakistan. The service itself was rather low down in the administrative hierarchy and rarely attracted people of calibre. It has been characterized by intense personal and factional rivalries in the post-liberation phase. Those in the senior echelons of the ministry have tended to be generalist bureaucrats. This has contributed to the low morale within the service.

Given the lack of continuity and inner contradictions, it was hardly to be expected that they could synthesize a philosophy from the contradictions and eclecticism of the regime. In practice, however, the ministry did not even compensate for its lack of direction by using its experience and virtuosity by improving the quality of its limited promotional efforts. It suffered from a singular incapacity to define its audience and to tailor the publicity efforts to a designated audience. As a result, its publications were poor in conception and presentation and occasionally counter to the explicit policy objectives of the regime. It was thus hardly possible to identify the ministry as a maker of communication policy since it failed to even conceptualize the idea of such a policy or to evaluate its significance for the development effort.

The Problems of Plan Formulation

Nowhere have these contradictions within the policy-making process been more apparent than in the preparation of the First Five-Year Plan. The plan document was prepared with great urgency within one year by the Planning Commission and published in November 1973. It sought to reconcile the socialist objectives of the regime proclaimed in the National Constitution with the fact that the ruling party had no real ideological affinity to socialist goals and its party workers had neither training nor commitment to these objectives.

The plan was built around an investment strategy and policy proposals that sought to redistribute income and consumption toward the masses and to extend their participation in the development process. It sought to reduce external dependence by emphasizing self-reliance through a restructuring of investment strategy and policies for improved production performance and domestic resource mobilization.

The plan was stillborn. Its publication coincided with the phase of unrestrained commodity inflation that afflicted the world economy in 1973 and 1974. Its investment goals and funding assumptions consequently needed drastic revision. However, the allocation strategies, redistributive policies, and policies for institutional changes for improved performance of the economy along with resource mobilization policies for self-reliance could have been initiated. But these policies needed a degree of single-minded political commitment and the use of a unified and motivated political machine to mobilize the people behind the plan. The planners failed to communicate the significance and imperatives of the plan to the political leadership. They, in turn, could get neither guidance nor feedback about their efforts because the regime's inner contradictions militated against any such direction or communication. It followed that in this orphaned state the plan could hardly be communicated to the people.

Projecting the Plan

The plan was published in November 1973. No clear program was chalked out either within the Planning Commission or the government to project the plan before the country. The publication of the plan at a press conference led to a short period of media projection for the plan, but this was largely unstructured. The media were left to project the plan as they deemed fit. This meant that the national press ran summaries and extracts. Some papers ran a few articles criticizing the plan, but little was done by the administration to orchestrate articles in the papers projecting the plan or even to highlight critical features of the plan as part of a policy of educating public opinion about the significance of the plan. The radio and television agencies ran a series of talks and discussions of the plan, but again, these were not carefully programmed presentations of the plan and emerged as rather eclectic in character leaving no clear image of the thrust or import of the document.

At the political level, there was no attempt to make capital out of the publication of a plan ostensibly embodying the development strategy of the regime over the next five years. The plan rarely found mention in the speeches of ministers or political workers. Even in the national parliament, debate on it was cursory. The prime minister when he on rare occasions referred to the plan did so to talk of its publication as an achievement of the regime rather than to highlight the strategy underlying the plan.

This casual treatment of what normally constitutes a significant statement of the personality and intentions of a government owed to contradictions inherent in the regime that have been discussed earlier. The plan as formulated by the Planning Commission failed to educate or mobilize the support of the political leadership. Some members had a limited perspective on the plan through objections raised by their secretaries on specific components within their sectors. However, the central elements of the plan, spelling out the strategy of the development effort, received no attention. The plan as it emerged was thus an exercise that embodied the work and aspirations of the planners to which the political leadership felt no commitment whatsoever. To the extent that the planners represented the radical contradiction within the government, a *cordon sanitaire* around the plan appeared a more convenient expedient than exposing the contradictions within the regime. Attempts to translate its policy components into Cabinet decisions largely stemmed from initiatives of the Planning Commission and inevitably came to nought.

Since the formulation of the plan had been done largely by government agencies, it could hardly invoke, in its own right, any popular support. It was an elitist document. The people had neither been consulted nor involved, and they therefore saw it as only remotely related to their immediate concerns. Its alienation from the people was a function of its lack of political support within the government. Although even if government support had been there, the process of alienation from the masses could hardly have been bridged since the regime was itself at that stage experiencing its own alienation. It follows that some attempt to project the plan through a scientifically designed communication policy would have widened its impact. But technical virtuosity, whether in the plan document or its projection, could not compensate for the failure to integrate the plan into the political compulsions of the regime and if not the regime, the masses.

Sectoral Communication Policy

The failure to project a central statement of policy such as the plan may have stemmed from the fundamental contradictions within the government that frustrated any attempt to project a clear-cut strategy of development. At a more disaggregated level, however, ministries and agencies of government were trying to project their programs. Here we will only discuss those sectors where communication was functionally an integral part of the plan. The three areas where this was critical were rural development, health, and family planning. In these sectors a critical element in the plan lay in using field-level workers to persuade people to behave in a particular way. By contrast, in other areas, development programs were more impersonal involving either expenditure plans or government initiatives in institutions building or policy implementation.

This dichotomy is, however, somewhat misleading and is used only to delimit the compass of this paper. All sectors and policies had a communication component either explicit or implicit in their implementation strategy. The road sector had a plan for local communities to invest labor in local road building programs for mobilizing underutilized labor in its area. This program could only have been carried through by intensive political mobilization of all segments of the village community as to the meaning of the program and the role of the people. The industries' plan aimed to raise productivity from installed capacity needed to mobilize factory workers to greater effort for this plan. This too involved political work among the working class, as well as managerial inputs into communication with their workers. When we therefore limit our discussion to these three sectors, it is more illustrative than definitive in its significance.

The Rural Sector

Within the program for rural development an important component is provided by communication policy. This implies that for the realization of plan objectives the agencies and government have to persuade farmers to modify their cropping and cultural practices and to associate themselves with cooperative efforts as organized by the government. While the government may use its resources to install irrigation facilities, provide fertilizer, pesticide, seeds, and credit, the individual farmers must be willing to use these facilities. This they may do by perceiving the benefits from government-sponsored programs and by being educated as to the adaptation of the new agricultural practices promoted by the government.

The Role of Extension Agents

The traditional method of communicating new ideas embodied in the development plans of the administration has been through the use of salaried extension agents. From preliberation days, the key person in this strategy was the Union Agricultural Assistant (UAA). Four thousand of them were distributed throughout 4,000 *unions,* the lowest administrative unit then and now in Bangladesh. The UAA was expected to educate the farmers about the value of the improved technology and the modalities of using fertilizer and pesticide, seeds, and irrigation water. In this task he was supposed to be aware of the natural conditions in his *union* and the problems of the farmers and to act as a point of direct communication between the farmer and administration. He, in turn, reported to the government on the state of the crop and other local problems. National statistics on commodity production were based on the visual estimates of the UAA on acreage and yield. The impact of crop failure, natural disasters, shortages in inputs, and even prices of commodities were fed to various echelons of government by the UAA who in effect became the eyes and ears of the government and a source of primary information on the state of the rural economy.

In this capacity the UAA was the key agent in the communication strategy of the administration, since through him the farmers had tangible contact with the intentions of the government in the field of development. But, even in preliberation days, doubts were expressed about the capabilities of the UAA in playing that critical a role. The UAA was then seen to be insufficiently trained and motivated to fulfill that central role. This was made evident in various field studies which sought to estimate the degree of communication established with the farmer.

In the post-liberation period the deficiencies of the UAA were recognized in the First Five-Year Plan. The rural development sector plan spelt out a fairly detailed program for upgrading his skills. The plan sought to expand the scope and quality of extension services by combining the UAA and progressive jute farmers, who also played an extension role and by recategorizing them as village extension agents (VEA). The plan aimed to have one VEA per 2,000 net cropped acres which implies that some 11,000 VEAs would have to be in the field. The plan aimed within the first plan period (1973-78) for a target of 7,500 VEAs to be concentrated in 15 million acres to be brought under intensive cultivation. Outside this area, the UAAs were to continue their position after having upgraded their skills. The VEAs were to be an improvement in the way of qualification and skills on the UAA, and an elaborate training and apprenticeship program was chalked out for the VEA.

In actual practice the program was stillborn and the UAAs are still in the field with very little in the way of upgraded skills. The problems of lack of training and instruction, along with insufficient remuneration and poor communication with the farmers, persist. In these circumstances the UAA continues to play his traditional role of linker between the local administrators and rural power elite.

In earlier studies indicated above it had become apparent that the UAA was hardly playing the communication role intended for him. In practice he became an agent for dispensing government-provided inputs. To secure access to these scarce inputs the rich farmers sought close relations with the UAA. He in turn secured his access to the village through the rich farmers. This alliance served to channel the scarce inputs to the affluent farmers who either used them to improve their yield or, as frequently, resold them to smaller farmers though appropriating the scarcity premium.

The Role of Political Intermediaries

In the post-liberation period of high commodity prices and acute scarcities, this relationship became even more critical. The local political leadership played an important role in intermediating this relationship so that the balance of power in resource distribution moved from the local administration to the local political leadership with the UAA becoming to a large extent the instrument of the local political forces.

In these circumstances the critical points of communication between the administration and the people were controlled by the local affluent farmers and among them by the dominant political groups. The masses were made spectators of this process whereby the medium of communication in rural development became the instrument of sectional interest groups. The scarcity of resources that limited the strength of the extension services and vitiated their quality also contributed to the scarcity of inputs and to the search for political power to extract the premium from prevailing scarcities.

The Role of Rural Institutions

Attempts to directly involve the people in the search to transcend the locally dominant social groups led in the 1960s to the Comilla experiment in cooperatives and its institutionalization in the Integrated Rural Development Programme (IRDP). This strategy sought to use the farmers themselves as their own extension agents through the training of *model farmers* who became the point of communication with other farmers in the cooperative. Studies of the preliberation experiment along with ongoing studies of the post-liberation period demonstrate how these groups came to be monopolized by the rich farmers in spite of the explicit objective of organizing small farmers. These institutions tended to become vehicles for securing scarce inputs and the struggle to control the UAA was extended to the struggle to dominate the cooperatives. The plan proposal to make local representative institutions central elements in the planning process and in promoting mass participation and mobilization for development was stillborn. Since the format for local self-government was never adequately worked out until the last days of the Mujib regime, the plan to make the IRDP cooperatives socially representative through compulsory representation of the village poor was overtaken by other efforts in this area.

These failures in popular mobilization culminated in the plan for compulsory cooperatives and decentralized local government. These were to be the key elements of policy in the new political changes ushered in by Sheikh Mujibar Rahman early in 1975 following the conversion of the Bangladesh polity to a one-party Presidential system. The plan for compulsory cooperatives, based on joint production and sharing of the produce by the landless and the landowners, had a significant potential for undermining the traditional structure of income distribution in the village. The system of district governors with greatly expanded authority for local development stood to bring development closer to the masses. The program was aborted by the murder of Mujib so one never knew if it carried any real potential for popular mobilization.

The current policy of "Swanirbhar" or local self-reliance seems to be dependent on the local power structure for its success. Even if it has an impact on output, what studies exist indicate that its very success may accentuate inequalities by concentrating resources on the rural elites and making them key elements in the program. It is, however, too early to warrant any definitive judgment on the nature, scope, and impact of the program.

In these circumstances, the medium of interpersonal communication through government functionaries and institutions is likely to remain an instrument of the traditional rural elites. Changes of power at the top cannot transcend the critical role of the dialectic of development at the local level. Here scarce resources are likely to continue to be appropriated by the surplus farmers even though new elements among them may directly benefit. The problem of communication with the masses is thus likely to persist.

Health Sector

The health sector is another area where government policies and services need to be communicated to the people. Traditionally, points of communication were disaggregated. Four thousand Health Assistants and Vaccinators, largely provided immunization against smallpox and cholera. Five thousand Malaria Supervisors carried out a spraying program to contain malaria. Their role was functionally limited and little was done to utilize them productively to communicate ideas of improved health practices and hygiene to the villages.

The First Five-Year Plan aimed to integrate these unipurpose services into a multipurpose health service embodied in the person of the Basic Health Worker (BHW). A planned target of 10,000 BHWs was set which aimed to train and upgrade existing unipurpose workers to perform this new role. Apart from playing a functional role of providing preventative health services to villagers, they were expected also to educate village households on environmental sanitation, water purification, family health, and family planning. They were also to provide a feedback to planners by communicating primary information on the health of the people.

These elaborate plans were again of limited impact. Latest estimates indicate that the BHW concept has taken some root and 12,000 such workers are in the field. But since they were drawn from other unipurpose schemes, the formal merger of their functions in a multipurpose health scheme cadre is slow to emerge. Shortage of support facilities has created further problems. While the provision of public health services is less elitist because the affluent in the villages and urban centers find the services too primitive for their needs, its coverage of the poor is still well short of their needs. No formal attempt has been made to mobilize and train the masses to cope with their own health needs.

There has, however, been a remarkably impressive program organized privately by a group of dedicated young doctors. This program, known as the People's Health Centre, has been set up so far only in *Savar Thana*. It seeks to train the village youth to provide medical services of a preventative and curative nature for the masses. The program seeks to enroll the masses, for very modest payment within their limited means, as part of a village health service. This provides them with household visits by paramedics who have been locally recruited and trained as barefoot doctors. These both provide rudimentary curative services and educate the villagers on matters of environmental and personal hygiene, family planning, nutrition, and even cropping practices to make them self-reliant in meeting the prescribed nutritional program. These paramedics now even provide tubal ligatures at the center where village women are ligated by these nonprofessionals and sent home within the same day. The key element in the plan aims to mobilize the masses themselves within the resources available, to equip and educate themselves to meet their basic health needs, and to participate in a unique family planning program.

It remains to be seen whether the project can multiply itself. The present project is heavily dependent on the commitment of the project organizers who are obviously making an investment in labor and dedication which will be hard to expand, at the price, on the open market. Its obvious success has also attracted considerable external assistance which has built up its capital stock. It is less clear whether such significant individual efforts in popular mobilization can survive and multiply within a social milieu which is basically inegalitarian and inimical to the liberation of popular impulses.

Population Planning

Population planning was yet another area where mass communication was seen to play a critical role in the viability of the plan program. To quote the plan document: "The first task is, therefore, to launch a major educational and motivational campaign to bring the seriousness of the population problem into focus. . . . Simultaneously, campaigns to motivate people to adopt the currently acceptable measures like pills and condoms and simple clinical methods should also be launched and group responsibilities to supervise implementation of such schemes initiated."

The emphasis on the communication component of the program emerged from the limited impact of earlier efforts which rested on the role of undertrained midwives and male motivators, who contributed little beyond serving as conduits for the limited flow of contraceptive devices into the villages.

The plan program aimed to train one male and female worker for every 8,000 couples in order to provide motivation and services as part of the health and family planning motivation program.

The lead role of the Ministry for Health and Family Planning was to be complemented by the incorporation of population planning motivation into the educational curriculum, using the field services of the cooperative department and the rural development agencies to communicate ideas on family planning, and finally, to use the media through a planned program for dissemination of information regarding population problems and family planning. Unlike other projects for communication, high-powered communication efforts for population planning were more readily funded by the external aid agencies.

As in the other sectors, the population communication programs have made only a marginal impact. To quote the Economic Review of 1974-75: "Publicity of family planning method and supply of proper materials for desired clinical measures have not achieved expected success." The institutional problems arising out of the need to merge various unipurpose agencies to provide an integrated service has afflicted the population planning program as much as it has the health program.

In the media some efforts have been made to put out publicity for the plan through Radio Bangladesh through lectures,

discussions, dramas, comic stories, poems, etc. Features of
the writers' bureau under the Ministry of Information brought
out articles on population regularly in newspapers. The film
division is being strengthened to tackle the same problem.

It is quite apparent that the gap between intention and
implementation is wide. However the communication program
again suffers from an inherent conceptual weakness. Because it
invests its effort in expenditure intensive top-down methods of
communicating, it is constantly at the mercy of budget cuts and
administrative inadequacies. Its fieldworkers are salaried government functionaries whose inflation-eroded wages are manifestly
inadequate to attract people of either ability or motivation into
the villages to communicate the message of population planning.
The supervisory chain in itself, and for the same reasons, is weak.
The result is that both the spread and quality of the effort is poor.

The use of the media is by definition restricted in its
orbit. Articles on family planning in the national dailies are,
from the evidence, directed to educated middle-class audiences,
but their rather pedantic presentation is likely to inhibit even
such readers. The chances of the masses reading such materials
is constrained by literacy levels as well as access to papers in the
villages. Where such a message does get across, it goes to the village affluent and educated elite groups, who are also the only ones
with radios to hear the creative efforts of the Ministry of Informatic

To the extent that the elitist strategy seeks to motivate elite
groups in the village to take the message to the rural poor, the impact and motivation of the elite are themselves questionable. Indeed, data from some field studies indicate that more affluent
families in the village if anything tend to larger families than the
landless, whose economic compulsions as much as the high mortality rate of their offspring keep their family sizes relatively
smaller. Studies which correlate high infant mortality with high
birthrates are now accepted in population studies as the result of
rational planning decisions of the poor who are unlikely to be
influenced by the feeble communication efforts of the media.

Obviously, a successful communication program in family
planning cannot transcend the problems of providing security in
old age, the options of wider economic opportunities, and the
involvement of women as equals in the decision-making process
through their economic emancipation. All these problems are
inherent in the social structure which limits the options of the
rural poor. The chances in Bangladesh of achieving any spectacula

breakthrough in the program by resource-intensive, aid-supported efforts, without a corresponding structural change in society is likely to emerge as an expensive pipe dream of donors and recipients alike. The charade of widely publicized family planning efforts which attract foreign aid and which sometimes constitute one of the preconditions for Western aid is likely to be the price Bangladesh has to pay for its structural constraints and consequent aid-dependence.

THE INFRASTRUCTURE FOR COMMUNICATION

Having selectively reviewed the role of interpersonnel communication in Bangladesh, it may be useful to look briefly at the communication infrastructure and the mass media as an instrument of development communication.

Education

The level of literacy and the state of education largely determine the impact of the written word. The impact of newspaper and the government's written publicity are constrained by the number of people who can read them at all. This in itself is likely to fall short of those who are actually reached by the written word but this will be discussed separately.

Available information indicates that growth in school enrollment is barely keeping up with population increase so that the relative state of literacy has tended to remain substantially unchanged. This is consistent with a growing number of literates with some education. Indeed the primary school enrollment increased by about 80 percent between 1960-61 and 1972-73 so that in the latter period 50 percent of children at primary school age (6-10) were getting some form of education. The price of expansion is paid in the erosion of quality in education leading to a high drop-out rate. Only 17 percent of those in the secondary school age group were in fact attending school in 1972-73.

Education serves as an important part of the infrastructure of communication. The access to education makes people more receptive to communicating the idea of development both because it gives them the technical capability of receiving knowledge and widens their perception of the world.

In Bangladesh society, education has traditionally been seen as a medium for escaping from the ranks of the masses into the hallowed world of the educated middle class. Generations of the rural poor have accepted any sacrifice to enable at least one of their sons to get enough education to break out of the world of their fathers and move "up" the ladder even if it is to feed at the crumbs left by urban society.

A culture which imposes its elitist perceptions onto the masses not only divides society in a most dangerous and unproductive way but also fills the masses with self-contempt for their lowly and underprivileged status in society. This culture unfortunately only contributes to the crisis of poverty. It generates aspirations without being able to fulfill them and equips people to become parasites rather than producers. This tradition so asiduously fostered by the British raj to produce the native infrastructure of their raj became a positive danger to the stability of an independent society. Pakistani rule did little to break with this tradition.

Today the educational system of Bangladesh perpetuates the colonial legacy and barely contributes to making people productive members of society. The abysmal quality of formal education imposed on the masses equips them to become underpaid clerks in a society which can never absorb the growing numbers of such people and in fact hardly needs them in the development process. The fact that in 1972-73, 58 percent of children in the age group 6-10 were classified as being in primary school should be seen as a problem rather than a gain for society because it means that so many more unemployables are coming on to the market to contribute only their frustrations to a society already under the strain due to the irrelevance of its educational system.

Therefore, to see the spread of literacy and education in its present form as a key element in the development process (because it might improve the communicability of such ideas to the people) is positively misleading. To the extent that our goal remains to release the full potential of the masses by regenerating confidence in the worth of their labor and their ability to participate in the building of society, an elitist education system that alienates the youth of the villages from their own world is an anti-development force in society. In this context, the literacy statistics as an indicator of development prospects is as sterile as is the faith in GNP growth as a measure of development.

The plan document had been fully conscious of this fundamental weakness in the educational system and articulated the need and the plan for making education more production-oriented and relevant. But in both conception and strategy it could not break out of the sociocultural straightjacket fashioned for society by generations of elitist directed policy-makers.

The Role of Nonformal Education

Considerable emphasis was put on the importance of nonformal education. The encouraging results of a number of local, privately initiated experiments in nonformal education pointed to the contribution this approach could make in supplementing the formal system and in making instruction more relevant to the needs of society.

The problem with the nonformal educational programs is that such efforts in Bangladesh tended to become hot-house creations—which lasted only as long as some dedicated local leaders could maintain the enthusiasm of the community or social groups targeted by the program. A recent study of nonformal education in Bangladesh has shown that such efforts instead of perpetuating themselves territorially and numerically tend to run down in resources and enthusiasm over the years.

This is hardly surprising if the thrust of the whole system is to impose on the masses an elite-oriented development strategy where the goals of success are measured in the pursuit of individual success outside the village since the same strategy has concentrated all the opportunities and the rewards of development in the urban centers. Indeed attempts to invest heavily in changing the structure of education in Bangladesh end up in serious structural imbalance illustrated by the graduates of polytechnics parading the city streets demanding white collar jobs while village roads and sanitation cry out for a technical input from their educated "sons."

In this system, the poverty of the farmers leads to a high drop-out rate. This is illustrated by the fact that out of 58 percent of school age students at the primary school level, only 17 percent get into secondary school, and 6 percent make it to college. A strategy which seeks to raise the retention rates of the system and seeks to upgrade the system by having more teachers to improve the quality of the clerks of urban society is hardly a gain. Thus, plans to use sophisticated techniques of radio and television and even satellites in support of education are irrelevant until such time as the educational system can direct itself to the first principle of development communication—to teach the educated to communicate with the masses, to learn from them before they can teach them, and to work with them rather than to sit at a desk.

The Telecommunications Network

The technical infrastructure to communication is provided by a country's telecommunications system. In a wider context a comprehensive and efficient telecommunications network is a vital element in integrating the country and bridging the gap between the metropolis and the backward rural areas. The ability to keep close contact between a national administration and the village base is valuable for supervising the development effort and making villagers feel that they are not living in a world apart. In a landscape where surface transportation is expensive and time-consuming the tele-link is of added significance.

Unfortunately, during the two decades of Pakistani rule, the telecommunications network was seriously neglected. In 24 years the average investment was only TK-20 million per year. As a consequence, at the outset of the First Five-Year Plan there were only 66,000 telephones in use in a country of 75 million people. These were based on only 237 telephone exchanges of which only 22 were automatic. A large part of the country remained outside the telephone network. What coverage existed remained largely urban oriented, with over two-thirds of the phones concentrated in the three main urban centers and those in individual households and offices. For the general public needs, there were only 700 call offices scattered throughout the country.

Fortunately the telecommunication links are well underway to covering the country, whose small size of 52,000 square miles makes this more feasible. The current plan has lined up most of the required external resources so that by 1978 a high capacity microwave link or coaxial cable network will link all major traffic centers. Medium capacity microwave or a VHF network will connect the remaining important centers while low capacity land lines or VHF network will be extended to all headquarters and other centers of economic importance. The telecommunications network will also fully cover the cyclone-prone areas of the coastal belt.

This basic grid will then enable the telephone and wireless link to cover the whole country, although progress to these goals may be interrupted due to budget constraints. The extension of telephone links was usually kept short of funds on the grounds that the urban centers were attracting all the telephones. The pressures of metropolitan-oriented development will continue to appropriate resources, even though the importance of linking up hitherto remote areas is of considerable importance. Here again, the biases of telecommunications investment will parallel the urban biases of the system. A decentralized mass-based development strategy would have to ensure, even for functional reasons, that all villages had both telephonic and wireless contact before one private phone was allocated to Dacca middle-class householders.

The country now has an earth satellite facility at Chittagong which will link up with the high frequency equipment under planned installation to link Bangladesh more effectively with the international circuits. No attempt is as yet envisaged to use the satellite for domestic communication.

THE MASS MEDIA
OF COMMUNICATION

Radio

The radio is the most widely used medium of mass communication in the country. The post-liberation regime has an ambitious plan to lay the infrastructure of a countrywide radio network with a capability for external broadcasting. The position at the beginning of the First Plan was that Dacca had the only station with substantial broadcasting facilities. Rajshahi and Chittagong had limited broadcasting facilities through a 10 kw transmitter. Khulna had a similar facility which was irrepairably damaged by the Pakistan army on the eve of their surrender in December 1971. It is now functioning as a relay station with a 1 kw emergency transmitter. Rangpur in North Bengal had a 10 kw transmitter with two emergency studios. A 5 kw transmitter installed as far back as 1938 in the Dacca suburb of Mirpur needs immediate replacement. Today a high power station at Savar in the outskirts of Dacca is operating with one 100 kw medium wave transmitter and two 100 kw short wave transmitters. A 1,000 kw transmitter has been recently installed under commission at Nayerhat near Dacca under USSR assistance.

This, when fully operational will ensure radio coverage for the whole of Bangladesh through a single channel medium wave program from Dacca and will also permit external service broadcasts to neighboring countries on the medium wave band.

Projects underway are designed to supplement the internal service and substantially build up the external broadcasting capability. An FM transmitter set in Dacca is under commissioning. A program for the full restoration of the Khulna broadcasting facility is underway with the objective of eventually having a 100 kw transmitter center there. A project to set up a 20 kw transmitter center at Sylhet is under implementation. A further project for 2 x 250 kw short wave transmission centers is at its first stage.

The fact that a small transistor radio with medium wave reception can be had for under US$10.00 has enabled radio to spread quite widely. It is, however, still well below its potential because indigenous manufacture and import of receivers remain severely constrained by foreign exchange shortages. Assembly plants operate well below capacity so that shortage of supply keeps prices much higher and thus limits demand and spread.

The present services provide for an average of 13 hours and 20 minutes of broadcasting per day from six stations at Dacca, Chittagong, Rajshahi, Sylhet, Rangpur, and Khulna. This covers the whole country. This is an increase from the 10 hours and 48 minutes of broadcasting time before liberation. A multilingual external service broadcasting in English, Nepali, Arabic, Pushtu, Urdu, Panjabi, and Hindi operates for 7 hours and 50 minutes daily.*

The facilities and service as they exist enable the voice of the government to reach out to the entire population. Planned facilities will obviously improve and amplify this ability. The significance of the radio is thus not without importance in a society where no other media have the capability for getting across to all the people and covering the whole country in the way the radio can. This facility has already been recognized as a political force, and as in most developing countries, control of the radio stations has become one of the first gambits in any power struggle.

---

*The estimated number of radio receivers in the country is one per 1,500 population.

A key element in fortifying the Bengali nation after the Pak army crackdown of March 25, 1971 was the seizure of the Chittagong broadcasting station and the historic broadcast of Major Zia Rahman calling the people of Bangladesh to armed struggle. The Savar facility was also seized and made a number of pirate broadcasts. Both became the first targets of the Pak army counterattack. During the liberation war the radio was the primary medium of contact between the struggle and the captive population within Bangladesh. "Swadhin Bangla Betar Kendra" (Free Bangla Radio Centre), the broadcasting facility of the Bangladesh government, became a source of hope to the oppressed Bengalis and mobilized their support for the struggle. This historic phase probably did more to expose the masses to the radio as mass media than any other event.

The importance of the radio as a political force can obviously be extended to more normal times when the government's and leader's political personality and intentions can be projected through this medium. Traditionally and in the post-liberation phase, significant statements of policy have been put out on a national hookup where the radio has served as the most powerful disseminator of the message. Since there is a total state monopoly over this facility, the government obviously has a powerful weapon for good or ill to indoctrinate the people.

This weapon was, however, being used in a more routine manner without adequate recognition of its significance. Thus all ministers took time on radio to project themselves and their policies. The radio was used both for political broadcasting and statements of policies and achievements by ministers. It also served as a sort of gazette notification of government programs. Thus the decision to demonetize bank notes and information about tendering the notes could only be disseminated by radio, which did so by spot announcements through the day. In this way these and other announcements of relevance to the people at large are put out over the radio.

More than in any other media the radio is used to publicize government achievements. Apart from television which has a much narrower and more sophisticated audience, radio gives the government an unchallengeable vehicle for projecting its messages, and guest speakers all have to submit their scripts for vetting in advance of going on the air.

Radio has been incorporated in the service of the development effort. Thus as has been indicated earlier, in the health, family planning, education, and rural development sectors, radio has been consciously used as an instructional and promotional medium.

However, the full potential of radio has been far from realized. The absence of a coherent social and political philosophy has been the overall constraint. There has been little conscious effort to break down the philosophy of the government either conceptually or in terms of programs and policies to be projected before the people. The Ministry of Information has never played the seminal role attributed to such ministries in more motivated regimes.

The background to this lack of ideological direction has been discussed earlier. The disability was however compounded by a lack of technical skill in communicating ideas and messages. Little attempt was made to explore techniques for communicating ideas in simple and comprehensible terms. To get a professor of agriculture to talk on new technology as if he were instructing a university class was hardly likely to motivate small farmers to adopt better farming techniques.

Some attempt was made, particularly in the rural sector, to use popular techniques of folk songs and plays to get across ideas. But this was sporadic and not part of any clearly thought-out strategy planned by the concerned ministries to get across a specific message to a specific audience.

At the root of the problem was the inability to get through to the masses. We have seen that the masses were largely excluded from the benefits of development or participation in its benefits. The media could hardly compensate for this fundamental contradiction. Its programs, thus while ostensibly seeking a mass audience, came to be tailored to the idiom and interests of the rural and urban elite groups and the language of the educated class. Since the idiom was tailored to their level, they became interpreters as well as disseminators of the news. Thus poor villagers may gather round the sole radio receiver of a rich farmer in a village and listen to a disembodied, alien voice, speaking a barely comprehensible language. It was the owner of the set or an educated youth who would tell the audience what the government was saying. The radio thus contributed to accentuating the dichotomy between the elites and the masses and in fact gave the elite an added instrument for perpetuating their domination.

Since the radio communicated a message of limited functional use and of little benefit to the masses, it was hardly surprisin that it flourished more as a medium of entertainment in their rather arid lives. Its musical programs became a point of attraction to the local tea shops and in this the radio served a social purpose. It is, however, evident that the potential for using radio was barely realized. Even within the limits of its elitist philosophy, more could be made out of radio as an agent of development. However, until it becomes a true medium of communicating with the masses, it will remain underutilized. And this level of communication can only follow when it communicates a policy designed for the masses.

Television

Television in Bangladesh is of fairly recent origin. In having a television broadcasting facility, Bangladesh is still ahead of many developing countries. Television was introduced in 1964 when a pilot station was commissioned from an improvised studio in a big office building in Dacca. This permitted a limited coverage within the environs of the metropolitan center. Beneficiaries were largely the urban elite who could afford to invest in TV receivers, although some were distributed for community use in places such as college common rooms and officers' messes.

This modest beginning was, however, merely the prelude to a bigger expansion program. A project designed to set up a modern television station in Dacca was put under way before liberation at a cost of TK 47 million. This was funded by Japanese assistance and aimed to provide modern equipment for two big studios and three small booths, an auditorium, a studio for educational television, one film production unit, and a staff training institute. The project was to be complemented by erecting four satellite stations to be located in the four corners of Bangladesh.

The new station at Rampara, Dacca, was commissioned in March 1975. The station is large and modern and has a broadcasting capability well beyond the limits of the current TV programs. The Natore substation for north Bengal is almost ready for commission, and the equipment for the other centers at Khulna, Sylhet, and Chittagong have already arrived.

The expansion of the TV facility has, however, been beset by ambiguities as to the scope and role of television in Bangladesh. At the outset the Planning Commission was even skeptical about permitting completion of the ongoing scheme.

It was argued that television in Dacca was the ultimate in elitist development. It catered to a mini-scale elite audience in Dacca. Its programs were tailored to this audience. Indeed its import of canned feature programs from abroad catered to an even narrower English speaking audience. The format of the talk show and other paradigms of Western television were all tailored to the interests of the urban intelligentsia of the metropolis.

The project only survived at that stage because the bulk of the equipment for the Rampura Station and most of the construction had been completed. The station was, however, commissioned much slower than planned because the project was the first to be pruned when there was a budget constraint. The substations similarly became casualties to this strategy and the Natore substation was only commissioned because the prime minister was sold as to its worth by the persuasive efforts of the very able chief executive of the Television Corporation.

From the outset these doubts about the need and relevance for television were apparent. Early in 1972 the Planning Commission sought to set up a interministerial committee to review the need and possible role of television. This move was frustrated by the jurisdictional objection of the Ministry of Information. To this day no corresponding interministerial effort to spell out a policy for television has emerged.

As a result the television authorities have been putting out their own notions of television use. In this they have sought to justify television as a medium with potential for mass communication aiming to visually communicate government development policies to the people. This objective has been incorporated in the First Five-Year Plan document which declares that: "The objective is not only to generate programmes for entertainment but also to produce educational, health and agricultural programmes for the benefit of the rural population." This implied the creation of facilities which would permit 8-10 hours of broadcasting a day, coverage of 80 percent of the population, and arrangements for reception of the program in the rural areas.

It follows that if the principle of a TV broadcasting facility is accepted then investments to relay the program and to receive it at the widest possible level is the only way to ensure access of the medium to the masses. While part of the delivery infrastructure was provided in the plan, the reception policy was severely contained by import restrictions on TV receivers and on assembly kits for locally assembled units, which were classified as a luxury item.

At the prevailing market price of TK 8000 for a small-sized TV set, it is not accessible even to the middle class who have an income of about TK 2000 per month. Currently televisions are largely coming into the country through people coming from abroad or through the home remittance scheme for expatriate Bengalis. This keeps supplies limited and prices up. Government efforts to widen viewing by distributing community sets is of very limited impact. In this context a policy of taking television to the rural masses appears to be in the remote future. Only a handful of villages are electrified, so that transistor television would be needed if the network gave coverage to adjacent villages. The spatial structure of village society would not make communal viewing around small transistor TV sets feasible so that only the very affluent, if at all, would be the beneficiaries.

This contradiction between the potential for television and the social and private costs of spreading its impact has not been resolved. It shows little future signs of being reconciled. As a result, television is destined to become an entertainment medium of the elite groups. Educational programs about improved agricultural practices when flashed on the screens of the affluent lead to sets being switched off. Educational programs cater to the children of the rich who have, in any case, access to books and good schools and need little compensation for the lack of literacy and educational facilities. We may thus witness the spectacle of all these major investments in creating a TV infrastructure, including well-designed development communication programs all getting through to a narrow elite whose main urge is to get more imported programs such as "Dangerman" and "Kojak."

Newspapers

The newspaper is second to the radio in its access to the people. Its spread is limited by the limits of functional literacy. Apparently many of those designated in census reports as literate cannot read a paper with comprehension of its contents. This however does not limit its spread to nonliterates since it is a general social phenomenon for the literate member of a social group to read out the news to an audience which includes subliterates as well as those who cannot afford to buy a paper. This indicates that the circulation of a paper is for all practical purposes well in excess of its sales.*

---

*The total daily circulation of newspapers is about 450,000.

The post-liberation period saw a proliferation of daily and weekly papers. Most of these had a short and precarious life since the economics of the industry only kept papers viable through advertising, since sales revenue was rarely adequate to sustain any paper. Since government advertising was a key and major source of funding, this gave the government considerable leverage in controlling the press. In the post-liberation period, extensive nationalization of the industry, trade and financial institutions drastically curtailed a private and fertile source of advertising revenue.

The government itself owned only two English language and two Bengali dailies which were inherited as abandoned property as a result of the absence of their owners after the liberation war. These were poorly run, in debt and hence lost circulation and professional staff. As a medium for projecting the image and policies of the government, they were singularly ineffective both as to the size of audience and quality of the message.

In contrast, privately owned papers rapidly gained ground at the expense of the state because they marketed the most salable product—criticism of the government.

By the end of 1974, the government's image in the newspapers was at its lowest ebb. With limited support of its own papers, the capacity of the newspapers to meaningfully project the policies of the government was virtually nonexistent. The use of direct and indirect sanctions of a legislative and financial nature may have imposed a modification in criticism but did little to promote any positive projection of the government's image.

The preliberation practice of "buying up" journalists and scholars to project government policies was used less successfully by a regime which felt that its popular credentials precluded such expedients. As a result what skills there were tended to be deployed in excoriating state policies. These produced occasional punitive actions against individuals and papers but scarcely refurbished the tarnished image of state.

The clientele of the press was largely made up of the urban educated classes, although at the village level the rural elites and educated people were also readers of the press. This meant that through the newspapers, these opinion-making classes were seeing the government projected in the most negative terms. Its policies were rarely projected except to highlight its shortcomings and achievements were inadequately publicized. Plaintive press notes issued by the Ministry of Information were, in this state of eroded credibility, rarely believed. Repetitious and tendentious speeches of ministers which were reproduced did little to improve the image.

Much of the "bad" press inevitably followed from the failings of the government, and efficient news management would have done little more than serve as a cosmetic since Bangladesh's problems were always too close to the surface to permit such disguise.

Thus the newspapers in private hands tended to be owned by social groups which were essentially hostile to the social tendencies of the government. Even though the government was far from radical in its policies, its few gestures in that direction had drastically alienated the classes which owned newspapers. At the other end of the spectrum, radical weeklies or a few opposition-owned papers were even more sharply critical of the government for its real and apparent failings. The journalists as a profession were generally hostile to the government both from a "left" and a "right" perspective.

In this situation, moves to curb the press were an inevitable tendency as the government's alienation increased. The Fourth Estate had been one of the more vocal and effective critics of the government in the post-liberation period. The constitutional changes which ushered in the one-party state were accompanied by drastic curbs on the papers. All papers were closed down and only two English and two vernacular dailies were permitted to continue under state ownership and direction. The situation in the post-Mujib regime has seen the restoration and revival of a number of private dailies and weeklies, but the nature of a martial law regime has not permitted any serious flowering of dissent.

The press had in the post-liberation period been the least suitable medium for communicating policies. It was the only medium to reflect within limits the dialectic within the polity. To this extent it focused attention on problems and served to educate the public about the weaknesses of government policy. Had this process been handled with more finesse even such a role could have played a positive role. A well-edited press highlights the problems of society, the failures of the government to tackle these, and the available options for society. It can thus create an informed public which can then be mobilized both against a bad government and for a meaningful set of alternatives. It can also provide feedback to the government about the problems and concerns of the people and the impact of various policies.

The nature of the dialectic and the calibre of the press, however, rarely enabled them to transcend their purely negative role. This in turn was, with limited exceptions, carried out in essentially tendentious tones which frequently substituted rhetoric and innuendo for hard fact. This resort to armchair editorializing—instead of sending journalists out to lay bare the facts of the crisis and its causes—deprived the people of a very vital source of education.

Government efforts to promote its development efforts in the press were nonexistent or counter-productive. The planning agency which in preliberation days had been a source of inexhaustible copy on the developmental achievements of the regime, was in the post-liberation phase, totally silent. Neither did it put out materials itself nor did it promote such efforts from outsiders. Indeed its own annual economic reviews were perhaps the most informative and trenchant critique of the government's failings in the development field and could have provided a major input into the press criticism of the government if the press had chosen to seriously study these documents rather than rely on the rhetorical style.

Efforts by the Ministry of Information of a more blatantly promotional nature produced such poor calibre copy as to be counter-productive. Poor content was rarely compensated by production techniques which could subtly and meaningfully project ideas.

Indeed, on many occasions the government press itself became an instrument to fight out interministerial battles which brought the contradictions of the government to the surface. This personalized use of the press by ministers, political leaders, and agencies in the department was part of a general tendency within the press to use the medium for personal gain. Thus a businessman press owner, cut out of a deal, did not hesitate to use his press to blackmail favors for himself. Even papers with no direct material stake lent themselves to such blackmail practices, where for personal or even factional gain they would lend their columns to a businessman trying to secure a benefit from a particular agency of government.

In these circumstances, the press as with other agencies has hardly reached its real potential as a medium for communicating development policy. By its nature it has a potential for promoting debate through the dialectical method. But as a medium it will remain restricted to a more limited educated class and can thus never be an instrument for mass mobilization. To the extent that it can keep the government in touch with popular concerns while it informs the educated elite both as to the facts of development and their role in both formulating options and conveying these to the masses, it has a considerable potential for the future as part of a mass-directed communication strategy.

Film

The medium of film may only be mentioned *en passant* since in the post-liberation period it has done little to promote development.* This is surprising since the government controlled Film Development Corporation has been a major source of assistance to the private film industry. In the post-liberation period very little has been done by the Film Development Corporation (FDC) to produce documentaries with a development bias. Traditionally when this was done it played to a limited audience in the urban centered cinemas.

The FDC has perhaps the best infrastructure for film making. It has a well-equipped studio in Dacca with another under commission. These are loaned to private producers, who also get film and other technical support at subsidized rates from the FDC.

It is hardly surprising that the self-abnegation of the FDC has seen the prospering of the private sector in the film industry. This has been one of the growth sectors in private industry, as witnessed in the spread of cinema houses and the profusion of locally made films coming on to the screen. A rabid degree of protectionism insulates it from any form of competition from imports and keeps local production profitable.

These films are pot-boilers in the best subcontinental tradition. They are, with rare exceptions, of limited social value and are purely entertainment designed to provide escape for the audience. They project a world of fantasy where middle class values can be acted out as pipe dreams for the urban poor.

To the extent that the FDC can utilize its own facilities to make worthwhile films they will tend to be limited to urban audiences since private cinema owners have not found it worth investing in the villages in the absence of electricity and other

---

*There are about 200 cinema halls with a seating capacity of 130,000.

facilities. Mobile vans and boats have a potential, provided that films designed to project a meaningful message to the rural masses can be made.

CONCLUSION

This paper has tended to move outside the traditional compass of a discussion on communication policy since it is premised on the irrelevance of such policy formulations outside of the social context of development. It has thus tried to spell out the social context of development strategy in post-liberation Bangladesh and the contradictions within society which constrained the development effort. The contradictions within the policy led to a failure to project a clear development strategy and was illustrated in the fate of the First Five-Year Plan. The limits of administrative effort in communicating various policies were examined and the tendency for the media to be conditioned by the elitist direction of policy was brought out.

The approach tends to articulate the inherent problems faced by those who seek to use communication policy as an instrument of development in Bangladesh. Obviously within the limits of the system there is scope for communicating policy objectives more efficiently, and these may be explored by policy-makers. However such efforts by their very success may succeed in alienating the masses, since the gloss of communication strategy can hardly compensate for the conspicuous failures of development strategy to involve and benefit them. Another paper of a more positive nature could be written spelling out a communication policy which is designed to sell a development strategy for the masses. This is hypothetical in the present historical context, but nonetheless of great relevance in spelling out the options open to a society such as Bangladesh in contrast to the constraints within which it has hitherto had to develop.

While such a redirection of strategy must grow out of Bangladesh's own social dialectic, the scholar interested in studying communication policy for Bangladesh may very productively direct himself to research more definitively some of the issues brought out in this paper. The specific role of the political media in both projecting and distorting the intentions of government can be specifically studied from published works and field research commissioned for this purpose. Field research to spell out the access to government resources by various social groups in rural society and the interpersonnel social contacts and consequences of the extension effort can be a useful area of enquiry. The social ownership base of the media—radio, television, and newspapers—as well as the social background of their audience can be usefully studied. The implicit and explicit sociocultural content of the message and its impact on specific social groups can be productively studied. Some of this information has been derived from field studies carried out in a different context and has provided the information background to this paper. But the time would appear to be ripe for a full-scale study specifically designed to examine the social background and impact of communication policy and to design a mass-oriented communication strategy in the context of Bangladesh. To the extent that similarly oriented studies from other developing countries can provide a perspective on how different social formations and development strategies influence similar or different communications policies, the Bangladesh study would be of even greater value.

PROBLEMS OF COMMUNICATION PLANNING IN INDONESIA

Astrid S. Susanto

INTRODUCTION

This paper combines data from the field with available information for communication planning purposes. Together, these sources show the problems faced during planning and also demonstrate that, in spite of manpower constraints, at least at the central government level, efforts are made to do some communication planning. The situation is favored by the political condition of Indonesia, where the development perspective of the country does not only cover economic, but also cultural development, based on a conviction that development should be enjoyed and be of benefit to the people. In the first place, persuasive communication is needed to make people understand the ways and means of development. But at the same time, development programs can only be successful if they are genuinely geared to the needs of the population. Therefore, upward and reciprocal communication are vital components in the process of development, and (communication being both an activity of society and a means of expressing personal needs) communication planning also becomes an integral part of the development process.

Inevitably, in this process, many constraints are met. They are experienced not so much because communication is not taken seriously, but more because developing countries have to perform development activities in innumerable field levels and sectors at the same time. In the case of Indonesia it is a considerable problem to answer at the grass roots level, the rising (though simple) demands of the peasants, and at the same time to plan and create the nation's future resources. The contribution of communication in bridging all these sectors in support of development is not only to satisfy short-term needs and for the sake of development alone, but also for the well-being of the citizen in the long run.

DEVELOPMENT PLANNING IN INDONESIA

The impetus of Indonesia's development support communication planning is directed towards its 58,164 villages. The main aim is to raise the standard of living of the village population, based on the following classifications:

• Subsistence villages (swadaya)	Isolated, traditional with a dominant subsistence economic system; 30 percent of the population have attended elementary school; yearly per capita income *below* Rp. 12,000*; a weak village administration.
• Self-activating villages (swakarya)	Still outside the reach of external influence, yet undergoing a change of life pattern; per capita income of Rp. 12,000 per year; 30 - 60 percent of the population have attended elementary school; improved village administration.
• Self-propelling villages (swasembada)	Not traditional anymore; influenced by external stimuli; integrated with nearby town; have left subsistence economic system; about 60 percent of the population *finished* elementary school; working village administration; yearly per capita income of Rp. 17,500.

---

* US$1.00 equals approximately Rp. 415.

Since it is planned that within 25 to 30 years all subsistence villages should become self-propelling, it is estimated that each national five-year plan must raise 11,400 villages to the self-propelling stage. This means, in turn, that each year the government has to support the development of 52 districts, or 280 villages, or four percent of the total number of villages. The problem becomes more acute if the 1,721 units called "pre-villages" are also taken into consideration. These units cannot yet be called villages (not even those reaching the subsistence stage), since their village borders are unclear and the people are still living in isolation. But generally it can be said that the villages of Java and Bali and some outer islands have reached the self-activating stage already. The situation, as described in a recent report by the Director General for Rural Development (1975), is summarized in Table 1.

The goals of village development are seen as:
1. Increasing job opportunities in agriculture, small-scale industry, and handicrafts
2. Population resettlement and transmigration
3. Improving the minus and critical-soil areas, and their population's living standards
4. Improving the standard of living of fishermen and the coastal population
5. Improving health conditions and education
6. Improving utilization of the soil and diminishing the dangers of erosion
7. Teaching the village population to benefit from village cooperations
8. Improving administration at the village level and rural adjustment to change
9. Improving the coordination and efficiency of local government

These efforts are concentrated upon developing popular skills and improving mental attitudes toward development. But at the same time the peasants have to be taught to find and use their resources for the development of their own village, thus reducing their dependence upon the central government and its allocations. It is within this frame that (according to the Statute no. 5/1974) village heads are given the following duties:
- to act as head administrator of the village
- to collect and maintain village data
- to plan for village development programs

TABLE 1. RURAL DEVELOPMENT TARGETS

level of village development	year 1972		year 1973		year 1974		year 1975	
	total	percentage	total	percentage	total	percentage	total	percentage
subsistence villages	790	1.5	1,163	2.0	1,745	3.0	2,614	4.5
self-activating villages	29,534	50.8	29,664	51.0	30,878	53.0	31,785	54.6
self-propelling villages	27,840	47.8	27,337	47.0	25,541	44.0	23,765	40.9

- to improve peasant participation
- to improve the village social forums (LSD or *Lembaga Sosial Desa*)

The improvement of the villages is not to be done in isolation, but based on the concept that some villages will have their district capital as a growth pole, while state-wise, district capitals will have their provincial capital as the regional growth center. At the same time, regional development is also based on resources, capacities, and needs. In this way, the government has divided the country, not only into regional growth centers, but also into areas with maximum, medium, and lower development capacities.

DEVELOPMENT COMMUNICATION

It is quite natural that, in this context, communication is viewed as a means to speed up development.

In the village development programs, the village communication forums play a decisive role, and these are also being promoted by the government. At the village level it is the *Lembaga Sosial Desa* which serves the internal needs of the village. Within this forum the village development programs are discussed, skills relevant to village needs identified, and cadres for village leadership trained. At the village level both formal and traditional leaders, and other influential persons, have to work and decide together what is best for their village; and via the LSD (in which the village head is member and chairman), programs concerned with development are explained. In this way the isolation of the village is diminished and interrelationships with the surrounding villages and nearest town encouraged. The village is conceived as a unit with an important contribution to make to the development of a larger area.

As all sectors of development aim at the development of the Indonesian people, it is the village, at the lowest end, which has to realize all these plans and at the same time be its own consumer. It is therefore through discussions at the village level, be it at the village meetings, the social development forum, or through discussions held at rural listening groups, that the real *coordination of information on all matters concerning development* should be coordinated and reinforced. At the same time the government has foreseen more integration of information through the Information Center (*Pusat Penerangan Masyarakat*) at a regional level, which has to be the last knot of integrated information from the vertical central government units before all information enters the villages. All digestion, interrelation, and coordination is done by the Information Center, which also supports a public library, where information booklets are available (the same materials that are distributed by the Ministry for Education, Scouts'movements, and other social organizations).

MASS MEDIA DEVELOPMENT IN INDONESIA

Newspapers

Mass Media development was foreseen in Chapter 29 of Indonesia's second five-year development plan. The second plan revealed that, at the end of the first development plan, newspapers' circulation reached a total of only 1.5 million people, out of which 1 million were covered by the 122 dailies. Out of these 122 dailies 17 were published in Jakarta (representing 56 percent of the total circulation); this means that only 44 percent were published outside the capital. It proved difficult to set an estimated circulation for the end of the second five-year plan, since newspaper reading depends very much on the capacity and capability of the press itself in the financial and editorial, as well as the marketing, field. Additional difficulties were encountered because the press covered the private sector. Furthermore, the government is very aware of the fact that newspaper reading is determined by the degree of literacy. Yet, some increases have been noticed since 1971 in the consumption of newspapers. If by 1973 the total daily circulation reached only 822,419 copies, by the end of 1974 it showed an increase of nearly one million to 1,860,280 copies. The reasons for this sudden jump still have to be found. A *Seminar on Graphic Training* at the end of 1974 made some estimates (based on an annual 2.5 percent population increase), that by the end of 1976 the total circulation of newspapers and magazines might reach 126,195 copies per day, if development continued at existing ratios. How far that estimate will be correct still has to be seen.

If the situation in Jakarta shows an extraordinary number

of people reading more than one paper, newspapers in the provinces have a worse problem of serving too large an audience with only a small circulation. As an example it can be mentioned that the *Surabaya Post* in East Java, which had a circulation of 60,000 copies per day at the end of 1975, had to serve an audience of 25 million people.

In order to overcome problems such as this, the press has, in various ways, approached the government for support, especially for the development of rural presses. It has been proposed that the government should buy a certain percentage of the circulations of the newspapers and distribute these free in the villages. The government has, understandably, discussed this proposal as uneducational (with illiteracy so high) and has sought alternative means. Some methods proposed are for general support, such as a reduction of telephone and telecommunication tariffs, facilities in newsprint import, and government support for training of the journalists. Furthermore, in order to pave the way for the future, the government has started a form of development bulletin in West, Central, and East Java. Rosihan Anwar, a noted journalist in Indonesia, stated in his paper "The Function of the Press in the Development of Rural Areas" (1975) that a survey held in West Java (at two regencies, Lebak and Bandung) proved that, although respondents also read other provincial newspapers, the government bulletin *Tandang*, containing development know-how and practical hints for the rural population, had the highest percentage score, 52.50 percent, whereas the leading provincial newspaper *Pikiran Rakyat* only reached 13.9 percent within the rural villages. He came to the conclusion that Indonesia's provincial press is still too urban-oriented, and therefore cannot meet the demands of the village people. But in view of the fact that government development bulletins in West, Central, and East Java are now looked upon by the press as too heavy competitors (being financed by the state), the government is looking for an option which is more acceptable to the press itself, called the rural press. The government publications mainly concentrate on development projects, the dissemination of skills and local development achievements. These publications are thought to be an incentive for the peasants to compete with each other in achievement. A correspondence column is included and through this column two-way communication is encouraged. At the same time it is hoped that, once he becomes used to these development bulletins, a need for general newspapers will automatically be aroused in the literate peasant.

It should be admitted here that the layout of the development bulletins is still too monotonous and serious and the print is too dull, using small characters and too few pictures and photographs. It is hoped that the improvement of printing facilities in 1976 will enable the Information Centers to publish better and more attractive bulletins, which will really stimulate the new literate. The fact that the bulletin is written in the local language already is a great help, but if the print is not attractive enough, even this relevant-to-village-needs-bulletin will have only a limited audience.

Whether the government or the private press should investigate and promote a genuine rural press is still undecided. Anwar suggested that the rural press should include: 10 percent national and international news, 30 percent practical information, 20 percent provincial news, 30 percent regional news, features, and others, and only 10 percent advertisement. Naturally the low percentage of advertisement (instead of the usual 40 percent) will cause other problems and it may be that the government will be asked to intervene and bear "the losses" of the 30 percent lost ads. This idea is already being discussed and, further development in Indonesia might be quicker than planned. If the rural press is to become a reality in Indonesia before the end of the second five-year plan, some other criteria such as circulation numbers for each province, or circulation percentages compared to the population, should be taken into consideration even at this stage. Anwar, in the same paper, proposed that the rural press enterprise should be private and have a circulation of 10,000 copies per region. The paper should be issued once a week in a four-page tabloid size, sold at a price not more than Rp. 10,—or US $0.025. It is obvious, from these calculations, that government subsidy cannot be avoided. Production costs are too high, and consumer capacity too low, for more press development to be carried out purely privately, but at the same time government interference or subsidy is construed as hampering press freedom. The situation is aggravated by rapid technological improvements in the printing world, which the private sector, naturally, wants to incorporate into the industry. Skills also have to be developed, such as technical, editorial, and managerial, as well as marketing ability. A survey in 1973, carried out by the Thomson-Group of England, disclosed that the difficulties of the local press lay not so much in its market, but in the fact that it catered for a different readership than the one available to it. Even its advertisements

were not really catering to local readership, but were rather looking for a more urban-Jakarta-oriented audience, which is very
limited in its geographical area. Even if the government helps in
training people for the graphical part of the enterprise (which is
done through the Graphic Training Center in Jakarta), the need
for editorial and marketing know-how is still essential.

In planning the development of the Indonesian press,
therefore, the government has to reconcile itself by giving support
and subsidy to enterprises which (politically) are likely to be its
opponents; it stands to reason that such planning (especially if
it has budgetary implications) will not be easy. Although the
rural press is an ideal medium for Indonesia, it looks as if we
have many difficulties to overcome before a rural press in the
sense of a "printed medium, with editorial columns focused on
the needs and wishes of a restricted part of the Indonesian population, living outside or around cities throughout the country"
can be realized   (Tack and Brunswel, 1975).

Radio and Television

The development of television and radio in Indonesia has
been "easier" than was the case with the development of the
press since television and radio are in the hands of the government which makes planning and decision making easier.

If the development of the press depended on the development of a reading capability, the development and extension of
television and radio depend on the development of electricity in
the country. Fortunately, technology offers some solutions
where electricity is not yet available (through generators and
battery transistors).

At the same time, the new technology has also helped
sidestep the problem of illiteracy, in such a way that for the
82.4 percent of the rural population, information can be disseminated via television and radio. In the field of television,
the five-year plan approved an increase of studios from six in
1974 to ten at the end of 1978/79. At the same time, the number of relays has to be increased from 25 in 1974 to 56 in 1978/
79. The coverage of television (being 82,600 square kilometers
in 1974) was to be increased to 1,216,000 square kilometers by
the end of the five-year plan. The number of television sets
(estimated at 370,000 at the end of 1974) was to be increased to
680,000 at the end of the plan. The realization of this plan had

been so much favored by the situation of the petro-dollar at the end of the 1974/75 fiscal year, that the government decided to proceed and rehabilitate what was necessary. The rehabilitation of radio and television covered 49 sites, namely 11 at Sumatra, 6 at West Java, 5 at South Kalimantan (Borneo), 4 at Central Java, 7 at East Java, 3 at Sulawesi (Celebes), 1 in Ambon, 1 in West-Irian, and 2 each in Bali, Lombok, and Timor.

As soon as the decision was made (and even before contracts were signed), discussions on technical assistance for the training of radio and television manpower took place. In order to staff these newly ordered facilities, Indonesia will need at least 1,500 personnel by the autumn of 1976. No training center is known to have this capacity, and thus Indonesia has also had to devise some crash programs. The Training Agreement for TV-manpower (with the Federal Republic of Germany) was extended for another five years, especially to cope with the introduction of color television in Indonesia. This TV-Training Center previously aimed at training 125 people per year; since the renewed agreement it has to train 250 people, at two levels (for beginners and advanced training) in two shifts. At the same time it is planned that some personnel trained during the first TV-Training Agreement with Germany, will tour the country and teach equipment maintenance "on the spot."

If manpower for the technical field is hard to secure, training personnel for the Information Centers is no less difficult. Recruitment from the universities is not adequate to supply the new 57 Information Centers scattered throughout the country, the more so because the "pull" is still to Java, and especially Jakarta; and those who have studied there are reluctant to return to their home-islands. It is hoped that modern equipment and that a position as head of the Information Center at the regencies will be attractive enough to draw communication trained people back to the villages, especially to the outer islands.

The fact that Indonesia is rehabilitating (and developing) its television and radio network has received a great deal of publicity (and criticism), and it is less well known that out of the transmitters for radio, for example, only the following capacity is available:

11 transmitters/studios with 90 percent capacity
46 transmitters/studios with 60-80 percent capacity
73 transmitters/studios barely working.

Many date from 1942-48 and need overhauling.
Although, theoretically, the extension of television will
reach all provincial capitals, and the extension of radio will cover
the whole country, technicians are of the opinion that Indonesia,
being a very mountainous country, has to cope with many
"blind spots." Thus, although theoretically the coverage of
television and radio can be complete in the five year plan after
1976, the truth still has to be found out.
Since the main objective of the extension of television
and radio was to reach the 82.4 percent rural population (immediately after the problem of hardware had been "solved" and
a temporary "way out" found for manpower development), the
problem of utilization became imperative. It is worth emphasizing that decisions on the supply and installation of hardware—for
communications as for other factors—very much depend on the
financial situation and possibilities faced by a country. Although
the five-year plan mentioned the development and extension of
the television and radio network, the realization of that program
had to wait until the financial situation of the country really
favored it and after other priorities with more direct impact upon
the population(social projects as well as agriculture) had been
partly fulfilled. Until then, the development of the communications infrastructure (apart from roads) was looked upon as a
luxury.
Once the decision was made to extend the television and
radio network system, plans had to be made for the receiving
end. The government could not contemplate an improved system
at the transmitting end without it being utilized at the receiving
end. So there was no other choice for the government but to
distribute radio and television sets to the villages as well. Since
Indonesia has 58,182 villages, covering 3,251 districts and 282 regencies, the government has allocated a budget for the year
1976-77 sufficient to distribute a number of television sets equal
to the total number of districts. Since the whole country cannot
yet benefit from television transmissions, at least this calculation
has enabled the yearly television distribution to be phased out.
In practice, the situation may be somewhat different, and one
district may be able to have more than one television set (taking
population density into consideration); more sets can be distributed to villages of the same district having a dense population,
or alternately to thinly populated districts, and the distances between the villages having television sets will be too big. For areas

not yet covered by television, the government continues to distribute 3-band radio-sets with recording capacities in a number equal to the districts to be served. The basic thought of distribution has therefore been based on an increase of receiving sets (either television or radio) each year, equal to the number of districts. In such a way, planning for the hardware and especially its budgetary implications can be more easily calculated.

UTILIZATION

Up till now, television has had only one channel (program) for each area, but the government now considers it necessary to have at least two channels (broadcast from Jakarta) in order to meet both the needs and absorptive level of the more modern population of Jakarta, and above all, of the rural population. The programs for the rural areas (nationwide transmission) will be known as *National Broadcasting*, avoiding the negative connotation often given to "rural broadcasting." (On the other hand the Jakarta studio will have a special program for the "spoiled" Jakarta audience.) The increase of television facilities was also meant to enable "two-way communication" from Jakarta to the regions. The regional studios are also encouraged to make independent programs and, using video-tape recorders, aim towards a national broadcast of their local productions. In this way it is hoped that the programs will be better varied than might be the case if only Jakarta had the production capacity. It is worth mentioning that areas like Yogyakarta (in Central Java) and Denpasar (in Bali) have also been chosen to become production studios, because these two studios can concentrate on cultural programs. By 1976, Jakarta studios will also have a color capacity, but as manpower for this new communication technology still have to be trained, it is considered more of a try-out phase for Indonesian color television, and it will only broadcast in color for one hour a day.

Further discussion on the planned effectiveness of television and radio programs at the receiving end will be discussed separately when planning for upward communication is analyzed.

PLANNING UPWARD-COMMUNICATION

Since the five-year plan stressed the need for more intensive two-way communication between government and the people and the increase of communication opportunities for horizontal communication, a seminar was held in April 1975 on "The Role of Communications in Development," sponsored by the Ministry of Information. Themes discussed were: communication at the village level, communication in urban areas, and the use of mass media in general in Indonesia. The starting point of discussions was that real development should be supported by voluntary participation and that this participation will only be possible if a harmonious and free communication is offered and secured by the government. Apart from that basic political thought, it was felt that communication had many other obstacles, that is, when a society is changing from traditional to a transitional stage, harmonious and open communication is more difficult to realize.

A series of seminars helped the government a great deal in pinpointing its policy on how to reach the mass of 82.4 percent of population in the rural areas and the 18.6 percent of population in the urban centers. One important decision was the extension of *Farm Broadcasting* to become *Rural Broadcasting;* another activity was the use of indigeneous media for information and two-way communication.

The intensification of *Rural Broadcasting* was realized via the extension of the German Technical Aid on Rural Broadcasting in 1975-76. This agreement will last for three years, giving assistance in training for manpower at the technical transmitting end, as well as at the receiving end by training the extension workers and information officers to lead the listeners' and viewers' groups. Rural broadcasting started as *Farm Broadcasting* in Indonesia in 1969, especially in West Sumatra, namely in Bukittinggi and Padang. First, it started with a weekly broadcasting schedule, with topics such as "Farm Variety," "Proper Farming," "Answers to Questions," and "Problems of Irrigation and Pests." Nowadays after seven years' development the same stations have 90 groups with 195 members. This explains that the same members are participants of more than one type of specialized listeners' group. The *Rural Broadcasting* programs are nowadays divided into the following groups: General Farming, Estate Products, Nutrition, Irrigation, Cattle breeding and Poultry raising, Forestry, the Farmers' Wives, Religion, Scout movement, Cooperation Fishery, Small-scale industry, and others. In 1975, through the whole of Indonesia there were 126 studios broadcasting *Rural Broadcasting* programs, out of which 43 were the RPI (government-owned stations) and 83 local government-owned studios. The central government studios transmit 114 hours/week and the

local government studios around 151 hours/week of their
Rural Broadcasting programs. Around 25 percent of the total
local government studios transmit their *Rural Broadcasting* programs six times weekly for 15-45 minutes each time. The most
common times are the hours after evening prayers. In South
Sulawesi (Celebes) *Rural Broadcasting* has a program after the
morning prayers.

The creation of new listening groups in a region cannot
be accomplished overnight. Some inventory of the number of
radios available (apart from the public radios) compared to the
population number should be the first consideration. In West
Sumatra, *Farm Broadcasting* was started when data showed that
there were 58,494 sets in the region for a population of 2.4
million people. This meant that an average of 40 people listened
to one radio; and if one family generally consists of father,
mother, and give to six children, then it could be said that eight
houses together had one radio to listen to.

As the habit of radio listening grew and the range of
topics of interest increased, sub-listening groups were set up,
according to the same division. Radio transmission alone, however, was not sufficient. Therefore, reinforcement was created
through (1) weekly visits made by the agricultural extension
officers, (2) answers given via radio and/or face-to-face to the
questions, (3) visits of the listening groups made to demonstrate
plots, and (4) films and supporting printed material distributed.
The development of the listening groups in Indonesia is shown
in Table 2.

TABLE 2. GROWTH OF LISTENING GROUPS

Year	Total Number
December 1969	83
September 1970	127
September 1971	11,268
September 1972	5,133
September 1973	11,875
September 1974	14,479
September 1975	15,212

It is generally known that not all registered listeners' groups kept functioning; some had to stop activities because organization and supporting material was lacking or poor in quality. A survey by a German team in 1973 disclosed that out of the 519 samples taken through Indonesia, 46 percent had stopped their activities, while at the same time new listeners' groups had come to life. Therefore, it can generally be said that the awareness and predisposition for such listening groups is at hand: it very much depends on coordination and it is government care that will decide how far these groups will keep on working.

One of the efforts to bring after-care resources closer to the groups is the Information Center (Pusat Penerangan Masyarakat) at the regencies. These Information Centers are equipped with the latest audio-visual and printing facilities, including mobile units as a source of supply for the listening groups. The function of the Information Centers will become more decisive as television viewers' groups come into existence. Since the government distributed some 600 public television sets (as a try-out) in 1975, their first reactions will be used to direct the "after-care" not only of listeners' but also of viewers' groups. It is at this level where it becomes obvious that sophisticated mass media have to adjust themselves and to use indigeneous communication techniques in order to be effective.

FOLK MEDIA

The use of indigeneous communication techniques was felt necessary since increasing opposition to the content of television was voiced. Criticisms implied that foreign influence is to be feared, and a loss of national identity was said to be "obvious," should modern mass media be introduced into the villages. This criticism naturally was addressed to the government, since the extension of the television and radio network was not meant to serve the needs of the "haves," but above all to reach the rural population. Thus, the government had to look for a solution.

Since film and television are audio-visual media, so the use of them shows similarities to actual performances. Besides the often forgotten fact that film was only possible after the factors of technologies were combined with factors of the entertainment (Wolf, 1975), the nearest solution was to use folk culture to fill the programs meant for the rural population. Although, nowadays, documentary and scientific films are often produced, it is still the entertainment film which has the largest production. In the Indonesian indigenous media, *Wayang Beber,* which used to be popular in Central and East Java, has the closest similarities to these techniques. A storyteller used to go from village to village with his stories painted on the scrolls, and as the story goes on, so the scrolls are unwound. Nowadays, the *Wayang Beber* is being filmed by the Ministry of Information; thanks to modern technology, it now has the advantage of being able to be shown at different villages at the same time. In South Sumatra the *Andai-Andai* is the local mixture of entertainment and education and a performance can last the whole night. South Kalimantan has its all night show of *Madihin,* and the islands of Riau have their *Randai.*

The *Andai-Andai* of South Sumatra is also an all night performance. The scenario is similar to the *Madihin,* but it has just one actor at the center of the audience-circle. This actor has a pillow on his lap and a huge sieve in front of him. He gets his inspirations from the shouts and reactions of the crowd, and speaks his rhymes and ballads accordingly. The language used is the local language. Themes touched upon are topics of the day presented in ballads and allegory. The topics can range from price increases for rice to the increase of divorce looked upon as a phenomenon of social crisis. Yet, the inventory of the dying culture of the *Madihin* and *Andai-Andai* disclosed that its actors had a low education, were often illiterate, and practiced their entertaining role seasonally between harvests.

An analysis of these folk cultures and their success in conveying special messages has pointed out that their effectiveness lay in the fact that indigenous culture has a strong interaction with the audience. The communicator must have empathy for the audience and be able to create the needed reactions and audience participation. It seems that modern mass media are lacking in this regard, and consequently need reinforcement; the incorporation of folk media content should be helpful, especially with messages for the rural population.

INFORMATION OFFICERS

All the above mentioned data should help the government in activating upward communication. Within this context, the role of the information officers is very decisive in finding out and recognizing these existing techniques and combining them with modern mass media in order to exploit their technical capacities to the full.

In order to investigate the capability and communication situation of information officers with respect to their audience, a survey was held in 1975 in six provinces (namely West Java, Central Java, Yogyarkarta, East Java, Bali, and the lesser Sunda Islands (Nusa Tenggara Barat). This survey revealed great difficulty in the training of suitable manpower. The 58,182 villages will need at least one information officer to serve two villages. But, the figures indicated that the area actually to be served is so large that an information officer usually visits a village only once in three months, owing to the size of his assigned area and problems of transportation. The results of that recent survey (Ministry of Information, 1975) were as follows:

- The most common means of communications is the village meeting; 78.28 percent of the information officers who were interviewed mentioned that public meetings were the most "popular" technique; yet around 33.45 percent of the village respondents (opinion leaders) thought this technique to be the worst. Furthermore, only 13.78 percent of the information officers thought face-to-face and interpersonal communication necessary, although 81.11 percent practiced home visits. On the other hand 47.93 percent of the interviewed opinion leaders thought home visits to be the most favored technique of communication.
- Apart from mass meetings at the village hall, around 50.34 percent of the information officers favored film and slides, yet only 12.76 of the opinion leaders were familiar with it.
- In order to know how the social relations were between the information officers and their audience, data was also sought on their village of origin. It proved that 93.33 percent of the officers were of the same region, although only 61.11 percent were close to their place of work. It was therefore not surprising that 88.89 percent of the information officers used the local language as their means of communications. Strangely enough, of the opinion leaders interviewed only 64.44 percent thought it necessary that local language was stressed, whereas the opinion leaders group showed a

lower percentage for this necessity, namely only 58.87 percent. It was earlier suspected that information officers were more "provincialistic" than their other counterparts. However, the effort to try to find the relevancy between age and "provincialism" proved not to be valid, because only 46.66 percent of the officers reached the age above 40, whereas the percentage for that same group for the opinion leaders reached 66.55 percent.

Seen from this situation it seems to be necessary to make a deeper study on this case since information officers are *thought* to be the *national link* between the regions and the central government.

- It is also noteworthy that the information officers as well as the opinion leaders come from the same "local elite." The information officers have their family background as 42.44 percent farmers and 30 percent government administrators; the opinion leader group as 39.66 percent farmers and 26.21 percent administrators. This data connects with the need for local language as the means of communications and the psychological cause that the information officers are using "provincialism" to maintain their status and attachment to the local population, whereas the opinion leaders (who are religious leaders and traditional leaders, apart from the village head) want to see in the national language a hold for more "power" in their village, to be more "national."

- The sources of information for the officers are:

	(percentage)
Ministry of Information	100
radio	78
newspapers	66
books	62
village talk	56
own sources	49
magazine	41
television	33
others	24

Only 80 percent of the information officers own radios. Their radio listening and television viewing habits are as follows:

TABLE 3. SHOWING INFORMATION OFFICERS'
MEDIA-USE HABIT

item	radio	television
	(percentage)	(percentage)
news	56.94	43.39
information	25.00	30.19
music and entertainment	6.94	13.21
drama	5.56	7.55
others	5.56	5.56

Of those information officers who watched television,
only 7.78 percent watch at home, 22.22 percent at
public televisions and 28.89 watch in other people's
houses.
Their newspaper reading habit is 45.56 percent daily and
54.44 percent irregular. This low percentage for those
daily newspaper readers might be caused by the expensive price of subscription and and at the same time their
level of education does not motivate them to find more
reading and information material. According to the
answers given by the information officers during that
same survey, their educational level was:

	(percentage)
elementary school	30
junior high school	12.2
senior high school	42.4
academy	14.45
university	1.11

In relation to equal administrators of other departments,
the information officers seem to have one of the lowest educational profiles. This makes it difficult for them to communicate with
their administrative superiors (for example, the district head, who
on the average is an alumnus of the Academy for Internal Administration [APDN] and thus has a B.A. degree). It is also one
of the reasons why they prefer either to approach the village
people via formal meetings at the village hall and shy away from
home visits (although reluctantly carried out because of instruc-
tions), preferring to mingle with people of their own level of
education. Their preferred sources of information and communication *partners* are:

	(percentage)
the village head	64
religious leader	36
teachers	10
schoolmasters	2
others	2

If we take the limited volume of information and topics of discussion at the village level, we can come to the conclusion that "information inbreeding" is likely to take place in villages, especially those far away from the information centers (like the district capital) or areas remote from the capital of Jakarta.

Their limited knowledge at the same time has given note to an extraordinary optimism, that "there are no communication problems with the people," (except for 22.22 percent respondent information officers who are of the opinion that problems of communication are caused by traditionalism among the population (14.44 percent), and populous apathy (7.78 percent).

These newly obtained findings show that development support at village level is still too much at the mercy of people with low education and limited knowledge and that therefore a new approach and program has to be planned for the recruitment of new information officers. Apart from the fact that the number and competence of the information officers will have to be increased, more vehicles have to be made available to them, psychological factors such as their communication patterns with the district heads have to be overcome, a balance between the use of the national language and regional languages had to be fixed, and more training in the use of simple audio-visual aids and interpersonal approaches has to be made available. If these facts are not taken into consideration when plans are made, the results of development support communication are likely to be very disappointing.

Discussion

The problems mentioned above form only a part of the problems to be tackled by communication planners. If training for the hardware is difficult enough, it is even more so for the software. Additionally, people with a communication science background are generally not in the planning field, but directly in information activities or other jobs such as public relations (for government departments, private enterprise, or the press). A great step has been taken through a new government regulation that ministries should have a Research and Development (R & D) unit. The R & D units (such as that of the Ministry of Information), which work together with the universities, seems not only to provide good data, but at the same time the units give an additional impetus to academic faculties to work in an interdisciplinary manner. Usually, the universities are well trained to carry out data collecting, although evaluation of the findings is very often still weak, and a great deal of re-interpretation has therefore to be carried out by the R & D units themselves to make results operational.

Finally, it is the financial situation of the country that will enable how fast the plans for recruitment or training can be carried out to provide the most suitable manpower. The "competition" in budget allocation depends on the priorities of the country, and this is a strong reason for a developing country.

Planning—especially in the communication field—is an overall activity, and within the context of scarcity, a communication planner has to be able "to give in" in some matters and to correct that same matter in an indirect way. One example might be to have a limited but good cadre of information officers, who at the same time are officers from other departments, trained additionally in the communication field. Communication knowledge *alone* does not suffice. Just as the planner at the central or regional level should have an overall plan, so the communication officer at each level should have that same information and be able to translate it into the needs and scope of his or her operational field. Planning at the central government level alone will not suffice. Only in this way can communications planning be successful in developing countries, where nearly all priority activities have to be carried out within definite constraints, such as available manpower, financial considerations, and the range and extent of knowledge.

Works Cited

ANWAR, R. 1975. "The Function of the Press in the Development of Rural Areas," Rural Press Seminar, Java, Indonesia.

Director General for Rural Development, Ministry of Interior Affairs. 1975. Paper to Rural Broadcasting Seminar. Jakarta.

MARTAATMADJA, S. 1975. Paper presented to Seminar on Rural Broadcasting. Jakarta.
Ministry of Information. 1975. *Laporan Penelitian tentang sikap juru penerangan dalam melaksanakan tugasnya untuk mensukseskan pembangunan.* Jakarta.

TACK and BRUNSWEL. 1975. "Production Problems." Paper presented to Rural Broadcasting Seminar. Jakarta.

WOLF, G. 1975. *Der Wissensharftliche Film in der Bundesrepublik Deutschland.* Bad Godesberg, 1.

NATIONAL COMMUNICATION POLICIES IN LATIN AMERICA: A GLANCE AT THE FIRST STEPS

Luis Ramiro Beltrán S.

INTRODUCTION

This essay is an account of the initial phase of the process through which the existence of national communication policies is being fostered in Latin America. It is a description and an analysis of the chief steps taken thus far in that direction as well as a discussion of the outlook for the immediate future.

The first section deals with the concept of overall national communication policies and the with the importance of these instruments for the developing countries. The second enumerates some policy decisions taken so far to bring about inter-American coordination of communication activities, mostly among countries in the Andean subregion of Latin America. An overview of the experiences of three countries—Perú, Venezuela, and Brazil—that have spontaneously made significant advancements toward the formulation and implementation of national communication policies is given in the third section. The fourth part reviews the international promotion of the initiative and traces its evolution across several recent meetings of experts—mostly sponsored by Unesco—that have provided some theoretical basis for the movement. The

The opinions expressed in this paper are solely the responsibility of the author and not those of the institutions for which he works.

opposition to the propolicy movement on the part of international media owner organizations is shown in the fifth part. And the sixth and last section depicts the confrontation of philosophies about the role of mass communication between the status quo-oriented and the reform-minded sectors and relates this to the historical next step in the process: the June 1976 Intergovernmental Conference on National Communication Policies for Latin America and the Caribbean to be held in Ecuador under Unesco's auspices.

NATIONAL COMMUNICATION POLICIES FOR DEVELOPMENT

A national communication policy is an integrated, explicit, and durable set of partial communication policies harmonized into a consistent body of principles and norms addressed to guiding the behavior of the institutions specializing in handling the overall communication process in a country.

Partial communication policies are sets of isolated behavioral prescriptions concerned only with given parts or aspects of the system and process of social communication. These policies are formulated, fragmentarily and independently, by owners of communication media, by communication professionals, and by government authorities, each naturally responding to their respective interests. As such, they often come in conflict with one another.

A democratic national communication policy makes the partial policies necessarily explicit, seeks to integrate them by reaching consensus or conciliation, and aims at having a reasonably sustained duration, subject however to continuous evaluation and adjustment.

The State's Leading Role

Understandably, the leading role in the formulation of a national communication policy is to be played by the state. For the democratic state, representative of the nation's community, is the public institution endowed with legitimate and appropriate power to formulate the policy and implement it on behalf of said national collectivity and for the benefit of all its components. As such, the state is to perform the roles of *stimulator, inhibitor, articulator,* and *arbiter,* just as it already uncontestedly does in other policy domains. It has the right and the duty to do so.

National communication policies constitute an innovation that is a newcomer in the young art of formal planning for national development. All over the world, the state—capitalist, communist, or other—already presides over broad policy-making in numerous areas of economic, cultural, and political activity. But still just a few countries in the world, and only very recently, seem to have come to grips with the need for national communication policies.

The Latin American countries themselves have evidently had for many years national policies on imports and exports, credit, foreign relations, and national defense, to name but a few. More recently, they have built policies on health, taxation, and land reform, among others. And it is only in the last few years that several of them have started to formulate national policies for science and technology, education, and culture.

The Need for Communication Policies in the Developing World

These countries are now beginning to think about having overall national communication policies. It is logical that they do so, for—contrary to the situation of the world's industrial powers—the developing countries demand policy-making on communication as a tool to attain development. This has been clearly perceived, for instance, by West Germany's Minister of Economic Cooperation, Egon Bahr:

> For the development of the Third World, media policy is a task which stands immediately after that of securing food and has, at least, the same importance as economic, monetary and demographic policy (1975, p. 20).

Wilbur Schramm, an internationally known development communication specialist, agrees: ". . . after the basic economic and political questions are decided—after a country decides how fast it wants to move, and what kind of national pattern it wants to develop towards—then it faces a series of ongoing strategic decisions directly on communication use" (Schramm in Lerner and Schramm, 1967, p. 31). Schramm further feels that "the really basic strategies of developmental communication are not merely communication strategies but are economic and political, and grounded deep in the nature of society" (*ibid.,* p. 27). This is why the national development policies and plans must have derivative and directly concomitant national communication policies since "in the absence of a clear national policy on any given issue, the communicator is in the position of a swimmer treading water just to keep from going under; he is unable to strike out in any direction" (Davison and George, 1961, pp. 437-38).

Ithiel de Sola Pool has underlined four central policy issues on which, in his view, most developing countries must make major decisions. First, how much of their scarce resources ought to be invested in building the country's mass media system. Second, what roles must be assigned to the public sector and which to the private. Third, how much freedom is to be allowed or how much control is to be exerted on the performance of the communication system. And fourth, how much uniformity is to be required and how much diversity is to be permitted (Pool, 1963, p. 234).

The very success or failure of development policies, plans, and actions can be seen in these countries as considerably dependent upon communication policies, plans, and actions. Indeed, as has been stressed by, among others, S.C. Dube:

> A series of costly and avoidable failures has shown the planner that even well-drawn projects of modernization fail to register with the people and to produce the desired results unless they are supported by an imaginative, adequate, and effective communication program . . . . (Dube, in Lerner and Schramm, 1967, p. 93).

Just as no society can exist without communication, national development based upon social change cannot take place without communication being organized in the service of the nation's goals. And organization, the rational and orderly investment of energy and resources, begins with policy—the polar opposite to improvization and anarchy.

The Opposition to Policies and Plans

However, until recently, and up to a point, still today in some places, the very organization of national development by the state, through national policies and plans is objected to by tradition-bent circles—conservative and liberal—in Latin America. They claim that this is an undesirable and undemocratic intervention of the government in the domain of private interests and into what is taken to be the natural and free evolution or progress of a country. Those circles are already objecting to the initial step taking place in these lands to formulate national communication policies and plans for development—another indicator of the inseparability of society and communication. Pertinent testimony by Brazil's minister of communication, Euclides Quandt de Oliveira, is telling:

> It can be said that only recently, with the enormous mass of knowledge accumulated and the social duty consciousness of the State before the Nation, it became a government principle to endeavor for organized development or, better, for a planned development adequate to everything and to all in the interest of the common good (1975, p. 5).

The minister added, "However, among us, Brazilians, efforts are already being made, and some with success, in the direction of designing convenient global and sectorial policies coherently envolving the whole system and the diverse phases of the economic and social processes" (*ibid.*, p. 9). By contrast, Minister Oliveira deplored that:

> . . . in what refers to mass communication, measures to rationalize their utilization are not felt yet. Media controlled by the Government, in different organs, although in a small number, still are not being employed coordinatedly. On the other hand, absolute liberalism, which is the predominant note in the private area of mass communication, determines that this media primordially take care of singular objectives, making difficult their utilization in the service of the broader objectives of social development (*ibid.*).

To be sure, a society that does not want to change in general will prevent changes from occurring in the extant communication system and process. Inversely, a society seeking generalized change should necessarily include in that process substantial changes in communication. According to joint Latin American presidential-level statements, all countries in the region want social change as a prerequisite for attaining general national development. Nevertheless, as Dube observed of the developing nations in general:

Little effort appears to have been made so far in these countries
to formulate a long-term image and value-oriented policy aimed
at building certain positive and forward-looking images and at
inculcating attitudes conducive to modernization. In other
words, the importance of communication as valuable social over-
head is as yet not sufficiently recognized (Dube, in Lerner and
Schramm, 1967, p. 93).

This essay is a succinct account of that "little effort" in
Latin America "so far."

COMMUNICATION POLICIES
FOR LATIN AMERICAN INTEGRATION

The preoccupation in Latin America with national communication policies at the country level was perhaps slightly
preceded by the preoccupation with the roles of communication in fostering integration among the states of this region. For
instance, in 1967 the Institute for the Integration of Latin
America (INTAL), a branch of the Inter-American Development
Bank, held a seminar in Buenos Aires on Latin American integration specifically addressed to communication experts specializing in public relations. However, for a while, the efforts
toward integration remained centered on economic activities
carried out through the Latin American Free Trade Association
(LAFTA) and, later, through the Central American Common
Market, the Andean Promotion Corporation (CAF), and the
"Pact of Cartagena"—the organization that evolved out of a subregional agreement for the economic integration of the Andean
countries (Venezuela, Colombia, Ecuador, Perú, Bolivia, and
Chile). The "Pact of Cartagena" was later accompanied by an
understanding for cultural, educational, and scientific integration known as the "Andrés Bello Agreement," an instrument
including communication concerns within its scope.

The "Andrés Bello" Andean Agreement

From its inception in 1970, the Andrés Bello Agreement established as one of its chief obligations that of "devot-
ing preferential attention to using social communication media
given their educational influence and to promoting the joint
production of audiovisual programs aimed at securing a healthy
formation and recreation of the people and at preserving the

ethical and cultural values" (*Impulso*, 1973, p. 60). Concomitantly, the institution obliged itself to foster, within the legal order of each country, measures to neutralize "the negative action that may be exerted over the formation of youth, the public morals and the mental health by certain contents of some means of social communication, principally, television, motion pictures, radio and printed matter" (Arizmendi Posada, 1974, p. 53). These policy interests of the agreement have come together with the promotion of information exchange among the Andean countries and the idea of establishing an Andean News Agency (*ibid.*). More recently, the institution has requested from United Nations Development Programme (UNDP), with the approval of its member states, supplementary financial support for the establishment of a Latin American Graduate School of Communication at Centro Internacional de Estudios Superiors de Comunicación para América Latina (CIESPAL), in Ecuador (SECAB, 1976).

The Andrés Bello Agreement also committed itself to cooperating with other international organizations—such as the Organization of America States (OAS), Unesco, and UNDP—in feasibility studies for a subregional system of education via satellite. These are finished and have been presented for the consideration of the governments. Some of the recommendations included in them were incorporated into a resolution of the Fifth Meeting of Ministers of Education held in 1974 in La Paz, Bolivia (Agudo Freites, 1975, p. 2). However, the secretary general of the Andrés Bello Agreement reported as follows his perception of a key policy position that resulted from this meeting:

> In general, the impression which the Ministers of Education have had in this meeting is that it is necessary first to strengthen the experience and the mechanisms working in the design, production and distribution of educational messages (such as teleducation, education by correspondence, utilization of the press for educational goals, etc.) before really being able to think about setting up a subregional system of education which employs the most modern means, among them the sideral antenna or the communications satellite (Arizmendi Posada, 1974, p. 54).

The Declaration of Cali

Of equal or greater significance have been agreements made by the ministers of communication at their first meeting

held in May 1974 in Cali, Colombia. Going beyond the hardware considerations that normally constitute the axis of their
concerns, these ministers approved a declaration and 22 specific resolutions that affect multicountry Latin American communication policies both in terms of hardware and software concerns.

One of the propositions in the Andean Pact of Cartagena
refers to the establishment of a Council of Social Communication. Another is to stimulate the formation of associations of
state telecommunication and television enterprises, along with
establishing a coordinated and joint postal and telecommunication policy. Other resolutions involve exchanging training facilities for radio and television production as well as for telecommunication and postal services; adopting compatible black and
white and, if deemed eventually convenient, color television
systems; and exchanging information for the rational utilization
of the radio-electric spectrum.

Integrative Efforts in Tele-Education

Along with official multicountry policy-oriented activities, some professional coordination efforts are also touching
upon questions of communication policy at the regional level.
This seems to be the case of the Latin American Association of
Tele-Education (ALTE) sponsored by Germany's Konrad
Adenauer Foundation through its Lima-based Institute for International Solidarity (ISI). In some seminars, the Latin American
tele-education specialists have made pronouncements not very
different from some of those recorded at the Bogotá and San
José meetings of experts or too far apart from the preoccupa-
tions voiced by the Andean government officials. For instance,
in Lima in 1969, they signed a declaration that included statements such as the following:

> We, the Latin Americans, live in a developing society whose
> present structures oppress and limit man. It is our challenge,
> as educators, to respond to this reality. Faced with the prevail-
> ing social injustice, education must struggle for a just society,
> in which man can fully and harmoniously develop as a human
> person (ALTE, p. 191).

Stressing the decisive importance of radio and television
for people's education, the participants in the Lima seminar

proposed that these media be put to the service of the collective effort and used to create "mystic and vocation" for development. They also manifested their will to help devise a socially sensitive tele-education methodology in substitution of the traditional educational systems, and they subscribed to the notion that modern mass media ought to be rationalized so as to help reaffirm superior human values (*ibid.*).

Coinciding with such purposes, the president of Venezuela, Carlos Andrés Perez, told a meeting of the Inter-American Association of Broadcasters (AIR) that the audio-visual media are not serving education, culture, and development. Thus he proposed "the creation of a Latin American network of radio and television which, both in its purposes and its implementation and dynamics, is at the service of the spiritual, economic, and social integration of the continent" (Agudo Freites, 1975, p. 7).

SPONTANEOUS INITIATIVES: PERU, VENEZUELA, AND BRAZIL

Every Latin American country has long had a few partial communication policies of one kind or another. The most common of these range from articles in constitutions down to specific norms operationalizing general laws, press freedom, and the granting of licenses to use the radio-electric spectrum. More recently, policy decisions were made on television ownership, with the private sector being the winner in all but a few countries: Bolivia, Colombia, Cuba, and Chile. *However, no country in this region has yet built the kind of master instrument that could truly be regarded as an overall national communication policy in the sense of being an all-enhancing, articulated, explicit, and durable set of coherent rules for the behavior of the totality of the communication system.*

The Three Known Exceptions

If Cuba has been able to do something of this nature, information about it is not readily available. There is, however, one country that has come closest to the ideal portrayed in this definition—that produced at July 1974 meeting of Latin American experts in communication policies held in Bogotá under

Unesco sponsorship (Unesco, 1974). That country is Perú. Next in importance is Venezuela, where a recently passed law establishing a National Council of Culture involves significant policy prospects, mostly in reference to radio and television. A third country, also quite active in radio and television policy and apparently beginning to lean toward an overall national communication policy, is Brazil.*

These three countries, with appreciable differences among them in their approach to the question, have entered the long and complex road leading toward overall national communication policies. And they did so on their own, that is, before international promotion of the idea acted as a mover.

The cases of Perú and Venezuela have been more extensively treated elsewhere by the present author. Therefore, in spite of their importance, their experiences will be mentioned in this overview only briefly. More attention will go to the case of Brazil.

Before so doing, however, it must be noted that these initial attempts to approximate the ideal of overall policies are taking place in very different political settings. While both Perú and Brazil are under military regimes, they are evidently polarized in ideological terms. Venezuela is under civilian rule but shares with Brazil a capitalist economy; and yet, different from Brazil, is run by reform-minded rulers seeking socio-structural change but not as swiftly and radically as in Perú. The significant thing about this diversity is that, regardless of it, the three countries appear to be among the few in the region having perceived the importance of counting on a communication system presided by a policy addressed to serve development.

The Case of Perú

In October 1968, after a lifetime of conservative rule of one kind or another, Perú was awaken by a military coup to

---

*According to official Venezuelan information (CONAC, 1975, pp. 54-60), Mexico and Argentina have also recently become very dynamic in the regulation of radio and television. However, this does not seem to be part of an attempt to reach the higher stage of an overall national communication policy. Colombia was one of the precursors in dealing with the regulation of these media and in conducting research leading to it, but the concern has not so far reached the government decision level at all. (See Fox de Cardona, 1975a and Ramírez Restrepo, 1974.)

what proved to be the most profound revolutionary transformation in its history. Rejecting both capitalism and communism, the government of the armed forces defined itself as social-democratic, nationalist and humanist, and pledged to liberate Peruvians from internal domination by the oligarchy and external domination exerted by foreign interests, mostly those of the United States (Perú, Oficina Central de Información, 1975). Since then, with considerable popular backing, the government has, radically but peacefully, acted to change the entire economic, social, cultural, and political structure of the country in the direction of full and just social participation. In so doing, it has not permitted activity of political parties or re-established electoral procedures. Instead it has promoted widespread and intense popular participation by facilitating the association of the population mostly around occupational groupings, in themselves different from those that existed until then. With their support, the government nationalized oil and mining companies; carried out a sweeping land reform; modified substantially the fishing industry, commerce, and cooperatives; and introduced a thorough democratization of education.

Prior to the revolution, the mass communication system of the country was almost exclusively in the hands of private enterprises; as a rule most of the big ones were directly linked with firms that concentrated economic power. Oligopolic media ownership; alienating, conformist, and mercantilistic mass media messages; indifference to national development needs; and penetration by U.S. interests, mostly through advertising, were the characteristics of such a communication system. (See Neira, 1973; *Textual*, 1973; and Gargurevich, 1972). The revolutionary government acted resolutely to correct this too. It adopted a series of concatenated policy decisions designed to transform the system so that it would serve the change-seeking majorities rather than the pro-status-quo elites.*

These measures, as a whole, diminished and controlled private power over communication and bolstered that of the state. But full nationalization of the mass media was avoided in favor of mixed enterprises in the case of radio and television

---

*See Ortega and Romero, n.d. and the following Peruvian documents listed under "Works Cited": 1971, 1974a, 1974b, 1975a, 1975(?)b, 1975c.

and "social property enterprises" in the case of the large dailies of national circulation. These dailies (located in the capital city) were expropriated and transferred to "national labor communities" of peasants, workers, professionals, educators, and intellectuals. A new press statute was implemented.

This was not done without strife since the affected interests fought against the reforms firmly and loudly. Because the expropriated dailies were affiliated with the Inter-American Press Association, known in Spanish as Sociedad Interamericana de Prensa (SIP), this organization condemned the measures as undemocratic and totalitarian and declared the country delinquent in terms of press freedom. But the reforms went ahead and were consolidated all the same. In fact, a telecommunications law completely reorganized and reoriented these services, including those of radio and television. These were to have at least 60 percent of their programming produced in the country and were to grant the state one hour daily for educational, civic, and cultural programs. Abuses in advertising, in orientation, length, and frequency were curtailed through a set of norms. No foreign ownership was to be permitted.

To give the state strength and coherence in matters of communication, a National Information System was created at the ministerial level. Under it, a series of decentralized agencies were established to take care of specialized activities, for instance, a government publishing house, a government institute for radio and television, a national telecommunications agency, a state advertising agency, and a telecommunications training and research institute. The basis for an overall national communication policy was established as a part of the National Development Plan.

The Case of Venezuela

In August 1975, the Congress of Venezuela passed a law creating the National Council for Culture. This broad policy instrument includes provision that should enable the state to reorient, reorganize, and substantially bolster the government's radio, television, and film producing facilities by establishing a State Radio and Television Corporation. This, in turn, should result in the implementation of a national radio and television policy, now formulated in a basic draft form (CONAC, 1975).

Bent on gradual socio-structural reform as the present social democratic government of the country is, the communication measures were concomitant and coincident with the nationalization of the huge oil industry from which the country obtains most of its now enormous foreign revenue. If fully implemented, the communication measures should put the state on a parity power base with private communication interests which had so far dominated the mass communication situation. In fact, under the law approved, the decentralized radio and television corporation, Ratelve, could come to be of such a technical and financial nature and magnitude that it should be able to do what private enterprise does not: *to use communication in the service of national development in general and, in particular, to promote culture and education for the benefit of the masses.* This will not involve nationalization of the private media although it should facilitate their control in terms of their becoming persuaded to behave differently and to modify the quality and intent of their messages.*

As in Perú, but even more vehemently, the private interests affected have attacked the government for these measures, labeling them undemocratic, totalitarian, and antagonistic to information freedom and human rights. But in contrast with Perú, where communication change readily took place within a situation of general social transformation, the Venezuelan government will have to fight a daily battle to implement its new policies. The private interests, significantly penetrated by foreign investment, are already being aided in the confrontation by SIP. In fact, the project for the law of culture was the object of a massive and concerted attack. The campaign was mounted by a number of private entities and coordinated by the national association of advertisers and of advertising agencies that according to Pasquali (1975), happen to be foreign in 65 percent and 76 percent of the cases, respectively. This time the campaign failed.

---

*For full information on the law and on Project Ratelve, see the Venezuelan official document (CONAC, 1975), along with the broader framework described by Agudo Freites, Gómez and Pasquali, 1975. For information on native and foreign domination of the communication system, see Diaz Rangel (1967, 1974).

President Perez and his minister of information have taken an open stand in favor of these and other reforms of the country's communication system. However, in spite of the extradordinary economic power the Venezuelan government wields today, the possibilities for effective generalized changes in that system do not appear to the eyes of some observers to be very high yet (Gómez, 1975 and Eliaschev, 1975). In support of their skepticism, they refer to these recent discouraging experiences:

1. The president announced in Congress that his government was studying the possibility of effectively applying the income tax to advertising revenues. Claiming that they would lose 30 million U.S. dollars and threatening to contribute to unemployment, advertisers and advertising agencies were able to stop this plan. The minister of information had to call it just a "vague" plan in order to appease the protesters.

2. The Ministry of Information announced a decision to establish a state corporation to provide provincial newspapers with credit and facilities for equipment renewal and newsprint acquisition. Again, under attack from, among others, SIP, the measures do not seem to have been implemented yet.

3. The minister of information announced the government's intention to set controls on the behavior of the advertising business so that it would cease to alienate and mercantilize the audience and would, instead, contribute to the creation of a "new Venezuelan man." Once again, charges of authoritarianism were made against the idea, the fate of which is yet to be seen.

4. An officer of the Central Office of Information announced that the government was considering the establishment of a national news agency, and President Perez, when visiting the president of Mexico, joined him in declaring that Latin America ought to establish its own regional news agency, but no positive action has been taken in either case.

The Case of Brazil

Brazil, the largest country on the South American continent, has over 110 million inhabitants dispersed over an area of 8.5 million square kilometers, and living under very different economic, social, and cultural conditions. This population is 60 percent urban, and 50 percent is under 20 years of age. The

Brazilian GNP has more than doubled in the last ten years, allowing the average per capita income to reach US$800 in 1974. However, great disparities exist. In the northeastern region, per capita income is roughly 50 percent of the national average. The southeastern region is by far the economic leader of the country with 70 percent of the Brazilian labor force, and 75 percent of its industrial production concentrated around the large metropoli of Saõ Paulo and Rio de Janeiro (Camargo and Pinto, 1975).

Mass media is basically a private enterprise in Brazil. The main activity of the government is media supervision. The basic legislation regulating the media is, according to Camargo and Pinto (*ibid.*) the following:

- *The Brazilian Law on Information* ("Press Law"). This ensures the traditional rights of thought, expression, and response for the Brazilian population; regulates the private media; and prevents abuses of freedom of expression. In addition, it establishes criminal procedures, civil responsibility, and general operational provisions for the media, such as the limitation of media ownership to Brazilians.
- *The National Council of Telecommunications.* Law 4117 of 1962 sets up a National Council of Telecommunications as a regulatory body to supervise the activities of government-granted concessions, to issue authorization and permits for the use of telecommunication services, and to apply penalties.
- *The National Institute of Cinema.* This is a federal organization set up under the Ministry of Education and Culture in 1966 to formulate and implement the governmental policy related to the development, improvement, and promotion of the Brazilian film industry.
- *The Brazilian Telecommunications Enterprise.* This was established to set up the basic operational network of the national system of telecommunications, including telephone, telex, data, radio, and international television. In addition, it handles relations with international systems of communication such as satellite systems.
- *Censorship.* Based on the National Constitution, it is present in all Brazilian media with regard to the

protection of ethical values and the dignified and
healthy formation of youth.

Researchers Nelly de Camargo and Virgilio B. Noya
Pinto conclude in their study *Communication Policies in Brazil,*
that:

> Today, circumstances have imposed a balance between freedom
> of communication and national order and security. Legislation
> tries to reconcile these exigences. . . . Many juridical formulas
> which are valid for a balanced and developed country demon-
> strate their insufficiency or even worthlessness in the develop-
> ing ones. The difficulty of matching ideals, interests and proper
> policies remains considerable (*ibid.,* p. 62).

The actual communication policies of Brazil, which have
been briefly reviewed above have been evaluated in a recent
study by Dov Shinar and M.A.R. Dias (1975), who put special
emphasis on the issue of a national communication policy in
that country. The authors concluded that, in spite of ample
lesiglation in the country in almost all areas of broadcasting and
other fields of communication, a systematic approach has not
yet been developed, nor found expression in the structure, operations, and output of communication in Brazil. In an analysis of
the goals of the communication policies, they found the following dominant: (1) national integration, (2) socioeconomic devel-
opmeht, (3) promotion of cultural and educational values, and
(4) financial profit for the private enterprises.

The study identified various problems that must be
overcome to achieve these goals. With regard to integration,
they found that the coverage policy of private radio and television was directed by commercial criteria rather than that of
national coverage. This produced undue concentration of the
media in the chief urban centers. Cultural goals have also suffered because of the commercial orientation. Only a small part
of the television programs are locally produced, and local and
regional content do not correspond to the cultural varieties of
the country. News was also found to be lacking for national
development purposes. The authors assessed the national development role of the media to be the weakest point of Brazilian
broadcasting, both commercial and noncommercial. Commercial goals were the only ones with a significant degree of achievement. However, this was found to be unevenly distributed
throughout even the commercial system, with the *O Globo* interests to be the real beneficiaries of the growth of commercial
broadcasting.

In summarizing their findings, Shinar and Dias noted
that the "short-comings of Brazilian broadcasting—partial
achievement of integrative goals, poor cultural performance,
insignificant contribution to processes of development and uneven distribution of commercial profits—point out the basic
problem areas related to broadcasting policy in the country"
(*ibid.*, p. 18). Brazilian Minister of Communication Oliveira
stressed a more specific problem: With the mass importation of
"can red" television programs, Brazilian television becomes a
"privileged vehicle for cultural importation, a basic factor in
the denaturalization of our creativity. . . . Commercial TV is
imposing on youth and children a culture which has nothing to
do with the Brazilian one" (1974, p. 46).
    Shinar and Dias concluded their study with the hope for
the "establishment of a national communication policy, that
would be global, whole and coherent . . . and would also create
mechanisms that would allow the use of communication media
instruments for the participation of the population in the definition, goals, and results of the development process" (Shinar
and Dias, 1975, p. 26). Minister Oliveira, keenly perceiving the
inconveniences of fragmentary and isolated policy-making, has
asserted:

> Mass communication is a key factor in the process of general
> conscientization in a developing country. It, therefore, is neces-
> sary and urgent that systematic, adequate and organized efforts
> be added to the formulation of communication policies (1975,
> p. 10).

    One step in the direction of the formulation and imple-
mentation of such a national communication policy is the project Radiobras (Brazil, 1975), submitted to the Brazilian Congress in October 1975. The objective of this project is to set up
a national telecommunications company that will administer
all public radio and television stations, including the radio station
of the Ministry of Education, in addition to the training of technicians in the field and special services to the state.
    In the document presenting the new law, the minister of
communication explained that one of the motives of this project was to bring the services of radio and television to those areas
of the country currently ignored by these media (*ibid.*).
    Another effort for the implantation of national commu-
nication policies is from the Ministry of Education, which

proposes the social use of communication media through the interlacing of the communication goals to those of the social and global development (Shinar and Dias, 1975, p. 27).

These two efforts represent a clear tendency to increase the control and influence of the state on the mass communication system of the country so that it serves development. In addition, both of these policy efforts contain a certain degree of centralization of the communication systems as a solution to the use of the media for national development ends. The question that remains to be answered is to what extent the continued concentration of the media system in that country, be that in public or private hands, is in itself beneficial to national development and the better distribution of wealth among the population, stated to be one of the premises of the Second National Development Plan for 1975-1979 (*ibid.*).

THE INTERNATIONAL PROMOTION OF NATIONAL POLICY-MAKING

Responding to the manifested will of the member states, Unesco has been fostering the existence of educational, scientific, and cultural policies for some 15 years now. It has in that respect provided technical assistance to interested governments, held meetings, and promoted research and literature useful for the countries to formulate, establish, and implement said national policies.

In 1971 Unesco began to do a comparable promotion job for national communication policies, in fulfillment of the express mandate it has received for from the member states. In fact, at its sixteenth session, Unesco's General Conference authorized in 1970 the director general *"to help Member States in the formulation of their 'mass communication policies' "* (Unesco, 1972). In presenting Unesco's Draft Programme and Budget for 1973-74 to the General Conference, René Maheu, the director general of the agency, stressed that:

> The espousal of the idea of a national communication policy . . .
> completes the process which, beginning with educational planning
> twelve years ago, has progressively geared the various parts of the
> programme to the task of systematically directing national efforts
> in the fields of Unesco's competence in pursuit of specific objec-
> tives, in a word, in furtherance of a policy which is itself an integral
> part of comprehensive planning for total development (*ibid.*, p. 1).

Acting to fulfill the mandate, Maheu told the General Conference: "The present Draft Programme assuredly constitutes no more than a first step in this direction and progress will be slow and difficult. But the very fact that this first step has been taken deserves mention because it represents an innovation which may have far-reaching consequences" (*ibid.*).

Paris, 1972: The First Consultation of Experts

As it is customary for international public organizations to do, Unesco consulted independent experts to begin exploring the conceptual avenues of communication policy-making with which the agency had until then no full familiartiy. Unesco's assistant director general for communication, Argentina's Alberto Obligado, invited 21 experts from 20 countries of different parts of the world to meet in Paris on July 17-28, 1972. The meeting of experts "was convened so that the Organization and its Member States may gain a clearer understanding of what communication policies and planning imply" (*ibid.*).

As noted by Unesco (*ibid.*, p. 2), those experts "represented a wide range of specialties: broadcasting (executives, producers, trainers, working in both public and private enterprises); press and news agencies, application of communication to rural development; educational technology, government administration with special reference to communication planning; mass communication research; economics, data processing, etc." In any case, these professionals were invited in a personal capacity and not as representatives of the institutions for which they were working. This was so in order to secure a fertile dialogue stemming from the uninhibited exchange of experiences.

Specifically, the Paris meeting was aimed at establishing the considerations that prompt public concern about communication, at defining the scope and limitations of communication policies and planning, and at suggesting manners in which these policies could be implemented at the national level (*ibid.*, p. 2). "*Recognizing the great differences in social and economic conditions as well as political systems throughout the world, the meeting did not seek to propose a single approach, but to indicate the key factors which may have to be considered within the specific context of each individual country (ibid.).*

That was, then, what the experts set to do as a group. The product of their effort was recorded in a report (Unesco,

1972) that Unesco put in worldwide open circulation at the outset of 1973 and that constitutes a composite of the knowledge and opinions of the experts and certainly not an official multigovernmental mandate. It was just a set of initial technical bases suggested as general guidelines for *voluntary* national government action.

Bogotá, 1974: The Second Consultation, Latin American Expertise

Just as it had done with other areas of promotion of national policy formulation—for instance, culture—Unesco decided to convene in 1975 an Intergovernmental Conference on Communication Policies in Latin America and the Caribbean. It thus made this region the first of those in the developing world to take up the matter at the highest political international level of decision making. Latin America was selected because it had demonstrated an outstanding preoccupation with the communication situation as related to development efforts, because it had already gained a significant accumulation of scientific research on communication problems (CIESPAL, 1975), and because it had shown on its own an active concern with communication policies and plans greater than that apparent in other comparable regions.

Much had to be done to properly plan and organize this high-level official international conference. Understandably, Unesco decided that a first step was to move from the worldwide level of the first meeting of experts down to a comparable gathering of Latin American and Caribbean experts, from which would emerge more concrete proposals, directly pertinent to the situation in this particular region of the world. Thus, the Bogotá meeting's goals were stated by Unesco as being:

> Firstly, to translate the findings of the previous expert meeting into terms realistic and applicable in the countries of Latin America, and secondly, looking forward to the meeting of ministers in 1975, to assist Unesco in defining the preparatory work which has to be done between now and 1975, in order that the policy-makers can have at their disposal valid information on which to make their policy decisions. . . . The function of this meeting was defined as that of showing governments and those responsible for mass communication media the urgent need to devise a coherent policy and to give the various national mass communication systems the best possible organization and structure having regard to national development goals (Unesco, 1974, pp. 4, 8).

Once again, this was a consultation of independent experts not invited as government representatives or delegates of national, international, private, or public institutions. There were 17 of them from 14 countries. They were "specialists in some particular aspects of communication such as economics, sociology, communication law. Professional journalists and broadcasters and managers of communication systems, the print media, the broadcast media, tele-communication systems, data-processing, rural communication problems, international relationships involving communication, community development and educational use of the media were also represented within the composition of the expert team" (*ibid.*, p. 4). Observers of seven international public organizations, both worldwide and inter-American, were also present.

Nine central themes were discussed by the experts in plenaries (*ibid.*, p. 6):

- The concept and definition of a communication policy: policy or strategy?
- The ideological context of a communication policy: role of the state in the formulation of a national, coherent, and corrective policy.
- Communication as an area of development policy.
- The situation of the mass media of communication in Latin America.
- Access to information and participation in communication.
- The difficulty of applying a national communication policy without the participation of the government and institutions: creation of national communication policy councils.
- The impact of the accelerated development of a communication technology and the priority of communication policy.
- The role of Unesco in the communication sector and the objectives of national and international cooperation.
- The need for research in the field of communication to make it possible to direct, formulate, and apply a communication policy.

In the first round of small group sessions, the experts dealt with the problems of defining, justifying, and establishing national communication policies, including aspects of formulation, implementation, evaluation, and adjustment of these. They did so seeking to blend the different specialty viewpoints and the varying conditions of the Latin American countries. They also concerned themselves with the promotion of the policies and with the organic structures for implementation, such as national communication policy councils, which would include representatives of all private and public sectors involved in communication activities.

In the second round of small group sessions, the participants tackled these areas of concern: (1) regional and international cooperation in relation to communication policies; (2) access to and participation in the mass communication media; (3) translation of communication policies into communication plans; (4) mass communication technology and policy; and (5) communication research related to communication policies.

In closing, the meeting recommended to Unesco that it perform a number of specific tasks geared to properly documenting the deliberations of the Intergovernmental Conference. The recommendations proposed summary descriptions of existing communication policies in six countries of the region, an inventory of communication resources in all countries of the region, and a document on the relationship between communication systems. They also proposed an experimental laboratory on development communication planning and the appointment for Latin America of a Unesco regional adviser on communication policies and plans, who would secure coordination of the field studies and promote, with the governments, attendance to and preparation for the 1975 Intergovernmental Conference, which would eventually take place in 1976 (Camargo and Pinto, 1975; Sommerlad, 1975).

A detailed discussion of the Bogotá meeting is beyond the scope of this paper.* But the point must be made that *the gathering was characterized not only by a diversity of skills, types of experiences, nationalities, and cultural backgrounds. It was also typified by a variety of political backgrounds and a plurality of ideological stands.* And it can be said that, in spite of those differences, the meeting apparently achieved appreciable consensus in:

---

*Detailed information about it is found in two Unesco documents (Beltrán, 1973; Unesco, 1974) and in an unofficial summary written by Fox de Cardona (1975b) for CIESPAL.

1. Perceiving the communication situation of Latin America as characterized, internally, by an acute concentration of message emitting and receiving options in the hands of private minority interests, as a rule unfavorable to social changes required to attain widespread national development (Beltrán, 1970, 1971, 1974 and Beltrán and Fox de Cardona, 1976).

2. Perceiving Latin American communications as unduly dominated by extraregional economic and political interests, mostly those of the United States.*

3. Believing that national communication policies are to be the paramount instrument to overcome such dominance by minority and foreign interests, which is unfair to most of the people and not conducive to democratic involvement in the development task.

4. Believing that those policies should be democratically and pluralistically formulated with the full participation of all sectors concerned, that is, media owners, communication professionals, and government officers, probably by representation on national councils on communication policy.

5. Believing that, regardless of its orientation and structure, each state has to perform, as a right and as a duty, the leading role in the establishment of the national communication policies, seeking to conciliate the interest of all segments of society and to serve the communal aims of national development, within each country's characteristics and possibilities.

6. Believing that all Latin American countries must also have joint policies relative to the behavior of international communication forces affecting their territories.

San José, 1975: Convalidation and Advancement

The report of the Unesco-sponsored Bogotá meeting circulated freely among interested institutions and persons in the region and steered the already significant preoccupation prevailing in it about the need for national communication policies.

---

*Venezuelan illustrations were contributed by Diaz Rangel, 1967, 1974; Agudo Freites, 1975; Gómez, 1975; and Pasquali, 1975. Wells, 1972, and Mattelart, 1973, have dealt in detail with certain aspects of the problem. At a broader level, Schiller, 1971, 1973, has concerned himself extensively with it. A recent overview of evidence of the situation is that of Beltrán and Fox de Cardona, 1976.

During April 12-19, 1975 another meeting of experts took place on the matter in San José, Costa Rica (CIESPAL, 1975). Unrelated to Unesco, it was organized by CIESPAL with the support of the Latin American Center for Democratic Studies (CEDAL), located in Costa Rica, and Germany's Friedrich Ebert Foundation. Once again, it convened experts on a purely personal basis and confronted them with a three section agenda: tentative communication policies in the region (experiences and projections), communication planning in dependent societies, and methodologies for the diagnosis of communication institutions addressed to providing fundaments to national communication policy formulations (Fox de Cardona and Beltrán, 1975).

Although only two of its participants also had attended the Bogotá gathering, the San José meeting showed a clear correspondence with the former in perspectives and propositions. The discussions culminated in a large number of specific recommendations to the Latin American governments and to pertinent regionwide organizations (CIESPAL, 1975). In recommending that the former establish national communication policies, the participants in the San José meeting called their attention to the following specific points:

1. The creation of state media as alternative to private ones.
2. Consideration of the social function of all communication media.
3. Consideration of the informative, educational, cultural, and recreational roles of the media.
4. Regulation of the activities of national and international news agencies.
5. Regulation of commercial advertising through the media.
6. Definition of the roles of telecommunications.
7. Definition of the contribution of tele-education to national development.

The meeting also suggested that the governments include in their plans measures to control the participation of foreign capital in the media and the importation of communication materials in their policies, along with stimulation of the national production of such materials. Furthermore, it recommended:

- That their policies be formulated and implemented in the service of development programs and plans pursuing social change.
- That their policies include among their specific aims that of contributing to the elimination of the relationships of dependence that affect life in the majority of the countries of the region.
- That state action be geared toward the elimination of mass media concentration, in terms of private ownership and of geographical location.
- That state action also be addressed to attaining a readjustment of the functions of the mass media to fitting the aims of integral development.

Among many other resolutions, the meeting proposed measures to increase and improve communication research and training, along with asking the governments to build "an adequate infrastructure for the coherent and coordinated implementation of all the measures involved in National Communication Policies" (*ibid.*, p. 5).

Quito, 1975: Toward Policies for
News Traffic

In June 1975, the capital city of Ecuador was the seat of a Unesco-sponsored Meeting of Experts on the Promotion and Exchange of News. This was another step in the preparation of the Intergovernmental Conference on Communication Policies in Latin America and the Caribbean that was planned for mid-1976. It was high time for such a gathering in Latin America, which was hosted by CIESPAL. In fact, CIESPAL itself has found that 93 percent of foreign news in 29 of the main dailies of the region were provided by United Press International (UPI), 50 percent; the Associated Press (AP), 30 percent; and France Press (13 percent).

John T. McNelly observed that "Latin America has seen less development of national news agencies than have Asia or Africa" (1975, p. 3). "The Latin American countries are covered by agencies that are foreign to them in the same way that Reuters was foreign to the United States," adds Peter Barnes (1964, p. 4). Thus this region "is left largely dependent on the big global news agencies" (McNelly, 1975, p. 3). A Latin

American researcher has concurred with these appraisals by U.S. analysts and has pointed to the roots and consequences of such a situation:

> Wire information depends on the United States as our economies depend upon it. AP and UPI have the decisive weight in opinion formation in the average Latin American country about the most important world events (Diaz Rangel, 1967, pp. 43-44).

"The past decade has seen mounting criticism of the flow of news in and out of Latin America and between countries in the region," acknowledged McNelly (1975, p. 12). Indeed all news traffic from the world to this region, from it to the world, and even among the countries in it, is chiefly handled by UPI and AP. And, in all directions, Latin America seems to be a loser since, as noted by Barnes, "the two American agencies which report Latin America . . . have their own interests to defend" (1964, p. 4).

As a consequence of this situation, the vision that the region has of world events is conditioned by the optics of the two agencies. Moreover, the image portrayed of the region in the United States and in other parts of the world is one that many claim that has little to do with the fundamental realities of life in these countries. Natural catastrophes and political instability are played up as a rule, whereas significant economic and cultural events receive little coverage. Picturesque or bizarre phenomena are preferred over events reflecting the struggle for social change. These are often down-played, ignored or grossly distorted. Information about highly developed regions of the world prevails over that relative to the developing ones. Even within the region, news traffic concerning three or four big countries is higher to the neglect of the rest.

There are a few small news agencies native to countries of the region and with a vocation to serve them. Some, however, are actually government publicity services and others are modest firms devoted to background or feature information. None of them has had so far a significant impact in the general system of news traffic. There is virtually only one agency resembling, in miniature, the structure of the large international ones: Latin, a creation of 13 of the big dailies of the region, has struggled since 1970 and is dependent upon the infrastructure of Reuters, the British agency. Evidently, to successfully enter such a heavily dominated market requires expertise, capital, and

facilities that Latin apparently cannot easily put together. And it also requires gaining clients from among those accustomed to the US agencies. Moreover, there is no clear indication that Latin itself has a news policy substantially different from that of the international agencies leading the trade.*
In inaugurating the Quito Meeting of Experts, Ecuador's minister of education, General Gustavo Vasconez, advocated for remedial action as follows:

> Latin America cannot allow the continued distortion of its reality and the distortion of its true socio-economic and cultural essence. The historic moment we live [in] demands an objectivity that will not be possible while the information that we receive from the rest of the world, as well as that which comes from our countries, continues to be handled with colonialistic ideological overtones of diverse tendencies (1975, pp. 1-2).

This meeting, again composed of independent experts representing diverse countries, disciplines, and viewpoints, arrived at several consensual recommendations. The main ones can be summarized as follows:

1. That the governments of Latin America and the Caribbean establish overall national communication policies "in as short a term as possible, under the pluralistic and democratic framework with which such policies were conceived in the Meeting that took place in Bogotá, upon Unesco's convocation in July of last year."

2. That the coming Intergovernmental Conference on Communication Policies "give the highest priority to the need for making explicit the national communication policies in what refers to the international flow of information in their respective countries."

3. That the need for creating a Latin American and Caribbean news agency be considered and that the coming Intergovernmental Conference on Communication Policies "proceed to constitute a Multinational Preparatory Commission

---

*Two comprehensive and up-to-date summaries of these problems have recently been contributed by McNelly (1975) and by Ordoñez Andrade and Encalada Reyes (1975). A previous one, which stressed a number of pertinent studies by U.S. researchers, is that of Beltrán (1970). A pioneer in demonstrating the questionable news flow behaviors of the international news agencies in relation to Latin America was Diaz Rangel (1967).

which takes into consideration what is expressed in the present
Document."

4. That the participating governments protect said
regional agency and support it against the competition from
extraregional agencies by means such as preferential tariffs and
the establishment of percentages of utilization of it by the
region's media.

5. That the governments promote, within their national
communication policies, the most expeditious establishment of
national, mostly public, news agencies, which, federated, could
come to constitute the regionwide agency envisioned (Unesco, 1975)

Initiatives such as that of establishing a regional news
agency have been voiced since at least the 1950s in several parts
of Latin America and in different circles. Political leaders, such
as the prime minister of Cuba and the presidents of Venezuela
and México have echoed this more recently (Mora, 1975). As
a rule, such manifestations have been met with censure from
United States-based international communication groups such
as SIP. According to Mora (*ibid.,* p. 6), the Associated Press
reported in March 1975 from El Salvador that the president of
the SIP's Commission on Press Freedom, German Ornes, alerted
the members about the possible creation of two agencies in the
region subsidized by public funds. And, still according to these
sources, Ornes said: "I believe we must condemn the idea and
agree that all members of the IAPA (SIP) should not contract
the services of those agencies" (*ibid.*).

Such agencies, however, do not seem to be in existence
at all yet, and whether or not the Quito recommendation to
establish a multigovernment one becomes viable in the long run
is something that remains to be seen. Nevertheless, if such an
agency is to in fact exist one day, it will be necessarily the product of concerted Latin American action. Something of this
nature is what the new director general of Unesco, Amadou
Mahpar M'Bow, stressed before the experts who met in Ecuador
in the message he sent to the closing of their deliberations:

> . . . It is illogical that such an important phenomenon as the flow
> of information passes to a large extent through a limited number
> of channels which moreover are determined by an ideology and a
> technology which do not necessarily correspond to those of the
> region. . . . In our judgement, joint actions at the regional and inter-
> national levels are, for the moment, the only answer to alleviate
> dependence of the information flow from technology and the status
> quo it tends to preserve (1975).

"At the same time," reported Antonio Pasquali (1975, p. 19), "the Interamerican Press Society [SIP] protested against a preliminary Unesco meeting—Quito in July of this year [1975]—in which the need to create national and regional news agencies for Latin America was discussed."

INTERNATIONAL OPPOSITION TO CHANGES IN COMMUNICATION

In the preceding sections, very brief mention was made of instances in which international private communication organizations had objected to state actions and expert meetings' recommendations proposing changes in the communication structures of some Latin American countries. In this section, a couple of major and recent cases of such opposition are discussed in more detail.

The Associated Inter-American Media Owners-Managers

There are two large organizations of this type: SIP and the Inter-American Association of Broadcasters (AIR—Asociación Interamericana de Radiodifusión). The former has more North American than Latin American members and is headquartered in Miami. Both are federations of media managers,, editors, and owners and operate in conjunction by virtue of a mutual defense agreement. "The Panama Doctrine, adopted by the organizations in 1952, provides that any aggression against either radio or the press will be considered an attack against both and will be resisted by all means possible" (Gardner, 1965). Together, SIP and AIR constitute a powerful international pressure group expressing the positions of the private print and electronic communication industry of the region and that of the newspaper industry of the United States.

SIP provides several technical services to its affiliates, grants the Mergenthaler Journalism Prize to outstanding Latin American newsmen, and has a yearly convention in the region. Its most noticeable activity, however, is the public presentation of the annual report of its Commission on Press Freedom. It is also its most controversial activity.

For over 25 years now, the commission has diligently

scanned the mass communication horizon of Latin America, identifying and denouncing cases in which, in its judgment, press freedom was being curtailed or suppressed by governments. Subsequently, through its network of affiliated dailies, it has launched individual attacks or full campaigns against such situations, and has had varying degrees of success and received praise as well as condemnation. In the most recent general assembly of SIP, held in São Paulo, Brazil in October 1975, the commission summarized its perception of the situation as follows:

> In what refers to freedom—and, very particularly, to press freedom in the American Continent, it is nowadays a dearth of islands of freedom surrounded by a roaring sea of oppression and dictatorships (SIP, 1975).

SIP and "Socialization" of the Big Press in Perú

One of the most recent and important cases with which SIP was strongly concerned was the expropriation of the main dailies of Lima, Perú, in 1974. A year later, these dailies were transferred by the government to "organized communities" of peasants, workers, cooperativists, teachers and intellectuals. A U.S. publication saw this as a "drastic measure . . . the most striking act of the 'Peruvian Revolution' since the take over of the International Petroleum Company" (Perú: Freedom of the Press, 1974, p. 233). And the same publication reported that within Perú "the expropriation of the conservative newspapers had become like the defense of the 200-mile (maritime jurisdiction) limit, an issue that all progressive sectors, including those generally opposed to the government, were bound to support."

Some applause came also from outside sources such as the Latin American Encounter of Journalists, which stressed that "in Perú, for the first time in the world, an experiment is being tried with the regime of press ownership." (Encuentro Latinoamericano de Periodistas, 1975, p. 23). Indeed, Peru's President General Velasco Alvarado, stressed on the occasion the view that:

> In expropriating the immense power of a press monopolized by small pressure groups, we do not transfer this power to the State. . . . Loyal to our democratic and participatory vocation, the Revolution transfers it to the social organizations of the

nation. Thus, we reject both the single model of private ownership of the press and the single model of State ownership. We
defend pluralism . . . with a clear preference for those modalities
of social ownership (1975, p. 2).

Criticism was far more frequent and noticeable than
praise. When the expropriation occurred, the voice of SIP
(known in English as the Inter-American Press Association—
IAPA) came in loudly in the words of its vice-president, Chile's
Rene Silva, who called the measure a "farce" (Comentarios
Mundiales, pp. 12-13), apparently implying that the announced
ulterior transfer to the labor communities was no more than a
subterfuge toward final state ownership. This proved so far not
to be the case at all. Nevertheless, from mid-1974 and almost
until the end of 1975, the SIP affiliates in Latin America and
in the United States heavily discharged their influential batteries
against the Peruvian government. Reacting to their criticism,
President Velasco Alvarado said:

There is an intense international campaign against Perú.
Those promoting it are those who have seen their interests
affected by the Revolution. Apparently the campaign is
directed by the Inter-American Press Society [SIP], the
organization which joins not journalists but the owners of
the printed Press of the Continent. . . . The Inter-American
Press Society is simply the spokesman for not confessed
economic interests which remain in the shadow. It is only
the puppet moved by invisible hands. . . . Behind the SIP
are those who had run away from Perú to escape justice.
But there are also the foreign consortia affected by the
revolution (Campana Internacional de la SIP, 1975).

"Few organizations have been so vilified and few have
received such an unqualified praise as the Inter-American Press
Association," observed in 1965 Mary Gardner, a U.S. journalist
and researcher (1965, p. 1). And she added in 1967:

On the basis of the evidence available, there seems to be no
doubt that the Inter-American Press Association has proved
to be an effective instrument in maintaining and perpetuating
freedom of the press in the Western Hemisphere (1967, p. 143).

Another U.S. researcher, Jerry Knudson, disagrees,
pointing out, for instance, that since 1952 the IAPA has censured
Bolivia for throttling freedom of the press under every progressive government but never under any repressive military

government which protects property and investment but not human life and civil liberties (1973, pp. 12-13). Concluded Knudson:

> In short, the IAPA seems to be using its arrogated power of censure—if the Bolivian experience is representative—to foster its own political ends. The IAPA judgments on freedom of the press in the hemisphere should not, therefore, be accepted without question (*ibid.*, p. 15).

AIR and the Bogotá Report of Communication Policy Experts

The other major case requiring attention here is that of the public objections raised by AIR to the report produced at the Unesco-sponsored Meeting of Latin American Experts in National Communication Policies held in Bogotá in 1974.

AIR's Commission on Cultural Action met in Argentina on September 12-14 (AIR, p. 2) with the specific mandate of examining said report. In closing its sessions, the commission evacuated an extensive evaluative document which was subsequently released to all mass media in the region and to the international news agencies.

The document starts by expressing AIR's feeling that none of the 16 experts convened in Bogotá represented any of the large private communication organizations of the region and that, with the exception of those of Cuba, Perú, and Trinidad, they were not even representative of state communication organizations. The document then stressed that the Bogotá report cannot be taken as expressive of either the thought of Unesco or of that of governments and suggested that, due to lack of information, Unesco might have attributed the title of "expert" to persons who are not.

Having derogated the source of the report, the document moves on to criticizing the style in which it was written. It labels it as "exuberant," "conventional," full of adjectives, unobjective, and intentionally obscure, but not sufficiently so to hide the central thought that inspires it. The commission asserts then:

> If we had to define this thought in a few words, we would say that the document in question identifies itself with a political line which, because it makes an extremely dangerous overestimation of the power of the State, it tends to build "a man for development" instead of building the basis for a "development policy for free men" (*ibid.*, p. 2).

The document then claims to reveal the "deepest intention" of the report locating it in the experts' proposal for the formulation of a "totalizing view of culture," from which the AIR Commission infers that these experts were virtually recommending "to set the basis for a Ministry of Propaganda, as those the western world knew in our century, to eliminate any possible free development of the communication media, and to anticipate that popular control over them be exerted not through democratic mechanisms, free from official pressure, but through 'regulatory mechanisms' created by the State itself."

This theme—the condemnation of the suggestion that private communication activity be submitted to state control—is carried on by the AIR document through several sections with slightly different arguments. Then, it rejects the experts' notion that private mass media, by their nature, are inept to serve the goals of development. Subsequently, it emphasizes again that "the unequivocal conclusion is that everything must be 'totalized', everything must be state owned, so that the myth of 'integral development' and that 'social change,' which is not defined, could fully take place." The next step in the line of analysis is to claim that the report is "destined to serve the aspiration of fascists and marxists" and that the "experts," on the excuse of proposing communication policies, "pretend to impose a specific ideological content to communication." It adds that the proposed policies are "openly contrary to the best traditions of our continent and, fundamentally, to the objectives permanently recommended by the Organization of American States."

The Bogotá report had mentioned alternative ownership policies in the case of radio, including the solely private format, the exclusively governmental format, and two formats mixing them. The AIR document appraises those as "modalities radically opposed to the American tradition, which made of radio an instrument destined to the exercise of freedom of expression" and as "four different manners for radio to become the new weapon of governing groups."

On that, the commission lays out its position in the following basic points:

1. The international community granted the states the administration of certain frequencies in the radio-electric spectrum.

2. However, the power of the state over those frequencies is not unlimited and thus it should reserve for

itself only the frequencies indispensable to fulfill tasks pertinent to public service.

3. Consequently, *"it is incorrect to affirm that private radio broadcasting constitutes a 'public service.' It is a private activity of public interest."*

4. If radio and television are conceived of as a means for the free expression of thought, their "utilization must naturally remain submitted to the same rules as any other medium addressed to the same end."

The commission then stipulated the roles of private broadcasting in this manner and order: *"to entertain, to inform, to educate, and to contribute to vitalizing the economic process."* In the exercise of them, the document claims, broadcasters *"have an undisputable right to freedom of programming."*

The AIR document ends in recommending remedial actions:

> The positions of that Meeting of Experts appear to us so grave for the survival, in Latin America, of all free media of social communication, that, in the Minutes of our deliberations, we proposed a series of actions which must be counterposed to its influence in the Intergovernmental Conference on Communication Policies in Latin America summoned for the present year (*ibid.*).

Apparently, one of these actions has been to contact Unesco's Paris headquarters and attempt to influence its behavior relative to communication policy promotion in Latin America. But the most noticeable action was the highly frequent press and radio attacks on the expert meeting's recommendations seeking to influence public opinion in relation to the coming Intergovernmental Meeting. The experts' report, a Uruguayan daily suggested, should be rejected by all those who still believe that the fate of freedom of expression "still depends, as in the past, on the existence of free enterprise in the domain of the information and opinion media" (UN Plan, 1975).

The experts who attended the Bogotá Meeting could not react as a group to the criticisms of their report as they disbanded on adjournment of this. If Unesco has had any official reaction, this is not publicly known.

Instead, SIP has reacted by joining AIR in the attack. The October 1975 report of the Commission on Press Freedom included statements such as the following: "Under the auspices of Unesco . . . a series of studies and meetings of alleged social communication 'experts' have been taking place, whose conclusion, of an eminently totalitarian fashion, will have to be very carefully analyzed by the SIP" (SIP, 1975a).

To do so, the 1975 São Paulo's general assembly of SIP instructed the president of it to appoint a commission in charge of studying the Bogotá report and present its verdict within 60 days. At the same time, it recommended consultations with executives of AIR about joint and separate action appropriate "to impede the approval of agreements harmful to the freedom of information and opinion" (SIP, 1975b).

This endorsement should help AIR to push ahead some principles in the region, agreed on at its twelfth general assembly held in Uruguay in March of 1975. Some of these principles are:

> that broadcasting . . . can only continue to be useful and beneficial to the people while dependent upon private entities, spontaneous representatives of popular opinion . . . and . . . that imposition by the State of programs of a nationalist sort, besides implying dangerous limitations, is against desirable competition in the media and constitutes an attempt against culture which must be universal (Pasquali, 1975, p. 18).

THE ISSUES AND THE INTERGOVERNMENTAL CONFERENCE

The divergence between the AIR and the officers and the Latin American communication experts is not a mere conflict of immediate and limited interests between mass communication media owners, managers, and editors, on the one hand, and communication researchers, critics, and planners, on the other. As two U.S. scholars recently observed: "Increasingly it is obvious that a right to communicate is deeply involved with present and future communication policies around the world" (Harms and Richstad, 1975, p. 1).

Indeed the attempts at formulating national communication policies in Latin America will have a growing and direct bearing on communication rights. For what these policies are seeking in the end is a redistribution of communication power so that opportunities for enjoying communication rights achieve an equalitarian level, benefiting all people rather than only a few.

In turn, pursuing such a democratization of rights is a movement that stems from a broader disparity between two increasingly opposite visions of society, conceptions of democracy and definitions of development.

Furthermore, the divergence is deeply rooted in the very nature of the general structure of economic, political, and cultural relationships characterizing most of the Latin American societies. These basic organizational arrangements favor the predominance of conservative minority interests, as a rule related to comparable extraregional interests, over the interests of the national majorities. Communication is an inextricable component of such an archaic and unfair social structure, being determined by it and acting so far to consolidate it. Thus, as has been underlined by Ortega and Romero (in press, p. 2), it is not possible for realistic policies to approach the communication phenomenon by severing it "from the social process as a whole, from the conflict of interests which takes place in the heart of society and, more particularly, from the existing relationships of production." In fact, as several studies have demonstrated, quite often those who own the means of production are also owners of the means of communication.

Another U.S. scholar, Herbert Schiller, summarizes this situation as follows:

> The struggle to overcome domination—external, where the power resides outside the national community; internal, where the power is exercised by a domestic ruling stratum—is the central, if not always recognized, issue in contemporary communications policy-making. Internationally, nationally and individually, the struggle, though often obscured, is between the forces of domination and those which resist and challenge it. All basic issues in communications today relate to this fundamental and increasingly intense confrontation (1975, p. 3).

The Philosophy behind the Mass Communication System

Because of its high frequency and consistency, the general creed inspiring the private mass communication system of Latin America is not difficult to synthesize. It can be said that, in essence, its basic principles are the following:

1. Freedom of information is the foundation of democracy. It is inseparable from freedom of enterprise and both involve, necessarily and preferentially, if not exclusively, private

initiative. Any attack on freedom of information is an attack on freedom of enterprise, and vice versa. And attacks on either or both are, ultimately, attacks on democracy, of which private initiative is the guardian.

2. Private mass communication enterprises are not public services. They are private businesses with public interests. As such, however, they are the spontaneous and legitimate representatives of said public interests and not solely of profit-oriented concerns.

3. Private mass communication enterprises have as their primary responsibilities those of securing the free flow of information and opinion and of promoting economic activities and growth. Thus, they are under no obligation to perform other communication tasks that are the responsibility of the state; that is, mass education.

4. Private mass communication enterprises contribute to national development not only in terms of providing information, opinion, and entertainment but also in fostering the increase and improvement of the production and consumption of goods and services.

5. In free-market, and thus democratic, societies, information is a merchandise like others, with the only difference that it is a cultural product. This difference, however, in no way justifies that the communication business be placed under any non-ordinary legal regime that may harm it.

6. In order to preserve democracy, mass media ownership must be essentially private. The state should have only few and modest mass media of its own, strictly to serve government objectives not serviceable by private enterprise, such as the text-long publication of legislative and executive dispositions. In addition, no state media, in general, should compete with private media and, in particular, the former must not be financed by commercial advertising which should only finance the latter. Likewise, state advertising itself should chiefly be channeled through the private media.

7. Furthermore, the state should not intervene in the activities of private communication institutions except in a very light and restricted regulatory manner that does not interfere with the uncurtailed exercise of the freedoms of information and enterprise. Any intervention beyond such minimal levels is to be regarded as authoritarian and totalitarian since it identifies itself with the undemocratic behavior of fascism or communism and conspires against communication rights.

8. Consequently, national communication policies are to be regarded as dangerous to democracy if they come to propose both increasing the communication power of the state and decreasing that of private enterprise through stronger government mechanisms of control of this latter, which would render information freedom inexistent.

9. In fact, even without such overall policies, communication rights are already gravely threatened, curtailed or eliminated by the majority of the Latin American governments who, in doing so, become themselves enemies of information freedom, and thus, of democracy.

10. Given such a situation, it is the right and the duty of the organizations grouping the major mass media enterprises of the Americas, to struggle, frontally and relentlessly, in defense of information freedom, communication rights, free enterprise and, ultimately, democracy in general. In so doing, these organizations represent the broad interest of the national communities as a whole and protect the universal principles of civilization.

The Philosophy Challenging the Status Quo in Communication

No one disputes the notion that information freedom is the basis of democracy. However, what increasing numbers of people are coming to realize is that in Latin America the existence of information freedom is today defended only as a privilege of powerful conservative minorities and that this, in itself, renders democracy largely mythical. Thus, everyone of the principles in the creed so actively promoted by organizations such as SIP and AIR is today being qualified, questioned, or rejected. This critical stand is not at all the exclusivity of isolated agitators and undemocratic extremists and it certainly does not propose that governments suffocate or eliminate all private mass communication activity. In fact, as SIP itself has acknowledged, only one of the region's more than 20 governments (Cuba) has a system of total state media ownership (SIP, 1975a). The rest have a mixed but uneven (private and public) system. All the governments are trying to do is attempt by legal means to bring the media to a balance that should secure fairness, rationality, and true service to the national community development aims.

The challenge to the traditional creed began, as is natural to expect, among professionals of communication themselves, since a number of them feel that they cannot indefinitely be utilized to blindly operate the media. The voices of scientists and intellectuals soon echoed them. Moreover, democratic political leaders—some performing as chiefs of state—have joined the criticisms and manifested a will to amend the situation.

The position of those who run the only regional center of social communication in this region, CIESPAL, can be taken as representative of that of many communication professionals. Indeed, Ordoñez Andrade and Encalada Reyes noted that:

> The old concepts of the freedom of expression of thought, of economic liberalism and the first attempts of an industrial revolution, weigh heavily in the role that communications have in society. But today, under the new circumstances of society, these concepts are obsolete and completely incompatible with the needs and attitudes which we must assume when facing new political, economic and social events. Secularism brought about angry discussions during the past century. Conservatives defended the thesis that education was a patrimony of God, which must be given by the Church or family at the most. Liberals proposed that the State assume the responsibility of all educational processes. Today, no one would doubt the right and obligation that the State has to clearly define its educational policies. Nevertheless, the discussion of the rights and duties that the State has to rule upon the use of communications continues to prevail. . . . The right to the freedom of expression of thought is an unquestionable and consecrated right. However, we should question the present communications system that allows groups closely linked with the centers of political and economic decision-taking to manage communication so as to derive profits from their investments, to strengthen the domination ideology that induces social groups to continue their consuming actions, turning them into mere masses of people who can buy the industrial production that these elite groups favor or endorse, without considering the cultural needs of those social groups (Ordoñez Andrade and Encalada Reyes, 1975, pp. 4-5).

The president of a democratic socialist state (as several of the Western European countries are), Finland's Urho Kekkonen, expressed a perception not different from that of the just mentioned Latin American communication specialists: "The traditional Western concept of freedom, which states that the State's only obligation is to guaranty laissez-faire, has meant that society has allowed freedom of speech to be realized with the means at the disposal of each individual. In this way freedom of speech has in practice become the freedom of the well-to-do. . . .At an international level are to be found the ideals of free communication and their actual distorted execution for the rich on the one hand and the poor on the other. Globally, the flow of information between States—not least the materials pumped out by television—is to a very great extent a one-way, unbalanced traffic, and in no way possesses the depth and range which the principles of freedom require" (1973).

Venezuelan communication scholar, Antonio Pasquali, agrees: "All the 'freedom of information' is concentrated in the oligarchic elites of information, contrasting with the social right to be informed; there is 'free flow' only in the non-reversible vector going from the informer to the receptor; democracy as the free interplay of public opinion is reduced to a mass opinion authoritarily manipulated with the help of imported engineering" (1975, p. 20). "A free flow of information is desirable, of course, but providing that Latin American nations have had an opportunity to determine its content and participated in its preparation, and that they have available the necessary institutionalized instruments for a feedback process, through which a clear balance of information can be achieved" (Ordonez Andrade and Encalada Reyes, 1975, p. 6).

Schiller has pointed out the habit of those who dominate the communication systems of identifying those opposing them as a threat to democracy. "If, for example, the 'free flow of information', processed and transmitted by a score of cultural corporations of a few Western states, is challenged, freedom itself is claimed to be imperilled" (1975, p. 25). He has also detected another of such tactics: arbitrarily equating property rights with personal rights and thus making the freedoms of communication businessmen synonyms with constitutionally guaranteed freedoms of individuals (1974, p. 113). Both tactics, have frequently been used in Latin America and, concomitantly, a third has been applied: presenting the interests of private mass media owners as necessarily equivalent to those of the broader national community. Thus when the former feel that their communication rights are being attacked, they defend them-democracy, which is being attacked.(Brunner, 1969). Juan Liscano, a foremost democratic* leader of Venezuela, objected

---

*This virtue of his has been acknowledged even by people who opposed the recently

to this tactic as being fallacious. In defending the director of the government's institute for cultural promotion from attacks launched on him by advertisers because he had strongly criticized commercial television, Liscano said:

> The insensitivity of the advertising world towards culture is really astonishing. . . . It is not true that a TV Law means an attempt against free competition or the democratic system. Countries of a democratic structure far firmer than ours, such as France, England, Italy, have nationalized televisions (not just regulated as is intended here), and [these] are among the best in the world. . . . (CONAC, 1975, pp. 277-278).

Earl Vance in an article entitled "Freedom of the Press for Whom?" (Summer 1945), had long ago already asked in the United States: "Is the freedom of the press to be conceived as a personal right appertaining to all citizens, as the Founding Fathers conceived it, or as a property right appertaining to the ownership of newspapers and other publications, as we have come to think of it largely today?" Questions of this nature were dealt with at a Unesco-sponsored meeting in Montreal in 1969 (Unesco, 1969). The participants' recommendations were rated as offensive to liberty of mind and speech by the Columbia Broadcasting System and the New York Times. (See Stanton, 1972, and *The New York Times*, 1972.)

Recently, this questions was asked again, in Latin America, by Ordõnez Andrade: "It is possible to ask, in any of our countries, for whom there is freedom of expression? For the marginated groups; for the political parties; for the journalists; or simply and exclusively for the groups which own the means of communication?" (1975, p. 5).

As a Mexican scholar put it, this region has not lacked "those who believe that, in order to attain a true democratic freedom, mass media ought to be exclusively private. This is not defensible because it would be equivalent to the famous laissez-faire, laissez-passer of the obsolete Liberal State, the failure of

---

approved Venezuelan law creating the National Council of Culture (CONAC), which has as one of its duties the state radio and television policy. For instance, Sofia Imber de Rangel, who criticized the project in the magazine *Visión*, acknowledged that "Most of the members who wrote the first project of law for CONAC are proven democrats, starting with their president, Juan Liscano" (Imber de Rangel, 1975, p. 40).

which has been blatant. *In this manner only anarchy or totali-
tarianism could be established.* . . . Within a more full and complete liberty, official means of communication must exist, as
well as private, granted that adequate equilibrium does not disappear. . . ." (Perez Vizcaino, 1971, p. 23; emphasis added).

The Position of Reform-Minded
Democratic Leaders

Carlos Andrés Pérez, the president of Venezuela, notes
that neither freedom of consciousness nor freedom of expression are limited only by governmental measures "but also by the
prevalence of interests over the essential context of the rights to
information that a country has " (1974, p. 7). Affirms the
president, "Liberty of information exists in our country in
what refers to the behavior and attitude of the government
which in no way interferes or meddles with it. But we could
not deny that this liberty of information does get meddled with
by partial interests in society. . . ." (*ibid.*, p. 5). Addressing a
SIP general assembly,* President Pérez stressed these notions as
follows:

> In the democratic regime, which accepts and fosters freedom of the
> press, liberty of information faces dangers, and grave ones, if informa-
> tion is in the service of certain interests. *This endangers the very free-
> dom that it defends, or that it pretends to defend, breaks the rules of
> the democratic game and threatens the legitimacy of the institution
> on which is founded* (1975, pp. 7-8; emphasis added).

"We believe that the State"—the president of Venezuela
furthermore asserts—"must have its own information media . . .
but of course not to subdue the people to a given ideological
trend or to serve the party in turn but to become an organ of
free, open, information that serves the integral interests of the
community." The President also said:

> The newspaper, the media of social communication of our days
> establish themselves as an enterprising organization, meets the
> needs of given interests and, in many opportunities, may be

---

*Several cases illustrating this latter have been reported by Diaz Rangel (1974).

contrary to the interests of the community that they serve.
*That is why we cannot define the media of social communication
as enterprises, but as a public service (ibid.*, p. 5; emphasis added).

Quito; June 14-23, 1976: The Decisive Step

As it is self-evident from the statements heretofore presented, significant opinion nuclei of Latin America are far from sharing the conceptual framework built and substained by SIP, AIR, and their affiliates. So it would seem that what some experts had recommended at the Unesco consultation meetings and at other seminars cannot be rated as a case of isolated and exotic thinking alien to genuine democratic principles. These recommendations fully coincide with positions already manifested by some no less democratic government leaders in the region. What they all seem to be saying is what Ecuador's Ordonez Andrade had expressed as follows:

What we are interested in is the definition of a global policy, of a policy that equally reaches the state, the institutions, the persons and the special groups of professionals, a policy that seeks to integrate communication to the countries' general planning and that, in addition, links the problems of communication with the processes of development and social change. . . . Then we would understand policy in its integral meaning and its global character (1975, p. 11).

This is precisely what the forthcoming Unesco sponsored ministerial-level conference of Latin American governments should be all about. When the pertinent ministers and their technical aids meet in Ecuador by the middle of June 1976 they will be faced with a complex agenda, abudant documentation, and a task as delicate as all historical undertakings are. Open to all viewpoints, they will have to make decisions crucial to the nature of the communication systems and processes in their countries as these exist today and as their sovereign states would want them to become from then on. If the decisions are going to be applicable, they will have to represent an agreement on all those basic policy criterion desirable for all countries of the region without disregarding the pecularities of each. The decisions will also have to seek an agreement around universal policy questions that should be embraced at the joint Latin American level vis-à-vis the problems of international communication, which so negatively affect life and development in this part of the world.

In both areas of discussion, what is to be seen in Quito, ultimately, is whether a majority of countries wish to have overall national and regionwide communication policies useful to perpetuate the prevailing communication situation or, on the contrary to substantially change it within legality and truly democratic behavior so that it may no longer represent another privilege of the few.

Works Cited

AGUDO FREITES, R. 1975. *CONAC: Sub-Comité de Radio y Televisión; resumen de disposiciones normativas.* Caracas: CONAC.
AGUDO FREITES, R., GOMEZ, L.A., y PASQUALI, A. 1975. *Políticas de comunication en Venezuela.* Caracas: Instituto de Investigaciones de la Comunicación.
AIR: ASSOCIACAO INTERAMERICANA DE RADIODIFUSAO, COMISSAO DE ACAO CULTURAL. Setembro 9, 1975. "Informe destinado a marxistas e fascistas." *O Globo,* Sao Paulo, Brazil.
ALTE. 1969. Seminario Latinoamericano para Directivos de Teleducación, 3o., Lima (Cieneguilla), Peru, 21 de Junio -21 de Julio, 1969. *Síntesis del trabajo realizado.* Lima: Instituto de Solidaridad Internacional-Fundación Konrad Adenauer.
ARIZMENDI POSADA, O. 1974. "Palabras del Secretario Ejecutivo del Convenio 'Andrés Bello' de Integración Educativa, Cultural y Cientifica de los Países Andinos." In *Reunión de Ministros de Comunicaciónes de los Países del Pacto Andino,* 1a. and *Reunión de Expertos en Comunicaciónes de los Países del Pacto Andino,* 2a., Cali, Colombia, Mayo 1974.

BAHR, E. 1975. "Tarea e importancia de los medios en los países en desarrollo; disertación del Ministro Federal de Cooperación Económica." *Carta a Nuestros Amigos.* Friedrich-Ebert-Stiftung (Alemania) no. 46.
BARNES, P. March 1964. "The Wire Services in Latin America." *Nieman Reports.*
BELTRAN, L.R. 1970. "Communication in Latin America; Persuasion for Status Quo or for National Development?" Ph.D. dissertation. East Lansing: Michigan State University.
_____. 1971. "Apuntes para un diagnóstico de la incomunicación social en América Latina; la persuasión en favor del status quo." *Razon y Fábula* (Colombia) no. 23.
_____. 1973. "National Communication Policies in Latin America." Paris: Unesco.
_____. 1974. "Rural Development and Social Communication; Relationships and Strategies." In *International Symposium on Communication Strategies for Rural Development. Proceedings.* Cali, Cornell University-CIAT.
BELTRAN L.R. y FOX DE CARDONA, E. 1975. "Hacia una metodología para diagnosticar instituciones estatales de comunicación; un ensayo en Venezuela como parte de la formulación de una politica general para los servicios públicos de radio y televisión." Documento preparado para la Reunión de CIESPAL y

CEDAL, con los auspicios de la Fundación Friedrich Ebert, sobre "Políticas Nacionales de Communicación en America Latina," San José, Costa Rica, 13-19 de Abril de 1975.

_____. 1976. "Communications Rights: A Latin American Perspective." Essay written upon invitation of the Right to Communication Working Group, Secretariat of the Campus of the University of Hawaii at Manoa in the Hawaii Research Center for Futures Study of the Social Sciences and Linguistics Institute.

BRASIL. LEYES, DECRETOS. 1975. "Radiobras, projeto no Congresso." O Estado de São Paulo, 5a-feira, 30 outubro, 1975.

BRUNNER, J.J. 1969. "El Mercurio, la educación y el orden vigente." Mensaje (Chile) no. 181.

CAMARGO, N. de and PINTO, V. B. 1975. "Communication policies in Brazil." Paris: Unesco.

CAMPAÑA INTERNACIONAL de la SIP. Comunicación y Cultura (Argentina) no. 4.

CIESPAL: Centro Internacional de Estudios Superiores de Comunicación para América Latina. 1975. Seminario Sobre Politicas Nacionales de Comunicación en América Latina, La Catalina, San José, Costa Rica, 13-19 Abril, 1975. Quito. Seminario realizado por CIESPAL con los auspicios de CEDAL y de la Fundación Friedrich Ebert de Alemania.

"COMENTARIOS MUNDIALES SOBRE LA NUEVA PRENSA." 1975. La Prensa: Hacia la Transferencia. Lima, Junio 28, 1975.

EL COMERCIO (LIMA) 1974. Editorial. El Espectador, Bogotá, Julio 28, 1974.

CONAC. 1975. Venezuela. Comision Preparatoria del Consejo Nacional de Cultura. Comite de Radio y Televisión. Diseño para una nueva política de radiofidusión del Estado Venezolano (Proyecto Ratelve) Caracas.

DAVISON, P.W. and GEORGE, A.L. 1961. "An Outline for the Study of International Political Communication." In W. Schramm (ed.), The Process and Effects of Mass Communication. Urbana: University of Illinois Press, 1967.

DIAZ RANGEL, E. 1967. Pueblos subinformados; las agencias de noticias y América Latina. Cuadernos de Nuestro Tiempo no. 3. Caracas: Universidad Central de Venezuela.

_____. 1974. Noticias censuradas. El Hombre y la Comunicacion. Caracas, Síntesis Dosmil.

DUBE, S.C. 1967. "A Note on Communication in Economic Development." In D. Lerner and W. Schramm (ed.), Communication and Change in the Developing Countries. Honolulu: East-West Center Press.

ELIASCHEV, J.R. 1975. "Los medios de comunicación; un país multimillonario en una nación extranjera." Crisis (Argentina) no. 32.

ENCUENTRO LATINOAMERICANO DE PERIODISTAS, CARACAS, VENEZUELA, OCTUBRE, 1974. COMISION DE LIBERTAD DE PRENSA, 1975. "Llamamiento a los periodistas de América Latina." La Prensa: Hacia la Transferencia (Perú) no. 4.

FOX DE CARDONA, E. 1975a. "Broadcasting in Colombia: Communication Structures and Regulatory Frames." Bogotá. (Preliminary draft.)

_____. 1975b. "Políticas nacionales de comunicación; resumen de la Reunión de Expertos sobre las Políticas y la Planificación de la Comunicación en América Latina, Bogotá, Julio, 1974." Quito: Centro Internacional de Estudios Superiores de Periodismo para América Latina (CIESPAL). (Mimeo.)

FOX DE CARDONA, E. and BELTRAN, L.R. 1975. "Towards the Development of a Methodology to Diagnose Public Communications Institutions; An Exercise in

Venezuela as Part of the Formulation of a General Policy for the Public Services of Radio and Television." Bogotá.

GARDNER, M. 1965. The Inter-American Press Association; A Brief History. Austin, Texas, The University of Texas, Institute of Latin American Studies. No. 26 Offprint Series. Reprinted from *Journalism Quarterly* (USA) *42*:4.
_____. 1967. *The Inter-American Press Association: Its Fight for Freedom of the Press, 1926-1960.* Austin, Texas.
GARGUREVICH, J. 1972. Mito y verdad de los diarios de Lima. Lima: Gráfica Labor.
GOMEZ, L.A. 1975. "Danza y contradanza de una política nacional de comunicación." Caracas: Universidad Central de Venezuela, Facultad de Humanidades y Educación Instituto de Investigaciones de la Comunicación.

HARMS, L.S. and RICHSTAD, J. 1975. "Right to Communicate: Human Rights, Major Communication Issues, Communication Policies and Planning." Papers presented at the Conference of the International Broadcast Institute, Cologne, August 31-September 4, 1975. Working Committee IV. Published in L.S. Harms, J. Richstad, and K.A. Kie (eds.), *Right to Communicate: Collected Papers.* Honolulu: Social Sciences and Linguistics Institute, University of Hawaii, 1977.

IMBER DE RANGEL, S. 1975. Mi punto de vista: La ley de cultura. *Visión* (Mexico) 45: 5.
"IMPULSO A LA COMUNICACION EN AMERICA LATINA." *Chasqui* (Ecuador) no. 3.

KEKKONEN, U. 1973. Speech. In *Symposium on the International Flow of Television Programs,* Tampere, Finland, May 21-23, 1973. *Proceedings.* Tampere: University of Tampere.
KNUDSON, J.W. 1973? "The Inter-American Press Association as Champion of Press Freedom: Reality or Rhetoric? The Bolivian Experience, 1952-1973. Philadelphia: Temple University, Department of Journalism.

M'BOW, A.M. 1975. "Mensaje de clausura del Director General de la Unesco." Quito. Mensaje presentado a la Reunión de Expertos para el Intercambio de Noticias en América Latina, Quito, Ecuador, 25 de Junio de 1975.
McNELLY, J.T. 1975. El establecimiento y desarrollo del intercambio de noticias en América Latina. Paris: Unesco.
MATTELART, A. 1973. Agresión desde el espacio; cultura y napalm en la era de los satélites. Buenos Aires: Siglo Veintiuno.
MORA, C. 1975. "Prensa latina and union de periodistas—Cuba." Quito. Paper presented at the "Reunión de Expertos para el Intercambia de Noticias en América Latina," Quito, June 24-30, 1975.

NEIRA, H. 1973. "El poder de informar." *Participación* (Perú) 2: 2.

OLIVEIRA, E.Q. de. 1974. "A televisao como meio de comunicacao de massa." Brasilia: Ministerio das Comunicacoes, Coordenacao de Comunicacao Social.
_____. 1975. Comunicacao e desenvolvimento; conferencia proferida pelo Ministro de Estado das Comunicacoes, por ocasiao da abertura do Seminario Latinoamericano de Comunicacao, Brasilia, 24 de Agosto de 1975. Brasília.
ORDONEZ ANDRADE, M. 1975. "La planificación de la comunicación en las sociedades en cambio." In Seminario sobre Políticas Nacionales de Comunicación en América Latina, La Catalina, San José, Costa Rica, 13-19 de Abril, 1975. Informe final. Quito, Centro Internacional de Estudios Superiores de Comunicación para América Latina (CIESPAL).

ORDONEZ ANDRADE, M. y ENCALADA REYES M. 1975. "International Communications and Ideological Pollution." Quito, CIESPAL. Paper presented at "Reunión de Expertos para el Intercambio de Noticias en América Latina," Quito, Ecuador, June 24-30, 1975.

ORTEGA, C. y ROMERO, C. n.d. Las políticas de comunicación en el Perú. s.n.t. s.p. (Versión preliminar resumida de la monografía preparación para la Presses de L'Unesco.)

PASQUALI, A. "On the Instrumental Use of Mass-Media in America for Purposes of Dependence." Caracas: Instituto de Investigaciones de la Comunicación, Universidad Central de Venezuela. Paper presented at the New World Conference, San Antonio, Texas, November 4-8, 1975. (Mimeo.)

PEREZ, C.A. Noviembre-Diciembre 1974. Discurso del Presidente de la República en el acto de instalación del Encuentro Latinoamericano de Periodistas. El Periodista (Venezuela).

_____. 1975. "Discurso en la instalación de la Trigésima Asamblea de la Sociedad Interamericana de Prensa, Octubre 1974." In R. Agudo Freites (ed.), CONAC: Sub-Comité de Radio y Televisión; resumen de disposiciones normativas. Caracas: CONAC.

PEREZ VIZCAINO, C. 1971. "La politica y los medios de comunicación en la integración de América Latina." In E. Ferrer et al. (ed.), Integración y comunicación colectiva; integración y derecho de la integración. Guadalajara: Universidad Autónoma de Guadalajara.

"PERU: FREEDOM OF THE PRESS." 1974. Latin America (England) 8:30.

PERU. LEYES, DECRETOS. 1971. Ley general de telecomunicaciones: Decreto ley no. 19020. Lima: Empresa Editora del Diario Oficial "El Peruano."

_____. 1974a. Estatuto de prensa y expropiación de diarios de distribución nacional: Decretos leyes nos. 20680 y 20681. Lima: Sistema Nacional de Información.

_____. 1974b. Normas de publicidad: Decreto Supremo no. 003-74-OCI. Lima: Sistema Nacional de Información.

_____. 1975a. Estatuto orgánico de la empresa de radiodifusión: Decreto Supremo 07-75-OCI. Lima: Empresa Editora del Diario Oficial "El Peruano."

_____. 1975(?)b. Ley orgánica del Sistema Nacional de Información. Lima: Empresa Editora del Diario Oficial "El Peruano."

_____. 1975c. Servicio de informaciones: Decreto ley 21173. Lima: Sistema Nacional de Información.

PERU. OFICINA CENTRAL DE INFORMACION. 1975. Bases ideológicas de la revolución peruana. Lima.

POOL, I. 1963. "The Mass Media and Politics in the Modernization Process." In L.W. Pye (ed.), Communication and Political Development. Princeton, New Jersey: Princeton University Press.

RAMIREZ RESTREPO, J. 1974. "Ensayo para un estatuto de la televisión en Colombia." Tesis de grado. Bogotá: Universidad Externado de Colombia.

SCHILLER, H. 1971. Mass Communication and American Empire. New York: Beacon.

_____. 1973. The Mind Managers. Boston: Beacon Press.

_____. 1974. "Freedom from the"Free Flow." Journal of Communication (USA) 24:1.

_____. 1975. The Appearance of National-Communications Policies: A New Arena for Social Struggle. San Diego: University of California.

SCHRAMM, W. 1967. "Communication and Change." In D. Lerner and W. Schramm (eds.), Communication and Change in the Developing Countries. Honolulu: East-West Center Press.

SECAB: Secretaria Ejecutiva Permanente del Convenio "Andrés Bello,": Bogotá 1976. "Acordado programa de capacitación e investigación en comunicatión social para los países andinos." *Boletín Informativo* (Colombia) no. 59.

SHINAR, D. y DIAS, M. 1975. "Problems of National Communication Policy in Brazil." Rio de Janeiro.

SIP: Sociedad Interamericana de Prensa. 1975a. Informe de la SIP; precaria la libertad de prensa en América Latina. *El Tiempo*, Bogotá.

_____. 1975b. XXXI Asamblea General, Sao Paulo.

SOMMERLAD, E.L. 1975. "National Communication Systems; Some Policy Issues and Options." Paris: Unesco.

STANTON, F. 1972. "Will They Stop Our Satellites?" *The New York Times*, October 22, 1972.

TEXTUAL (Perú) Diciembre 1973. Revista del Instituto Nacional de Cultura, Lima.

UN PLAN LIBERTICIDA. *El Pais*, Montevideo, Octubre 24, 1975.

UNESCO. 1969. Meeting of the Experts on Mass Communication and Society, Montreal, June 21-30, 1969. *Report*. Paris: Unesco.

_____. 1972. Meeting of Experts on Communication Policies and Planning, Paris, 17-28 July, 1972. *Report*. Paris: Unesco.

_____. 1974. Meeting of Experts on Communication Policies in Latin America, Bogotá, Colombia, July 4-13, 1974. *Report*. Paris: Unesco.

_____. 1975. Reunión de Expertos para el Intercambio de Noticias en América Latina, Quito, Ecuador, 24 al 30 de Junio de 1975. Documentos. Paris: Unesco.

VANCE, E.L. 1945. "Freedom of the Press for Whom?" *Virginia Quarterly Review* (USA) 21:3.

VASCONEZ VASCONEZ, G. 1975. Address by the Minister of Education of Ecuador at the Inaugural Session. Quito. Presented to the Meeting of Experts on the Development of News Exchange Arrangements in Latin America, Quito, Ecuador, June 24-25, 1975.

VELASCO ALVARADO, J. 1975. "Libertad de expresión y libertad de prensa; fragmento del mensaje a la nación dirigido por el Presidente de la República...." *La Prensa: Hacia la Transferencia* (Perú) no. 4.

"VISAS FOR IDEAS." *The New York Times*, November 24, 1972.

WELLS, A. 1972. *Picture-tube Imperialism? The Impact of U.S. Television on Latin America*. New York: Orbis Books.

COMMUNICATION POLICY AND PLANNING
IN CANADA*

Robert Rabinovitch

INTRODUCTION

I should begin by stating both my background and my bias; I admit that I am a trained economist who is trying to escape from the shackles of being a trained economist. Nevertheless, I find that being one is probably the best preparation possible for what I am now paid to do—namely, to be a policy analyst. My current responsibility happens to be to advise on policy related to communications, and in particular the use of communications, including broadcasting for social service delivery purposes. I am not a communication researcher; I hold no credentials in the area and I know very little about it. But, I should stress that in the Canadian Department of Communication, we do depend upon communication research at least as a starting point in the policy developing process. Without it, I am willing to admit, we would be like the blind leading the blind, even though we do have our problems, as policy analysts, with communication research and communication researchers.

---

*Transcript of an oral presentation at EWCI conference on communication policy and planning for development, April 1976, Honolulu, Hawaii.

PLANNING IN CANADA

This conference is about communication planning, and to take my confessions a stage further, I should say that planning in Canada, in the general sense, does not occur. There is no economic planning. There are some regional plans, but they are essentially designed to complement and to help direct market decisions. Essentially we are a market-based economy; we understand that there are certain problems with the market place and that from time to time it needs a slight push in a certain direction, but basically we accept it as the means of allocation of resources.

In Canada, we put about a billion dollars each year into regional development, and yet there is still no real plan. Essentially, these are inducement payments; we try to induce industry to locate in areas which have been defined as showing a level of regional disparity, where we believe that industrial development would be of assistance. As an illustration based on my own experience, I once had to evaluate the various policies and plans of the government which were designed either to move people to centers of population or to move them away from centers of population: in other words, to relate regional decentralization policies to urban-directed manpower training programs. It turned out that there were 17 separate programs, and they each pulled in a different direction.

A CANADIAN OVERVIEW

You will probably need to relate these comments to a brief overview of the Canadian scene. Canada has approximately 23 million people, 15 million of whom would consider English to be their first language, and 8 million French. But while its population is relatively small, geographically it is hugh. It covers five and one-half time zones, and it is approximately 4,000 miles wide. It stretches from the 49th parallel to the Arctic Circle. It has a mix of large cities and huge half-empty spaces. The large cities are certainly huge—like Toronto, three million; Montreal, three million; Vancouver, over one million. But from that point on, city populations reduce dramatically.

Politically, we are a federal system, with power split between ten provinces in the federal government. Unlike the American system, these provinces are quite sovereign, and with respect to communication, one can genuinely ask who has control. If we were devising a multiple choice examination we would need to include the following options: *nobody, Bell Canada, the federal government,* or *the provinces.* The correct answer is all of the above, or none of the above. It is really a very complicated system, where nobody fully agrees with anyone else on who has the power. Suffice it to say, however, that the federal government claims a jurisdiction and is trying to exercise it where it can. Provincial governments have jurisdiction in certain areas, for example where they control or own the telephone company. In the sphere of broadcasting, essentially the jurisdiction at the present time (and I should underline "present time," as one does not know where it will go) is in the hands of the federal government.

COMMUNICATION AND NATION-BUILDING

Both communication and transportation have always been the key to nation-building in Canada. It has always been cheaper, for example, on a straight economic basis to move on a north-south axis, or to use southern links to link up the east and the west of a country, yet we have fought going that way from the day the country was created, and essentially we have experienced a tug of war between United States and Canadian influences, in both an economic and a cultural sphere. That war continues today, and in some cases it is even heating up, especially in issues of border broadcast stations, the flow of programs into Canada, and so on. Communication and communication flow are a crucial point of disagreement between the two countries at the present time, and this goes right back to the beginnings of communications history. We do not even agree on when the telephone began. We in Canada believe that the first telephone conversation in history occurred between Bramford and Paris, Ontario initiated by Alexander Graham Bell in 1876. The Boston telephone directory says it happened another way.

POLICY STRUCTURES
FOR COMMUNICATION

The Department of Communication itself, for which I work, is an agency of the federal government, established in 1969 to improve efficiency in monitoring communication systems and facilities. The basic objective of the department is to ensure that all Canadian citizens have equal access to communication systems at equitable prices. It is a *hardware* oriented department, with no responsibilities whatsoever in terms of government information dissemination and only now is it developing certain responsibilities in the area of broadcast policy. The primary responsibilities for broadcast policy lie in the hands of the independent regulator, the Canadian Radio and Television Commission; and essentially they rest with the public and private broadcasters. It is only in the last two years that the government has attempted to reassert a limited degree of control over the actual policy-making process in the broadcasting sphere. New legislation is about to be introduced, which will reinforce the role of the government in the development of specific broadcast policy. This seems, in fact, to be a classic case of overreaction. In the early 1960s, the government became perhaps too involved with broadcasting policy and since it had a very weak regulator, it overreacted by establishing a very powerful independent regulator. It is now attempting to redress the balance between the two. Whether it can be done, I do not know. Some people in the regulatory business say that once you shackle the regulator, by second-guessing him in terms of the policy, which he makes simply by taking decisions, at that moment that regulator will cease to have any courage, enterprise, what have you. There are others who say, no: it is absolutely crucial that the political masters have real influence in the policy-making process. The debate continues. . . .

The Department of Communication, soon after its creation, realized that it would have to make a great effort to undertake studies in consultation with the public, if it were to develop a rational planning policy-making process.

STUDIES OF COMMUNICATION POLICY

What was evolved was a participatory process, beginning with a major study known as the Tele-Commission, initiated at the end of 1969 and culminating in a series of 40 reports and studies which were integrated into a final publication known as *Instant World*. This permitted collaboration between the federal government and provincial departments and agencies, universities, private companies, and associations. The Tele-Commission, in turn, prepared the way for the publication by the government of a "Green Paper," in 1973, entitled "Proposals for Communications Policy for Canada." This paper has been broadly used in recent years to stimulate discussions between and among all interested parties, in trying to elaborate agreed objectives which may form the basis for appropriate policy and legislation. The first piece of legislation which came out of this process was a bill which merged the two regulators in the area of telecommunication. There had previously been separate regulators for broadcasting and for the telephone; these have now merged into one under the title "Canadian Radio, Television and Tele-Communications Commission." We took a similar approach to analyzing computer communications, and even before the Tele-Commission had issued its final report, a special task force was formed to concentrate on concerning the computer applications. The result, in a two-volume report, called "Branching Out," was a number of recommendations which generated widespread public discussion and, frankly, very little else. A third task completed in the same area was a report entitled "Computers in Privacy," which was a basic study of the effect of computers as used for data linkages and data bases on the privacy of the individual. This report has had more success, and a subsection of a bill now in the House is designed to protect the individual against unauthorized linkages. It is interesting to note that the report came out in 1972, and had its most immediate impact upon other countries, including the United States (where it was used by drafters of legislation on privacy) and the Organization for Economic Cooperation and Development (OECD). We are now very involved with the OECD in a follow-up study in this area, concerned with information flow and in particular with the development of data havens.

We have also undertaken, and are continuing to undertake, projects on remote community communication. One, entitled "The Northern Pilot Project," was designed to help native people, Indians and Inuit, to define their own communication needs and to identify priorities for the provision of basic communication services. This experimental project has proven particularly useful in the development of policies for the extension of communication services in the north. The second major project which is going on right now concerns an experimental, high-powered satellite, known as the Communications Technology Satellite. It was launched at the beginning of 1976, and a number of technological and social experiments are scheduled to take place during the following two years. Hopefully these will serve as a basis for policy elaboration in the area of social service delivery to remote areas by satellite, in particular, tele-medicine and tele-education services.

DELIVERY SYSTEMS
OF COMMUNICATION

At this point, I should say something about delivery systems. Ninety-seven percent of all households in Canada have at least one telephone, one radio, and one television set. Fifty percent of all Canadian households have cable television services, and 75 percent of Canadians could have cable access if they wanted to. In most countries of the world, with the exception of the United States, telecommunication services are provided by the state; but in Canada, these services are provided by a combination of private and state-owned organizations. For example, among the telephone and telegraph companies, some are private, some are state owned. Broadcasters, again, are partly private, partly public in ownership, although the cable operators are all private at the present time.

Telecommunications

Among all Canadian industrial corporations, Bell Canada is the second largest in terms of total assets, and it is the principal telecommunications carrier. The corporation, apart from providing service to a majority of people in Ontario and Quebec (which are the two largest provinces) also holds the majority interest in companies serving three of the maritime provinces. Taken as a whole, the Bell group controls 60 percent of Canadian telephones, and 94 percent of the telephones in the east, although a second important grouping in the telephone sector is under the control of General Telephone and Electronics of New York, which owns almost 12 percent of the telephones in Canada through the British Columbia Telephone System (BC-Tel) and Quebec Telephone. Bell Canada and BC-Tel are the

major federally regulated telephone corporations, but another,
entitled Canadian National-Canadian Pacific, is a consortium
which controls and dominates the telegraph sector (and is involved in a competitive situation with Bell in the data sector).
Two other important carriers are Tele-Globe Canada (a crown
corporation established in 1949 to operate external telecommunication services) and Tele-Sat Canada (a mixed corporation
in which the government owns one-half of the shares and the
telecommunication carriers the other half). The latter's main
objective is to establish satellite telecommunication systems on
a commercial basis serving locations within Canada.

Broadcasting

Turning to broadcasting, the structure of the industry is
really quite complex. On the one hand, there is the public
element, known as the Canadian Broadcasting Corporation. It
is made up of 300 television stations and nearly 400 AM and
FM stations, and it runs two completely separate services: a
French service and an English service, now available in almost
all parts of the country (except in Vancouver). It also runs the
AM and FM radio services in both French and English. There
is additionally a private network composed of 300 TV stations
and a similar number of AM radio stations. However, some of
these private stations belong to the Canadian Broadcasting Corporation's network for network programming purposes: in
other words, they are private stations, making use of the public
network for the purpose of program delivery.

Cable Television

Cable television operators in Canada total approximately
400 separate undertakings, each holding a license from the
Canadian Radio Television Commission and a technical certifi-
cate from the Department of Communications. The CATV
operators in Canada are expected to program a channel with
community programming, but this is not (as in the United
States) an access channel, at least not at the present time.

SOME PROBLEMS

In this quick overview of communications structure, I

should highlight a couple of problems which we now face. We are essentially talking about a mature system, yet even in a mature system coverage is not complete. The Canadian Broadcasting Corporation (CBC) is under a mandate to extend its service to all parts of the country, and it is hoped that once they finish their current accelerated coverage plan, 99 percent of the public will have the CBC service, at least in one language (that is, the language of the majority in each area).

We are also, as a group in the Department of Communications, becoming more involved in questions of communications-transportation trade-off, and we are increasingly concerned about the use of communication for social service delivery. We believe that communication could prove to be cost effective for the delivery of social services, especially to outlying areas of the country. But we do run into very significant roadblocks from the existing structures in the communities with which we deal, and by this I do not mean communities only in terms of remote communities, but also professional groups of doctors and nurses, etc.

A continuing problem with us is our relationship with the United States. On the one hand we need American programming, and there is a significant demand for it. On the other hand, American programming does undermine audience sharing , and since ours is a system that depends to a significant extent on advertising revenue, the ability of Canadian broadcasters to achieve both programming and extension service objectives is also undermined. So, the importation of American programming and American stations can have a very deleterious effect upon an indigenous system. Pay television is another issue with which we are very concerned at the present time. On the one hand, it is seen as a threat by private broadcasters, but on the other we see it as having tremendous potential as a new system of program delivery, especially if pay television takes a form different from that being perfectly marketed in the US (namely the marketing of an entire channel). If pay television moves to a system based upon a fee-per-program rate, then we can see it as becoming an important instrument for the delivery of minority programming. We also see a potential to assist the development of the Canadian production industry (one of our major problem areas, both for broadcasting and for film). One final problem. In Canada we have traditionally looked to hardware as the answer to our problems. In fact, at another meeting we coined the phrase that

Canada has a "hardware fetish." We have more networks
(especially educational broadcasting networks) examining more
information than any country in the world (and I think used
less than any country in the world). I am personally not convinced, nor are many other people, that this is the way we should
have gone, or even the way we had to go, but it seemed to be an
efficient and speedy way to solve our problems. It has succeeded
to a certain extent, but it has created many other problems at
the same time. If we take a situation like that of Toronto, that
city now has cable systems deliver its 17 channels. A lot of them
are redundant. They repeat themselves, or they give the same
program at a different time. And what does that do to the
indigenous system? What does it do to the ability of our system
to generate programs which will tell people, for example, that
there is a difference between a district attorney and a crown
prosecutor? Everybody in Canada thinks that the crown
prosecutor is a district attorney, because they watch too many
American programs. It is a significant cultural problem with us,
and having chosen the hardware solution, we are now paying the
costs.

WHO PLANS HAWAII'S COMMUNICATION FUTURES?

Richard J. Barber

INTRODUCTION

This paper is intended to give a general understanding of the way in which the state of Hawaii has attempted to plan its communication futures. Planning (Drop, 1971, p. 95) in this context is used rather loosely—a condition necessitated in part by the dearth of comprehensive plans addressing this topic. Communication is taken to cover the wide spectrum from tele-communication, to print, to verbal. Due to the saliency of interest and technological development, much of the discussion will focus on telecommunication issues.

A broad view of Hawaii's history with a focus upon its recent communication setting is followed by an overview of many statewide planning efforts. Particular attention is then given to activities which focus on communication; a brief summary and look ahead complete the document.

While Hawaii as a "case study" is probably difficult to compare with other societies, it is hoped that some of the particular problems and approaches will be of interest to researchers and planners elsewhere. Communication planning in Hawaii mirrors the way such planning is carried out in the rest of the United States where it generally takes the form of a response to an immediate problem. Persons responsible for the making of plans (problem solving) come together on an ad hoc basis primarily from industry and government to draw up what are usually short-range plans. Such plans often lack the desirable input from other sectors of the society.

Nationally, we seem to avoid comprehensive, long-range planning, preferring to let the market forces determine the shape of the future. Aside from the regulatory processes as applied to the use of the radio spectrum and the protection of authors via the copyright laws, this avoidance of planning seems especially prevalent in the communication field.

However, at the federal level there are signs of discontent with this state of affairs. The current discussions revolving around the Consumers Communication Reform Act of 1976 may be reflective of a growing awareness of the importance of governmental action in telecommunication matters during a time of rapid technological change.

HAWAII AND THE COMMUNICATION SETTING

Some History

Hawaii, a very small part of the United States, is composed of seven inhabited islands located more than 2,500 miles from the US mainland. Its population of about 900,000 is concentrated on the island of Oahu—the city and county of Honolulu. The cosmopolitan character of the residents, as well as its warm climate and natural beauty, attract hundreds of thousands of visitors each year, with tourism now the leading "industry" in the state.

The history of Hawaii since the coming of Captain Cook in 1778 has been characterized by a series of major social, economic, and political changes. Briefly, Hawaii has been a kingdom, an independent republic, a territory, and a state of the union. During World War II it was placed under martial law. Major economic forces have included whaling, sandalwood trade, pineapple, sugar, military spending, and tourism. The native Hawaiian population reported by Cook to be about 200,000 to 300,000 was decimated by Western disease and reached a low of 54,000 in 1876 (Atlas of Hawaii, 1973, p. 99). Immigration from China, Japan, North America, the Philippines, and other areas, primarily for employment purposes, contributed to the island's unique ethnic mixture.

Although geographically far removed from the US mainland, Hawaii was early to enjoy the more recent technological

advances. In 1878, less than two years after Bell obtained his
patent, a three-mile phone link was in operation on Maui
(Simonds, 1958) and by 1880 more than 40 phones were in
operation on Oahu. Telegraph service begain in Hawaii in 1901,
newspaper printing, public and private education systems, complex judicial systems, and other forms of modernization were
in evidence at a very early stage of Hawaii's exposure to the West.

Communication Setting

TELEPHONE SERVICE IN HAWAII

At the end of 1974 there were 544,718 telephones in
service, statewide. Some 1,078,658,000 local, 4,564,049 interisland, and 8,619,719 transpacific calls were completed that year
(DPED, 1975b, p. 195). Since 1890, monthly rental charges
have been increasing to the present US$9.50 for residential
(Oahu) private line and US$24.15 for (Oahu) business phone.
Proposed monthly rates would go to US$11.40 and US$29.05
respectively (Hawaiian Telephone Co., 1975, p. 2, attachment 6).
(Neighbor island rates are significantly less.)

Long distance rates are considerably higher than those
for comparable distances on the US mainland. Current efforts
to have Hawaii included in the domestic rate averaging will be
discussed in more detail later. It might be noted, however, that
it took the advent of the domestic communications satellite to
cause Hawaii to seek an alternative to being treated as an "international" stepchild.

Four undersea cables, three to the US mainland and one
to Canada, link Hawaii to the mainland. Two cables link Hawaii
with Asia and the Pacific with a third now being installed to
Japan via Guam. Two Intelsat satellites provide for additional
telephone circuits. Current capacity is far in excess of demand.

Hawaii has recently gotten direct distance dialing service
between islands and overseas. WATS (Wide Area Telephone
Service) has been available interisland but is just now becoming
available between Hawaii and the mainland.

The Hawaiian Telephone Company is the sole statewide
operator. In 1967, it became a wholly owned subsidiary of
General Telephone and Electronics Corporation. Shortly after-
wards Hawaiian Telephone began to operate the military telephone
facilities on the island of Oahu (Legislative Auditor, 1975, p. 61).

Total company revenue in 1974 was over US$146 million and total company assets approach US$500 million, making Hawaiian Telephone a major economic factor in the islands.

TELEGRAPH

Telegraph (Western Union Hawaii), telex, and record and data communications have been provided by international carriers. Only recently has Hawaii obtained electronic mail service —but on an interim basis provided by a group of carriers.

A number of smaller firms supply radio, voice, and data transmission services primarily to industrial customers. For instance, Radiocall Inc. provides radio paging and telephone answering services, and Honofed Inc. supplies data communication services to financial institutions in Hawaii.

BROADCAST RADIO

Commercial AM broadcasting began in 1922; FM in 1953. Now Hawaii "enjoys" 26 commercial AM and 5 commercial FM stations plus 1 educational FM station (DPED, 1975b, p. 197). Most of the radio programming consists of popular music, advertisements, news, and public service announcements. In the past, certain stations have promoted "talk shows" with listener participation. A few stations specialize in catering to foreign language audiences (The Public Radio Study, Part II, 1975).

Plans are now well underway for the inauguration of a public radio system in Hawaii under the auspices of the Hawaii Public Broadcast Authority which operates Hawaii Public Television. Because Hawaii has adequate AM radio spectrum available, it will be possible to create a statewide system. In addition to the AM signal, one FM and up to two FM-SCA (subisidiary communications authorization) channels are envisioned. Hookup with National Public Radio, talk shows, educational programs, special services to the blind etc., are mentioned in promotional material.

BROADCAST TELEVISION

Broadcast television in Hawaii consists of four commercial outlets and one public television system. In most cases, main transmitters are on Oahu with rebroadcast occurring on neighbor islands. Almost all programming is originated on the mainland

and transported to Hawaii by airplane for delayed broadcast. Some local shows, including parts of newscasts, are produced live. Certain sports events and major news events are brought in live via satellite or satellite delay for more timely local broadcast. On March 1, 1976 one station "at great economic expense" began to bring in a live East Coast news broadcast five days per week. About 90 percent of Hawaii's households have television. This is similar to mainland patterns. Of residents with television nearly 49 percent watch three or more hours per day (The Public Radio Study, Part III, 1975).

CABLE TELEVISION

Cable television began in Hawaii in 1961 with a system in one of Oahu's newer suburbs. In 1970 the state acted to regulate the industry and divided the islands into a dozen franchise areas. To date, all areas, with the exception of perhaps one, have been franchised. Under terms of the new franchises, the cable operators are being required to offer free channels for public access, government, and education with connections provided at public schools. Provisions are being made for return cable capacity and at least one of the Oahu systems can accommodate 30 television channels outgoing and 2 television channels return.

Original estimates of installed capacity growth now seem too optimistic with the cable operators caught in the squeeze of trying to attract customers with inadequate cash flow. Currently, of the households with television in Hawaii, about 28 percent are on the cable. In 1972 the reported figure for Oahu sets on cable was 15 percent (Hwang, 1972, p. 20).

NEWSPAPERS AND PERIODICALS

Paid daily circulation of Hawaii's two major newspapers dropped slightly below 200,000 in 1974. Daily circulation of a Hilo-based newspaper is over 15,000 (DPED, 1975b, p. 196). The two Honolulu dailies share production and advertising facilities under the controversial Newspapers Preservation Act.

Maui and Kauai have weekly papers and there are also two Japanese and two Chinese language papers. Windward Oahu is served by the *Sun Press*; some two dozen or more other civilian publications are aimed at certain geographical areas or at target audiences—tourists, construction, business, politics, etc.

PUBLISHING

Several independent commercial publishing firms produce a variety of books, journals, and other materials—much of it related to Hawaii and the tourist market. The University Press of Hawaii follows in the tradition of publishing scholarly materials. It also publishes East-West Center books and further serves Hawaii's special needs by engaging in cooperative publishing and exchange arrangements with Asian and Pacific presses.

POSTAL SERVICE

Hawaii is served by the US Postal Service. The number of post offices has decreased from 88 in 1958 to 76 in 1974. At the same time, gross receipts have more than quadrupled to nearly US$30 million. In 1974, some 233 million pieces of mail were handled in Hawaii, about 259 pieces of mail for each resident (DPED, 1975b, p. 194).

LIBRARY SYSTEM

Through its statewide, centralized public education system, the State of Hawaii funds and operates public libraries on all islands. Books per capita in public libraries grew from 0.8 in 1950 to 1.1 in 1967. Books per pupil in public schools numbered 7.0 in 1967 (State of Hawaii, 1970, p. 20).

The University of Hawaii maintains libraries on each of its ten campuses; the Manoa campus has special collections related to graduate study, the Pacific Islands, Hawaii, Asia, and government documents. Interlibrary loan systems and library exchanges are in existence. Special information retrieval systems such as ERIC, MEDLINE, POPINFORM, and Census data are currently operational through the University library system.

The East-West Center maintains special collections of materials relevant to the foci of their institutes. The most extensive collection is in the field of communication.

OVERVIEW OF STATEWIDE PLANNING

This section outlines Hawaii's recent efforts to identify and alleviate problems and to shape its future through the use of general or sectoral plans.

The first State General Plan to include land use, transportation, public facilities, and population density was mandated by the legislature in 1957 and completed in 1961. As a 20-year development plan it made many very specific recommendations for land use, economic development, transportation, etc. The state legislature, however, chose to adopt it only as an "interim policy guide."

In 1967 the General Plan was updated in the *State of Hawaii General Plan Revision Program* (6 volumes). Included was a "description of the State planning process; State planning goals; a description of the State Economic Model used for analyzing economic policies; economic and population planning projections; general land-use, transportation and public facilities plans; a description of newly developed Oahu land-use model; and a recreation plan. . . .

"Since 1967, with emphasis on 'process' and 'products of the State planning process,' the State Administration has continued to develop planning projects which provide the framework for what might be called a continuing State General Plan" (DPED, 1974, p. 4).

It is recognized that contradictions exist between some of the recommendations. It should also be noted that some areas, while seemingly covered, such as agriculture, have not been subjected to rigorous planning efforts (Ghali *et al.*, 1975).

The more recent State planning and policy considerations have dealt with "slowed growth," "population dispersal," "immigrant problems," and transportation—highway and mass transit on Oahu and interisland ferry questions. Housing, welfare, health, and more recently tourism and energy, claim much of the policy-makers' attention.

A new Hawaii State Plan is currently being drawn up by the State Department of Planning and Economic Development. Mandated by the 1975 state legislature, the report is due during 1977. Act 189 mandates the plan to be

> . . . a composite of proposed and already developed State policies and programs relating to the development of the land and the development of natural, environmental, recreational, scenic, historic and other resources within the State. The State Plan shall establish both long and short range goals and general implementation directions for the State which shall include but not be limited to the following areas, provided that emphasis is given to their relatedness:
>
> (1) Cultural development; human, ethnic and community identity; individual rights; and social problems;

252

(2) Ecology, energy, natural resources, open space, and agriculture;
(3) Education, recreation, and leisure time;
(4) Physical, mental, and public health; safety; and related environmental protection;
(5) Land use and transportation/communication systems;
(6) Housing and urban design;
(7) Public utility and governmental services;
(8) Population size, density, and distribution;
(9) Economic development and employment diversity and
(10) Rate and location of public facilities and community services.

Planning director Hideto Kono recently outlined the various state and county planning efforts as follows:

The State Legislature and the Governor have directed my Department to produce the following products:
—A State Policy Plan by January, 1977.
—A Coastal Zone Management Plan by June, 1977.
—A State-wide Housing Plan by June, 1976.
—A Land Use Policy Plan by June, 1977.
—A Interim Tourism Policy Plan by January, 1976.
—An Overall Economic Development Plan.
—A State-wide Comprehensive Outdoor Recreation Plan update.
—Alternate Energy Sources for Hawaii.
—Urban Design and detailed Land Use Maps for four Oahu districts.
—A Carrying-Capacity Study and data base improvements to help support the development and refinements of these plans.

He then went on to list current major planning efforts in the State.

Department of Planning and Economic Development: Hawaii State Plan; Coastal Zone Management Plan; Tourism Policy Plan; Growth Policies Plan; Overall Economic Development Plan; State-wide Comprehensive Outdoor Recreation Plan; Alternate Energy Sources; Energy Conservation Program (for State agencies); Pacific Region Energy Resource and Development Plan (proposed).

Office of the Governor: State-wide Comprehensive Law Enforcement Plan; Windward Oahu Regional Plan (with DPED and other agencies).

Office of Environmental Quality Control: Hawaii Carrying Capacity Study; Solid Waste Management Study and Plan (Solid Waste Energy Resources Task Force).

Hawaiian Homes Commission: Hawaiian Home Lands General Plan.

Department of Land and Natural Resources: Hawaii Water Resources Regional Study; Water Development Project Planning; Historic Preservation Plan; DLNR Recreation Plan; Mauna Kea Master Plan; Forest Management Plan; Wildlife Recovery Plan.

Department of Health: Water Quality Management Planning; State Air Quality Implementation Plan; State-wide Comprehensive Health Facilities and Services Plan; Comprehensive Master Plan for the Mentally Disabled.

Department of Transportation: State-wide Transportation Planning Program, including Inter-Island Surface Transportation Planning; Master Plan for Honolulu Harbor.

Department of Social Services and Housing: Correctional Master Plan.

Department of Agriculture: Task Forces Planning Program (For Kohala, Kauai, Molokai); State-wide Agricultural Development Plan.

U.S. Corps of Engineers: Kaneohe Bay Urban Study; Hilo Bay Urban Study (proposed).

County Planning Activities: These include Resource Recovery Planning; Sewerage System Planning; Drainage and Flood Control Systems Planning; Community Development Planning Programs; General Planning and G.P. Revision Programs; Federally assisted "701" Planning Assistance Projects; Hawaii: Kailua-Kona Urban Design Study; South Kohala Community Development Plan; Hamakua Master Plan; Puna Community Development Plan; Kauai: Lihue Development Plan; Kauai Urban Design and Building Height Study; Kauai Open Space Recreation Plan; Kauai Urban Design Study (1975-76). The Counties also maintain Shoreline Protection Planning and Public Transportation Planning programs (DPED, 1975a).

One can readily see that Hawaii does not lack for planning studies and recommendations. What has been lacking, however, is any measurable concern with communication as a resource which can be or should be planned.

The great amount of attention given to transportation should have triggered some thought to communication as a supplement if not an alternative. It has only been in the legislation for the new Hawaii State Plan, as noted above, that communication appears as a topic of planning: "Land use and transportation/communication systems."

Communication does appear in several studies, primarily as a possible "non-polluting industry" to broaden the state's economic base.

It is too early to say what will come out of the new plan relative to communication planning.

Several causes for this lack of attention to communication may be suggested. The first is probably not unique to Hawaii, namely that communication in the United States has generally been the domain of private industry, albeit under government regulation in many cases. The available technology and the market economy have been the major factors determining what kind of communication systems are built and at what cost.

Second, while Hawaii has tended to look at communication as something to be regulated in the public interest, its position *vis à vis* the federal regulatory bodies has been rather weak. The legislative auditor of the state of Hawaii in 1974 charged that "there is no consistent, coordinated program for the representation of Hawaii's interest before federal regulatory agencies on matters affecting the utilities in Hawaii" (Legislative Auditor, *op. cit.*, p. 4).

Third, there is no *one* state agency clearly charged with the responsibility for communication issues, except in the matter of regulation through the State Department of Regulatory agencies. About two-thirds of the states in the United States do have offices of communication or telecommunication policy. With Hawaii's heavy dependence upon communication, it would seem a natural trend to follow.

A further possibility for the lack of coordinated planning in this field is a general acceptance of "the way things are." For many years Hawaii has been treated as an "international" place in terms of overseas telecommunication rates and services (FCC, 1972). It has only been in the past several months that policies and rates are beginning to equate those of the other 49 states. Services such as WATS (Wide Area Telecommunication Service) and electronic mail are just now being made available here. Pressure for this had to come from the governor's office and from our Washington, D.C. delegation (Legislative Auditor, *op. cit.*, p. 73).

While there is a lack of any overall approach to Hawaii's communication needs, various studies, experiments, proposals, criticisms, and plans have been carried out. Some of these are reviewed in the next section.

COMMUNICATION-RELATED ACTIVITY

A number of politicians, government officials, academicians, and lobbyists have sought to plan, to influence decision making, and to shape public interest *vis à vis* communication. These efforts taken together illustrate a fairly recent but growing concern with this topic. As noted above, however, there is still lacking an overall view of the problems and possibilities.

For purposes of illustration, some of the more visible efforts are outlined below.

A series of actions have been taken relative to the domestic communications satellite and the high transpacific rates for mainland-Hawaii calls. The controversy involves the designation of Hawaii as "international," the USA-INTELSAT agreement, rate averaging for Hawaiian Telephone, etc. A comprehensive discussion of the case is covered in FCC dockets and in other papers (Barnes, 1976).

From the discussions of the rate issue it is possible to glean information regarding planning issues and ideas about communication planning's status in the state. In September 1971 Senator Daniel Inouye of Hawaii requested information from the US Department of Commerce about telecommunication service to be provided to Hawaii via the proposed domestic communications satellite. Concern was expressed over the fact that some proposals before the FCC (Federal Communications Commission) for the domestic satellite excluded Hawaii from coverage. Senator Inouye specifically requested information on:

1. How will inclusion affect the State of Hawaii?
2. What effect will inclusion have on Hawaii as a user of international communications?
   a. How do the rules, regulations, and statutes governing international communication affect Hawaii?

I would appreciate the inclusion in any such consideration of:
1. The economic effects on our State as it relates to international trade and tourism.
2. The effects, if any, on Hawaii's political role in the Pacific (Lathey, 1971, p. i).

The findings of the Department of Commerce study, published in December 1971, included many obvious points—that Hawaii pays higher rates and that technically we could benefit from domestic satellite telecommunication. But more pertinent to this discussion, the report stated that "the study group was unable to find, outside the Hawaiian Telephone Company, any single source of quantitative information sufficiently comprehensive to permit accomplishment of the task (requested by Senator Inouye). Such a capability is particularly valuable to state government in view of the need to protect the public interest and to assure efficient telecommunications support to government operations" (*ibid.*, p. vii).

The report further stated that during the study, "continued efforts were made to obtain statements of requirements in quantitative form in order to determine the degree to which domestic communications satellites could serve as a part of the total telecommunications resources available to the State of Hawaii" but that *"little quantitative data was obtained.* That which was obtained was either so slight in quantity as to make it of little value for requirements determination or it could not be used for quantitative analysis because of the lack of other information against which to consider it" (*ibid.*, p. 43, emphasis added).

According to the report, statements made by those interviewed indicated that:

> **a.** Government and business (excluding Hawaiian Telephone Company) in the State of Hawaii are highly dependent upon telecommunications services, but the extent to which this is so cannot be stated by those interviewed in terms of communications services used, the extent to which these services provide economy and efficiency in operations, and the extent of their respective costs for telecommunications services.
>
> **b.** Government and business (excluding Hawaiian Telephone Company) in the State of Hawaii are not generally aware of the many types of telecommunications services available throughout the U.S. Mainland (wide-area telephone service, data-phone, private line networks, teleconferencing). Consequently, their demands for new telecommunications services are relatively few.
>
> **c.** Continuous comprehensive telecommunications planning by large users of the telecommunications resources available in the State of Hawaii is practically non-existent.
>
> **d.** Business users of telecommunications in the State of Hawaii feel that higher telecommunications costs prevail in the state than are experienced on the U.S. Mainland and that these costs hamper expansion of their corporate activities in the state (*Ibid.*, p. 49).

In short, the Department of Commerce study served to point out the requirement for more attention to needs assessment and for the collection of pertinent data for planning purposes

The potential for telecommunication rate reductions, and perhaps the Department of Commerce report cited above, spurred the state to hold a meeting in April 1972: The Governor's Conference on the Future of Telecommunications for Hawaii. The conference was designed primarily to bring government and industry together to better understand the needs of the state, down to the level of the consumer, and to gain knowledge of what the industry can provide.

Most of the conference was devoted to representatives of industry (Hawaiian Telephone Co., COMSAT, RCA Global, ITT, Hughes Aircraft, IBM, Xerox, etc.) speaking of the services they could offer (through the proposed domestic satellite) or of the normal services in which they engage. Very little was said of state needs, apparently because very little was known.

In Governor John Burns' opening remarks he indicated an awareness of our need for more information:

It is my hope that those representatives from our State agencies who attend this conference will benefit from your deliberations and will learn about new technology and services available today. I expect this knowledge to be applied to effect further economies in running our government.

If we can save on travel by using more effective and economical communications, our operations will be more efficient and less costly. If we can avoid delays by using new technology and services, we should endeavor to do so since the net result will be a reduction in cost to the taxpayer.

I am, therefore, initiating a survey within the State government along these lines. Each department head is asked to determine who (sic) new communications devices and services can cut the cost and improve the efficiency of our government.* In short, I am hoping that the wisdom of those who appear at this meeting will bring dividends to this Administration (Governor's Conference, 1972, pp. 5-6).

Mr. Rex Lee, then an FCC commissioner, used the occasion to urge the state to take advantage of the fact that it is "underdeveloped" in terms of telecommunications and to plan for the best of modern systems "because Hawaii is *now* recognizing that something needs to be done, you are provided with an excellent opportunity to assess your present and future communication resources and plan their implementation" (*ibid.*, p. 4).

The ongoing effort of the state to obtain equitable telecommunication rates and services led to the creation in 1975 of a Governor's Task Force on Telecommunication User Requirements. A primary objective is to better inform Hawaii's businesses, government, and consumers of the potential services available; and to obtain from the consuming sectors a sense of how much use would be made of new services and how much traffic would be generated through lower telecommunication rates. At the present time, it is difficult to be optimistic about the task force's chances of producing useful material or of bridging the information gap between supplier and user.

Another government report linked to Hawaii's telecommunications problems is the Legislative Auditor's report on the state's management of its public utilities (Management Audit of The Public Utilities Program Vol. II). In general it is highly critical of The Public Utilities Commission's lack of aggressiveness in protecting the interests of Hawaii's citizens—both in its dealings with Hawaiian Telephone (and other utilities) and in its

---

*I have been unable to locate survey results, if in fact a survey was made. It is reported that a survey has been carried out in 1976 to determine present and future telecommunications needs.

actions (or lack of action) *vis à vis* the several relevant federal
regulatory bodies.
Of specific concern with planning, the report states in
relation to environmental matters that "the utility regulators
have never engaged in any long-range planning." And "consistent
with the inaction with regard to long-range planning, the public
utilities agency has no program for research and development to
determine how environmentally compatible utility industries
might be created, nor is there any requirement that the utilities
themselves engage in such research and development. At a minimum, the regulators should be able to identify what the research
and development needs are in the fields subject to their control
and regulation, but they are not doing so" (Legislative Auditor,
p. 125).
The report also criticizes the lack of regulation over
capital improvements and marketing promotions, charging that,
"there are no rules, standards, criteria, or guidelines and no administrative mechanism by which the utilities capital improvements programs and projects might be fully reviewed, evaluated
and controlled" (*ibid.,* p. 93).
In a section entitled Regulation of Cable Television in
Hawaii, the auditors' report traces the history of CATV "planning" in Hawaii. Both Hawaii's rough terrain and decisions to
include CATV as part of two large subdivision developments
gave a good start to CATV by the late 1960s. However, regulatory difficulties with FCC's jurisdiction over wide spectrum
telephone lines (which were being used by cable operators)
brought a halt to CATV development. A special legislative committee recommended a franchising arrangement under the jurisdiction of the director of regulatory agencies (*ibid.,* pp. 140-141).
Questions were raised about the acceptance of mainland
standards for local operators with little discussion of local needs.
The report asked whether or not control of all CATV operators
should rest with the state. What about community control? It
also speculated that the state was encouraging the formation of
just a very few large cable operators.
A number of other issues were raised, but this should
suffice to indicate a lack of systematic planning for the introduction of CATV for the benefit of the consumer.
Hawaii's public television was called upon by a 1971
Legislative Auditor's report to conduct audience research and
program evaluation. This call echoed the FCC's urging of all

broadcast stations to assess community needs and interests. A study was conducted on Oahu in 1972 for the purpose of collecting "relevant data on Oahu's ETV viewers and potential ETV viewers, and to canvass the needs and concerns of the community for programming planning" (Hwang, p. 5).

A very recent effort to plan for public radio in Hawaii also utilized survey research techniques (statewide) to ascertain interests of potential radio listeners, to learn the demographic characteristics of the potential audience, and to obtain views regarding community problems (Public Radio Study Part I, 1975).

Such efforts to ascertain audience concerns are useful if properly conducted and if the results are judiciously interpreted. They do seem to fall far short of any meaningful ongoing public participation in programming decisions and should not be seen as a substitute for that kind of input. The two studies cited are, however, certainly superior to some of the relicensing "surveys" conducted by commercial broadcast stations.

Library planning in Hawaii has as its landmark a commissioned study by Booz, Allen and Hamilton (State of Hawaii, 1970) which outlined a statewide ten-year plan for library development. A later plan for 1973-78 (Hawaii State Library System, 1972) has been issued and reorganization plans are currently in process. The 1970 study with well-developed goal statements, comprehensive survey of user and non-user needs, cost estimates, location recommendations, and future projections is not matched in any other Hawaiian communication-related planning document. A study of library user needs has been contracted which will survey library users in selected parts of the state.

In addition to the "official" plans and studies, several research/experiment efforts at the University of Hawaii should be mentioned in this section.

In 1971 an attempt was made to assess the telecommunication needs of the University of Hawaii faculty and staff. Data was gathered for a 13-month period and a rough picture emerged of which units tended to spend the most on toll calls. Attempts to measure telegram and mail volume, however, proved to be rather fruitless. Interviews with a broad spectrum of University employees both in Honolulu and in Hilo (on the island of Hawaii) elicited interesting but predictable comments —for example, if it were cheaper or if it were even possible we would communicate more (Costa, 1971).

PEACESAT (Pan Pacific Education and Communication Experiments by Satellite) experiments have been carried out over

NASA's Applications Technology Satellite One (ATS-1) for the past several years through a program started by the University of Hawaii. This system utilizes two-way voice communication between low-cost ground stations on several islands of Hawaii and a number of island communities in the Pacific area. Joint programs can also be carried out with the US mainland including Alaska. Experimental in nature, the project, which is funded by state and national agencies, has been concerned with user needs for such low-cost communication systems.

The project has gained widespread acceptability in many countries of the Pacific, with a special network being used by the University of the South Pacific, a regional university based in Suva, Fiji. Its "success" as an experiment within Hawaii has been considerably less, however. This may be due in large part to the availability of other means of communication between islands and the relative ease of travel between islands (Peacesat, 1975).

ALOHA system experiments and research through the University of Hawaii have concentrated on experimental use of computer-satellite networks for information sharing and communication and in experimental work on packet-switching and radio-computer interconnections. The ALOHA system is currently applying for funds to develop interisland computer interconnection via microwave. Considerable technical expertise in satellite communication technology has been built up through this and related projects.

Three proposals to initiate research in the general area of telecommunication experimentation have been unproductive in terms of obtaining funds for research, but have had the effect of raising the awareness of communication potentials for the state.

One proposal involved the study of telecommunication/transportation tradeoffs in education in Honolulu and two other cities. Another, submitted to the National Science Foundation for the design and evaluation of experiments using two-way CATV for government and public interactions, involved persons from political science, communication, law, continuing education, sociology, psychology, and engineering.

A third proposal for social experiments in Hawaii using Applications Technology Satellite 6 in its third year of operation achieved the green light from NASA for time on the satellite. However, funding for the necessary local infrastructure and equipment was not forthcoming. In the process of identifying potentia experimenters—mainly for interisland video teleconferencing, training, meetings—we obtained enthusiastic endorsement from many state department heads, many of whom saw the possibilities of increased communication ability, better data flow, and a decrease in the need to travel.

In an attempt to bridge the gap between academia and the lay community, a paper, "Issues in Communication Planning for Hawaii" (Barber *et al.*, 1975) was prepared with support from the Hawaii Bicentennial Commission. The paper is currently being used as a focus for discussion in the community. Briefly, it states that to do proper planning one must first examine needs, in this case communication needs. It then discusses communication as a "resource," and outlines the history of Hawaii's communication systems. It goes on to discuss some of the major current issues in the state. (These are listed in the Appendix.)

Some of the community groups concerned with communication and Hawaii's needs include the Pacific Association for Communications and Technology, the Broadcast Commission of the Hawaii Council of Churches, the Citizens for Community Cable, the Childrens' Television Coalition, and the State-wide Telephone Users Committee. There are also, of course, the various professional associations of broadcasters, journalists, etc.

The Honolulu Media Council is involved in the study of both national and local communication problems. A public policy dialogue on the right of everyone in Hawaii to communicate is currently under way. Funded by the Hawaii Committee on Humanities, citizens and "academic humanists" are discussing such issues as openness in government, access to the media, etc.

SUMMARY AND A LOOK TO THE FUTURE

It seems fair to say that government planning for communication in Hawaii has been piecemeal at best, and in most cases nonexistent. Of the many volumes of statewide and county-wide plans and studies, the attention given to communication is negligible. Communication as a subject, as a need, as a resource has generally not been considered. While Hawaii prides itself on its statewide statistics, those needed for communication planning seem to be lacking.

As evidenced by university research and by civic activity, a number of knowledgeable and interested citizens and researchers seem willing and able to assist in the communication planning process. However, a central responsible and responsive state agency seems necessary to provide focus for these efforts.

What are the prospects for communication planning in Hawaii's future? In a recent article the Acting Director of the US Office of Telecommunication, John M. Richardson, depicts three possible communication futures: one shaped by technology, one by public policy, and one by the market. He speculates that over the next 10-15 years market forces will predominate in communication decision making and then "policy makers will fully realize the greater impact that telecommunications is having on the world" to cause the future to then be shaped by the policy-makers (Richardson, 1976).

With Hawaii's past dependence upon market forces to supply it with adequate communication resources—and a consequent lack of policy guidance based on long-range planning—it is difficult to envision a rapid move into a "policy-driven future." On the other hand, with Hawaii's history of comprehensive planning it is easy to speculate that with some encouragement and resources the state could in fact begin to actively and positively shape its own communication futures.

Hawaii has seen great fluctuation in its economic and social history and there is no reason to expect that the rate and magnitude of change will be any less in the future. With communication coming to be viewed as a resource (*Intermedia*, 1975, p. 1) and with the projected rapid changes in communication technology, it would seem that Hawaii's long-term interests would be well served by an investment in this area of planning.

APPENDIX
PLANNING ISSUES

Many issues arise when we set out to plan communication resources for Hawaii. Three starting points are identified:

- Communication is an essential resource, the development of which can be planned.

- Communication as a resource has a unique characteristic; when communication is cooperative, information sharing does not deplete or use up the shared information and quite often increases that information; communication resources should be abundant rather than scarce.

- Communication resources can be used to conserve, develop, and manage other essential resources; telecommunication can sometimes be used to conserve transportation; communication resources can support the development of economic resources; communication resources are required for the management of energy and most other resources.

Below are listed some of the communication planning issues likely to be important in Hawaii.

Specific Issues

1. Should there be an equity in communication service throughout the state of Hawaii? Should the residents of Kauai, for example, have generally the same communication services as the residents of Oahu? Is there a very good policy reason why the communication services should *not* be equitable?

2. Should all citizens of Hawaii have equal access to the means of communication (CATV, newspaper, broadcast, library, etc.) regardless of geographical location or ability to pay?

3. Should local review boards be established for hearing complaints about and license renewal applications of local radio and television stations? Presently, all such actions are handled by the Federal Communications Commission (FCC) in Washington, D.C.

4. To what extent are public/private agencies responsible for determining the communication needs of the members of the community? At present, very little effort is expended to find out about communication needs.

5. What communication resources are needed to enhance Hawaii's role as a center for think industries?

6. Who in Hawaii should undertake the necessary experimental pilot projects to demonstrate and evaluate the potential of new communication technologies?

7. Should the state of Hawaii require all schools to train students in a full range of communication skills—not only listening, speaking, reading, and writing, but also the use of cameras, typewriters, video-tape, computer terminals, and other newer technologies? How will these communication skills be tested?

8. Should public officials assume the responsibility of providing alternate means for participation in public meetings? Room space and transportation considerations limit attendance of interested citizens. Should the possibility of "telecommunicating" to public meetings be developed?

9. Should the state of Hawaii, because of the difficulties in obtaining information from outside the state, assume a special responsibility for providing information for the residents of the state? Should the state subsidize certain information services? If so, which ones?

10. Under what conditions, if any, should an individual or a group have a *right of access* to public communication media?

11. What are the responsibilities of public officials in providing information to the public?

12. Who should take the responsibility for exploring the public, private sector media, and government priorities for near-term and long-term communication improvement for Hawaii?

13. Should a special "clearinghouse" for information about our communication resources be established?

14. Who should be responsible for planning the fuller utilization of existing but underused communication resources, for instance, the "extra" channels on CATV, especially those dedicated to public access, education, and government?

15. Should the government encourage the use of public media in Hawaii to enhance the cultural solidarity of minority groups?

16. Should the state of Hawaii subsidize the experimental uses of new communication technology?

17. Should the state of Hawaii launch its "own" communication satellite or lease satellite channels for "public" uses?

18. Who in Hawaii should be entrusted to determine our communication needs?

19. How should we determine what our future communication needs will be?

20. Should we establish in Hawaii an independent *Communication Council* to conduct in depth studies on basic issues on communication planning?

Works Cited

ATLAS OF HAWAII. 1973. Honolulu: University Press of Hawaii, 99.

BARBER, R., GRACE, D., HARMS, L.S., and RICHSTAD, J. *Issues in Communication Planning for Hawaii.* 1975. Honolulu: An Occasional Paper of the Hawaii Research Center for Futures Study.

BARNES, B. 1976. *Telecommunications Discrimination and Hawaii: A Battle on the New Frontiers of the Right to Communicate.* Honolulu: University of Hawaii Law School.

COSTA, A. December 1971. *Telecommunication Service in Hawaii's System of Higher Education: An Examination of Current Volume and Projected Needs.* Masters Thesis. Honolulu: University of Hawaii.

DPED: Department of Planning and Economic Development. 1974. *State of Hawaii, Growth Policies Plan: 1974-1984 General Plan Revision Program,* vol. 4. Honolulu: DPED.

DPED: Department of Planning and Economic Development. 1975a. *Hawai'i,* 12.

DPED: Department of Planning and Economic Development. 1975b. *The State of Hawaii Data Book: 1975, a Statistical Abstract.* Honolulu: DPED, 195.

DROR, Y. 1971. *Ventures in Policy Sciences.* New York: American Elsevier Publishing Co., Inc., 95.

FCC: Federal Communications Commission. March 22, 1972. "Domestic Communications—Satellite Facilities," *Federal Register.* 37, 5891-5892.

GHALI, M. *et al.* 1975. *Agricultural Planning for Hawaii: A Study in Methodology.* Honolulu: University of Hawaii Center for Governmental Development.

Governor's Conference on the Future of Telecommunications for Hawaii. 1972.

HAWAII STATE LIBRARY SYSTEM, LONG RANGE PROGRAM 1973-1978. 1972. State of Hawaii, Department of Education, Office of Library Services.

Hawaii Telephone Company. 1975. *Company Docket No. 2585.* Direct Testimony of Exhibits of Hawaii Telephone, 2.

HWANG, J. 1972. *The Viewing of Public Television on Oahu.* Prepared for Hawaii ETV Network, 6.

INTERMEDIA. 1975. *3:* 1.

LATHEY, C.E. 1971. *Telecommunications and the State of Hawaii.*
Washington, D.C.: U.S. Department of Commerce, i.
Legislative Auditor of the State of Hawaii. 1975. *Management Audit of the Public Utilities Program,* vol. 2. Hawaii, 61.

"Peacesat Project, Early Experience, Report One." (The Design and Early Years of the First Education Communication Satellite Experiment.) October 1975. Honolulu: University of Hawaii.
PUBLIC RADIO STUDY, PART I: A STUDY OF THE NEEDS AND INTERESTS OF THE AUDIENCE FOR PUBLIC RADIO BROADCASTING IN HAWAII. 1975. Honolulu: Survey and Marketing Services, Inc.
PUBLIC RADIO STUDY, PART II: A STUDY OF CURRENT BROADCASTING PROGRAMMING IN HAWAII, AND PUBLIC RADIO'S POTENTIAL IN COMPARISON WITH OTHER MEDIA. 1975. Honolulu: Survey and Marketing Services, Inc.
PUBLIC RADIO STUDY, PART III: A SURVEY OF PUBLIC TELEVISION VIEWING IN HAWAII. 1975. Honolulu: Survey and Marketing Services, Inc., 2.

RICHARDSON, J.M. February 1976. "The Technology Driven Future, The Public Policy-Driven Future, or the Market-Driven Future," *Communication News,* 18-19.

SIMONDS, A. 1958. *The Hawaiian Telephone Story.* Honolulu: Star Bulletin Printing Co.
State of Hawaii, Department of Education, Office of Library Services. *Planning for Libraries in Hawaii.* 1970. New York: Doubleday and Co., Inc., 20.

INSTITUTIONAL LEVEL
COMMUNICATION
POLICY
AND PLANNING

Communication policy development and planning go on in most (if not all) sectors and at a variety of levels within public and private organizations. All of these policy and planning activities are interrelated, composed of guidance mechanisms for the "communication system" of society. As yet, however, we only dimly perceive the broad outlines of this system, finding it necessary to use broad and ambiguous labels for large, amorphous parts of it in our research.

One such label is "institutional-level planning." In one sense, this label defines by exclusion: it includes all communication planning which does not take place as part of higher-level national planning. In another sense, it defines by organizational level: it includes planning at ministerial, sub-ministerial, and regional levels—and their equivalent in the private sector. Institutional-level planning can also be thought of as differing from national-level planning in *process:* the former is more tactical and operational; the latter more strategic and policy oriented.

All of these distinctions help somewhat. Examples, however, probably convey most clearly what is meant by institutional-level planning. Here are a limited few: extension education, campaign planning in support of development, nonformal education utilizing communication media, use of broadcast media to support formal education, political campaigning, and advertising. Communication activities of this sort require explicit planning, but tend to be carried out within resources and policy parameters determined at other, higher levels within the social/organizational structure.

In this section we have papers on four different types of institutional-level communication planning. John Middleton reports on planning for instructional television in support of formal education in Canada and the United States. His paper shows how existing policy and organizational structures, namely the extremely decentralized nature of control of education in these two countries, force a particular approach to communication planning. In this case, decentralization requires a uniquely cooperative approach to planning, and well-developed strategies of organizational coordination.

Rogelio Cuyno discusses planning for communication in support of an integrated rural development program in the Philippines. The strategies employed were aimed at establishing a "common framework among the many organizational systems involved. . . ," reminding us that communication planners must think of the communication needs within their own organization as well as needs to be met through provision of communication services to external audiences. That Cuyno lumps education, training, and communication together in describing strategies further alerts us to the possibility that distinctions between these terms may come to lose meaning.

Eddie C.Y. Kuo deals with yet another kind of communication institution as it faces a particular problem. His study of language policy for radio and television in Singapore points again to the potentially powerful role of mass media in achieving national integration, a theme appearing in other papers in this volume. His analysis of the relationship between language policy, communication policy and planning, and national integration as a goal highlights the contextual nature of communication policy and planning at the institutional level—where it exists in order that some other, larger social goal may be achieved.

Alan Hancock's paper deals with yet other aspects of institutional-level planning. As does John Middleton, Hancock writes about planning for educational media. Here, however, the context changes from decentralized to centralized, from a cooperative model to a technical assistance model. The differences in planning process that come with these different contexts are important. In particular, the strategies for involvement of key policy-makers in the planning process appear to have worked out differently. Hancock's account of how a planning process was designed and operated, and the constraints which altered its shape is a useful contribution to understanding of the reality of the planning process.

INSTITUTIONAL LEVEL COMMUNICATION PLANNING UNDER CONDITIONS OF COORDINATION: PRELIMINARY REPORT OF AN HEURISTIC CASE ANALYSIS

John Middleton

INTRODUCTION

The study of communication planning is in its infancy. As researchers and practitioners, we are only just beginning to recognize the importance of the process of communication planning as a key variable in the purposive use of communication to achieve social goals. We have little research that has been directed specifically toward our subject. And as we have little direct research, we also lack theory and methodology. If these assertions are correct, we are at that point in the research process where we must identify the important questions about communication planning and methodologies for finding answers.

At the same time, we do not begin with a completely clean slate. There is a great deal of research and theory on each of the components of the phrase "communication planning." Communication has been studied rather extensively from various perspectives, yielding a substantial body of theory on communication media, the communication process at various levels of society and on communication effects. While considerable work remains to be done, we can begin our study of "communication planning" with a variety of conceptual tools useful in understanding the "communication" half of the term. These tools

The author gratefully acknowledges the support of both the Agency for Instructional Television and the East-West Communication Institute in the conduct of the research. Opinions and interpretations expressed in this paper, however, are the sole responsibility of the author.

are drawn from psychology, social psychology, linguistics, sociology, and still other fields, making communication an exceptionally interdisciplinary research area.

Similarly, a significant body of research exists in the planning and policy sciences. As with communication research, study of the planning process draws from a number of disciplines and models, including many of the disciplines relevant to communication research, as well as other areas—such as organizational science, public and business administration, educational planning, and economics.

Purpose of the Paper

Consequently, as we embark on the study of communication planning, we face two generic problems. The first is to identify the research questions and methodologies necessary for the study of the communication planning process. The second is to draw wisely from the wealth of related research, theory, and methodology available to us from communication and from planning.

In this paper, I will attempt to deal with the first of these problems in a very tentative and exploratory way. I will report briefly on a case study I am conducting of an American communication institution which plans and executes instructional communication projects within certain policy parameters and through mechanisms involving a great deal of coordination between organizations. This case study thus falls within one of the several initial categories for study of communication planning at the institutional level that has been tentatively developed at the East-West Communication Institute as a first framework for our study of communication policy and planning. These categories, briefly, are: (1) policy development and national level planning and (2) institutional level communication planning in several configurations— planning in media institutions, instructional communication planning for formal school systems, and planning for extension communication (or nonformal education). We are also interested in the question of interorganizational coordination in communication planning under each configuration and, of course, linkages between the policy and institutional levels.

The focus of this case study is on the *process* through which communication projects serving consortia of agencies are planned and carried out. The *effects* of the communication are

FIGURE 1. INITIAL FRAMEWORK FOR STUDY OF
COMMUNICATION POLICY AND PLANNING

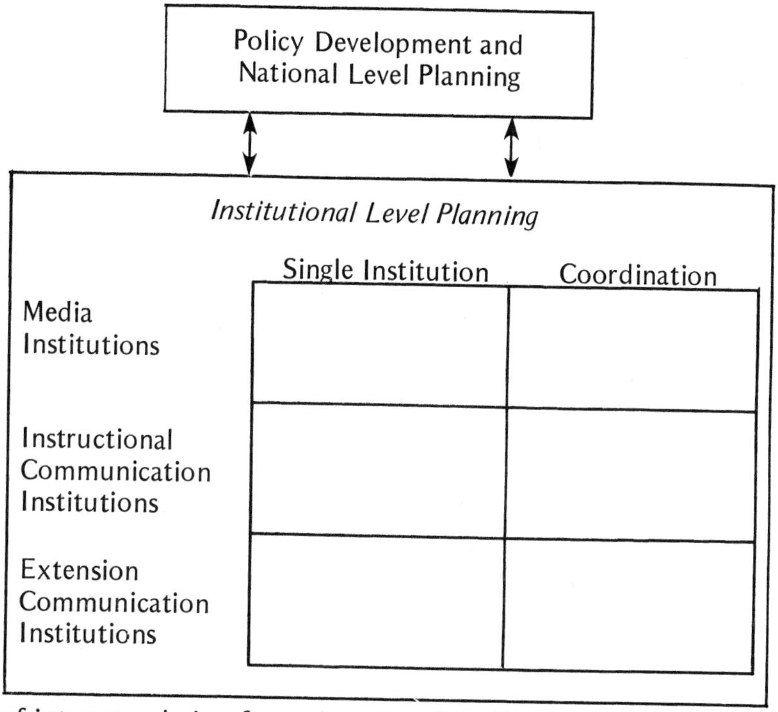

Policy Development and National Level Planning

Institutional Level Planning

	Single Institution	Coordination
Media Institutions		
Instructional Communication Institutions		
Extension Communication Institutions		

of interest only insofar as data already collected by others indicate that the planning process is successful. Moreover, within the planning process, the emphasis falls equally on software, or program planning, and on organizational planning and coordination strategies.

The case study is considered *heuristic*. That is, a major purpose of the study is to identify research questions as well as methodological issues that can form the basis for more systematic inquiry. The study is also about a *successful* example of communication planning. While the study is not complete, I will report here some preliminary findings that appear to explain this success, as well as a few notes on methodologies.

Caveats

A few early disclaimers are in order. I am not attempting to develop a theory of institutional level communication planning.

A case study provides a sample of one—hardly the basis for generalization. Moreover, the case study itself has been conducted without much formal theoretical underpinning. It is primarily a search for questions. The findings may be framed as statements, but these statements hold only for the single case. They may, however, serve as questions for consideration in the development of more systematic studies.

Second, the study is not complete. A number of steps remain, primarily to cross-check or "validate" the findings. Thus these must be taken as tentative at this point.

BACKGROUND OF THE STUDY

In 1973 a significant event in the history of instructional television in the United States took place with the incorporation of the Agency for Instructional Television (AIT). AIT was created to institutionalize a process of cooperative development of television-based learning materials for educational institutions in the American states and Canadian provinces. This process had been begun under the organizational predecessor of AIT, the National Instructional Television Center (NIT). With the creation of AIT, cooperative development of school television was given a formal organizational base and was connected in formal and important ways with the structures of education in Canada and the United States.

In the succeeding three years, the agency has evolved a planning and development process with a number of unique features. Through this process, it has created a number of high quality communication products (integrated learning materials based on television) which are widely used in schools. In the words of one of the key instructional television administrators in an American state, the AIT approach has ". . . enabled school television to take a major leap forward towards widespread acceptance as an important component of education."

In the summer of 1975 AIT asked me to conduct a study of their management and planning processes. The report of the study is to be used by the agency to explain its procedures and "style" to its clients. There is some hope that the study will be of general interest in the field of instructional television. The study will also parallel, in some ways, recent studies of the Children's Television Workshop, producers of "Sesame Street" and the "Electric Company," two highly successful instructional television projects (Land, 1972; Polsky, 1974).

METHODOLOGY

Data Collection

As is often the case with case studies, the main methods of data collection have been interviews and examination of records. In addition, considerable attention has been given to the relationships between various documents developed at different stages in the planning for a particular project and the end products of that planning. Emphasis has been given to identifying changes that have occurred in the nature of the communication product as it evolved—and to the sources of these changes.

Interviews have been conducted with the staff of the agency and with officials in client organizations in eighteen states. These interviews have been relatively unstructured and iterative. First questions grew out of examination of planning documents. Initial interviews with agency staff, both individually and in groups, led both to answers and more questions. In the first round of interviews, notes were taken, and information cross-checked with different individuals. Data from these first interviews were synthesized as the basis for a set of written questions given to respondents a week prior to a second round of interviews (some four months after the first round). The second interviews were tape recorded and transcribed onto three-by-five-inch cards for organization around a structured outline for the report.

Data from the first round of interviews were also used as the basis for a first outline of the study, which was discussed in detail with agency staff and modified accordingly.

Interviews with clients were conducted by telephone, following the mailing of a set of basic questions. These questions were used as a starting point. Respondents were encouraged to go beyond the questions to provide additional information. These interviews were also used to cross-check information gathered in staff interviews.

A further dimension of data collection has been added by virtue of my participation, as a consultant, in an ongoing project. Status as participant-observer in the process has added additional insight.

Final stages in the methodology (yet to be completed) involve review of draft versions of the report by agency staff and clients.

Hence the overall model has been to develop information on how the agency works as a basis for further interviewing and to cross-check information with different individuals and organizations. In addition, two rounds of interviews with staff members made it possible to repeat questions at two points in time, with the interval being used for refinement of the inquiry. My experience has been that a certain basic level of understanding of an organization's planning process has been necessary before questions can achieve clear focus. What people say about the process, and what the products of the process indicate, has been supplemented by the investigator's observations as a participant in the process.

Analysis

The study was undertaken without a formal theoretical framework. However, in organizing and analyzing the data, some framework was necessary, particularly for those aspects of the study dealing with planning and development procedures for the instructional materials. A modified version of a general instructional development process (Kaufman, 1972) has been used as a general conceptual tool for ordering and understanding these procedures. In addition, the basic input-process-output model from systems analysis was also used in organizing data.* Basic theoretical constructs from research on interorganizational coordination have been useful in interpreting data on coordination aspects of the planning process (Beal and Middleton, 1975).

Fortunately for analysis, the record of successful communication projects at AIT is not unbroken. Planning for a project now in production broke down seriously at a critical stage. The basic planning process for this particular project was modified considerably from the general model followed for other

---

*Approaching a case study of a program through systems analysis has precedent. See Serena Wade, "Hagerstown: U.S.A.," *New Educational Media in Action: Case Studies for Planners,* vol. 1 (Paris: UNESCO/IEP, 1967). Case studies of the *process* of educational innovations have used systems models as well. See *Case Studies of Educational Innovation: IV. Strategies for Innovation in Education.* (Paris: Centre for Educational Research and Innovation, OECD, 1973).

efforts. In analyzing the causes of this breakdown, it has been possible to trace much of the difficulty to these modifications. The project has been put back on line by returning to the basic planning and development model. Thus limited comparison of "good" and "bad" cases within the total study has been possible.

CONSORTIUM PROJECT DEVELOPMENT: THE FUNCTION OF AIT

AIT has been created as an instrumentality of the educational agencies of the states and provinces to create television-based learning materials which meet significant and widely shared needs for curriculum improvement. The stated goal of the agency is to strengthen education through television and other technologies.

Projects are funded by consortia of state and provincial agencies, each of which contributes financial support at levels determined by the number of pupils enrolled under its jurisdiction. Pooling of resources has made possible production at significantly higher standards of quality than is possible through local production of materials. It has also enabled agencies to obtain materials costing upwards of three-quarters of a million US dollars for investments ranging from 2 to 5 percent of the total. From the point of view of these agencies, this is felt to be a tremendous bargain.

THE POLICY CONTEXT

Instructional television for school use must be developed within the context of two policy structures: education and public broadcasting. Analysis of the policies in either field is clearly beyond the subject of this report, and in any case has been done elsewhere (Mielke et al., 1975 and Katzman, 1975 for broadcasting; ASCD, 1971 for educational policy). For the purposes of this paper, however, it seems important to identify the major policy parameters within which AIT plans school television.

Education

1.   DECENTRALIZATION IN EDUCATION

A long standing tradition in American (and to a somewhat lesser extent, Canadian) education is local control of schools. The

Constitution of the United States does not mention the topic of education; and in American constitutional law this reserves to the states all powers over education. In all but one state (the exception is Hawaii), control is further decentralized to school districts, usually with elected boards. State agencies exert influence in the process of choice of curriculum, for example, but the decision on what to teach on any given day may often be left to the classroom teacher.

This tradition has resulted in fear of any attempt to establish a "national curriculum." The idea is that federal control might lead to "politicization" of the schools. Consequently, federal aid to schools has relatively few "strings" as related to curriculum. And federal policy is generally against funding of any materials or curriculum project which will be used nationally as part of school programs. (Pilot or research efforts are fundable.)

The result is that agencies such as AIT which seek to work at the national level must be responsive to local needs and able to operate with local funding. The consortium approach to materials development fits well with this policy. However, as projects increase in size and cost, there may be pressures to seek federal funding.

2. FUNDING PATTERNS AT THE STATE LEVEL

State education agencies are funded, at best, for two years at a time by state legislatures. Their funds for educational materials, notably for television, are quite small, and must stretch to cover rental fees for the large number of telecourses used. This leaves relatively little money for new materials, and there is constant competition for these funds from a variety of sources, including textbook publishers and agencies such as AIT. Moreover, school television is often viewed by legislatures as having secondary importance.

AIT and other agencies in the school television business are therefore handicapped in attempting to finance costly projects, even through the consortium approach. Small budgets make large investments difficult. And the pattern of funding from legislatures makes the alternatives—small investments over a number of years—difficult as well.

3. ORGANIZATIONAL PATTERNS FOR SCHOOL TELEVISION

The task of forming consortia to fund and utilize school television projects is further complicated by the variety of organizational patterns for school television. In some states, school television is the responsibility of the department of education. In some states it is the responsibility of a state-level educational broadcasting network. In yet other situations it falls under the authority of councils representing a number of organizations. In consequence, AIT must be thoroughly knowledgeable of these different organizational patterns. Moreover, the consortium approach, in particular funding policies, must adjust to these different patterns—not the reverse.

Broadcasting

1. DIVERSITY OF STRUCTURES

Katzman (1975) has reported on the variety of organizational structures for the public television stations that broadcast school television, identifying five broadly distinct types. These types range from regional network arrangements, through large and small stations supported largely by viewer donations, to stations run by school boards and colleges. The processes of program choice vary with these structures. Planning for utilization activities to accompany the introduction of a new AIT project (teacher in-service, community awareness/public information activities) must take these differences into account.

Depending on the nature of the organizational arrangement for broadcasting and for school television, public broadcasting agencies, not education agencies, may be the principal consortium member agency for a given state. This raises further problems of coordination with the education agency in the needs determination process as well as in utilization planning.

2. STATION REACH, TV SET DISTRIBUTION, AND OTHER PARAMETERS

A final set of constraints on the AIT planning and development process stems from the related facts that not all schools are reached by open broadcast; and that many schools have one or no television receivers. (Mielke reports data showing that about 25 percent of all schools have no TV receivers, 1975, pp. 26-27.) Some schools have closed circuit systems using a variety of technical video formats; others must rely on films. Thus to make the product as widely useful as possible, AIT must produce and distribute in a variety of video-tape formats and in 16 mm film. The product, in short, must be adjusted to fit with available media.

THE ORGANIZATIONAL STRUCTURE

There are two wings to the agency. The consortium development process is managed by a Development Division with a core professional staff of six. A larger Operations Division is responsible for a large acquisition and distribution program for several hundred television courses acquired from other production agencies. There are four regional offices, and there are central support offices for publications and administrative support.

The agency is governed by a Board of Directors which represents the top leadership of AIT clients—the state and provincial agencies of education and educational broadcasting. The board sets organizational policies and, importantly, makes final determination of priorities for agency projects. The establishment of this Board of Directors when the agency was formed created strong links between the agency and its client groups. This linkage is important particularly in the process of determining the area of the curriculum where needs are widely shared, and for which television-based materials are appropriate. Governance and priority setting by leaders of client organizations have important legitimization effects, in addition to helping to ensure that priorities indeed reflect the status of needs in the 60 states and provinces.

AIT staff essentially manage a communication planning and production process. As communication planners, they have developed a framework for detailed planning by expert committees to conceptualize a project, to design communication materials (including television programs and related print materials), and to plan public information programs and materials, as well as teacher training materials, used to introduce new projects into school systems. The framework includes a variety of mechanisms designed to involve user agencies in the planning process. Actual production is subcontracted to television production agencies, with central quality control from AIT.

THE PLANNING PROCESS

The planning process rests on mechanisms for identifying areas in the curricula of state and provincial education where commonly shared needs for improved materials exist. The underlying philosophy of the process is based on the concept of surviva in the "marketplace." The reasoning goes something like this: if real and significant needs are identified, agencies will commit funds to projects designed to meet these needs. Moreover, these projects will be well and widely utilized. Thus a decision to fund is interpreted as verification of the importance of a curriculum need, at least as perceived by educational administrators. It is also seen as an important commitment to utilization.

One of the primary effects of this orientation is to create two operational criteria for success. The first is project funding. As long as projects attract funding, AIT stays in business and can consider itself successful. The second criteria reinforces the first. If projects are widely utilized, they are considered successful. Thus there are two measures of goal attainment, one early in the process, and the other at the end.

A General Model

The first thing that must be said about the way AIT develops school television is that the process never seems to work the same way twice. The flexibility with which the basic system is adapted to meet different and changing circumstances makes it difficult to say, with any certainty, that this is the way the system is—and always will be.

However, there are broad structures and general approaches which undergird the procedures followed in all projects. The diagram in Figure 2 has been developed as an aid to understanding this basic structure. This picture is quite abstract, reflecting only the underlying structure.

As shown, there are three general phases in planning and development. The first is *initiation,* which encompasses activities to determine needs and to conceptualize a project once a priority need has been determined. Needs are identified through regional meetings of educators and educational broadcasters, at which AIT staff present preliminary analyses for a number of project areas. These meetings result in priority lists of curriculum areas where materials are wanted. These lists are analyzed and synthesized by an independent advisory group of experts, which in turn makes overall recommendations to the AIT Board of Directors. This board, which itself represents highest leadership in the field, makes the final determination of priorities. This process is repeated every four or five years, when existing priority projects have been completed.

FIGURE 2. A GENERAL MODEL OF THE AIT CONSORTIUM DEVELOPMENT PROCESS

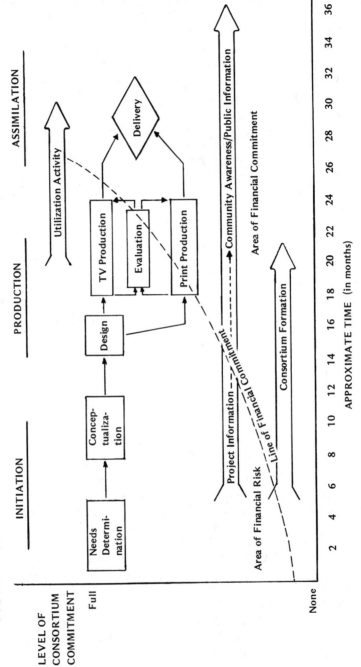

Once a need has been determined, an expert committee of content specialists is assembled to prepare a project prospectus, which outlines the conceptual basis for the project and its general scope. Preliminary versions of this document are circulated to client agencies for feedback, which is incorporated into a final prospectus. The prospectus becomes the formal plan for the project and is the document against which agencies commit funds.

During the *production* phase, the conceptualization is translated into designs for TV programs and related print; development of the materials takes place; and evaluation activities go forward. As shown, evaluation is formative, with results feeding back into the TV production activity.

Design activities are also undertaken by committees under the supervision of AIT. Products of this stage include themes for television programs and specifications for print materials. These specifications are in turn passed to production agencies, which develop materials under central control of AIT staff. Designs, scripts, and specifications are reviewed by consortium agencies by mail and at periodic meetings during the production phase. Early versions of television programs are also reviewed at these meetings, as are results of testing of programs in classrooms. Feedback from clients is taken seriously. Programs are changed and redone. On at least one occasion, an entire project was halted, redesigned, and begun again based on this feedback.

During production, educational specifications (the designs) are passed to creative production people, who have the responsibility of creating materials which meet high artistic and quality standards while achieving the objectives of the designs. AIT staff maintain strong central control of quality in both respects. Writers and producers of television programs typically carry out considerable formative research of an informal nature with the intended target group (various age groups of children) in schools, testing concepts, language and formats in scenario, script, and rough-cut film form.

The third phase, *assimilation,* covers activities intended to promote the integration of materials into the curricula and programs of consortium agencies, including teacher in-service and orientation (utilization) and community awareness/public information programs.

Three of the activities on the chart are shown as continuing efforts. One of these is a complex series of communication efforts designed to keep consortium members informed of progress and to assist consortium members with community awareness/ public information activities as projects go into utilization. Utilization activities comprise a second ongoing effort to support consortium members' teacher in-service and information programs. Third, and forming the base and touchstone of all work, is the formation of a project consortium.

The time scale in months is approximate. Depending on the size of the project, the degree of new conceptualization required, the rate at which the consortium is formed, and other factors, the total period of time required varies. Moreover, the needs determination process results in the identification of several priority areas at once. Practically speaking, work begins on the highest priority, then the next, and so on. This results in longer periods of time between needs determination and the beginning of conceptualization activities for later projects.

The chart also shows how the materials development process is carried forward while a consortium to fund the project is being formed. Again, the relationship demonstrated by the "line of commitment" is a general reflection of the process as it has operated so far. It is clear, however, that AIT is at considerable financial risk through most of the early phases of project development. Thus far, no consortium has been fully formed, no project budget fully funded, when production of the television program began. Only the existence of a small revolving fund created with grants from industry and a foundation loan makes these early activities possible.

The fact that money is going out before the project is fully funded stems from the AIT philosophy that the mechanisms of consortium development must adjust to the way in which state agencies function. Some agencies can move quickly; others cannot. As a result, cash flow becomes an important aspect of AIT planning.

In sum, there are three broad phases of planning—initiation, production, and assimilation. Clients (consortium agencies) are involved in planning throughout. The activities of these phases are carried out simultaneously with the political process of consortium development. The two streams of effort are linked by careful planning and by a small AIT staff team bound together with strong commitment to school television and to the consortium approach.

TENTATIVE FINDINGS

The foregoing description of the consortium development process at AIT is exceptionally brief, and fails to convey the complexity of a communication planning process full of subtlety and nuance. Hopefully, however, it will be sufficient background against which to view a number of tentative findings in the study.

The findings are presented in two parts, one related to the organizational aspects of the planning process, the other to components of the planning process more closely related to communication. In reality, of course, these components are quite interrelated and mutually influential. In fact, a major point of interest in the AIT planning process is the degree to which political/organizational factors have been integrated with more technical aspects of planning communication products.

Taken together, these findings may be read as a statement of hypothetical planning principles which appear to be at least partially responsible for AIT success. As noted in the section above on methods of analysis, comparison of the planning process in successful projects with the process in a project that broke down strengthens, somewhat, the degree to which these principles may be generalizable. Generalization, however, is not the purpose here. Rather, the principles should be seen as hypotheses on the process of communication planning, under conditions of coordination, which can be fed into the design of more systematic studies of other institutions. The extent to which such additional studies confirm these hypotheses, and develop new ones, will determine the generalizability of these findings.

The hypotheses below are often stated in terms of relationships between an aspect of the planning process and "success." The success criterion in this instance is the one agreed upon by AIT and participating agencies: quality of products and wide utilization. In other institutions the success criterion may be defined differently (see No. 9 below).

AIT Organizational Findings

1. THE DEGREE OF COORDINATION VARIES DIRECTLY WITH THE DEGREE TO WHICH PARTICIPANTS IN THE PLANNING PROCESS SHARE A COMMON GOAL

AIT was created because of agreement among client organizations on two ideas: first, that school television would not reach its potential to strengthen education unless materials met high expectations for educational and production quality; second, that quality of this level could be attained only through pooling of resources. This agreement was reached at a national meeting attended by representatives of virtually every state and provincial education agency, and the resolution from this meeting provided the direct impetus for the creation of the agency.

The purpose of the agency has been clear from the beginning. Importantly, this purpose was articulated by users of agency products. There is substantial continuing agreement on the goals of AIT as an agency, and consequently on the ends toward which planning is directed.

It is also important to note that the degree to which this goal is commonly shared provides a common criterion for success. Thus users of AIT projects know what they want, and can reach general consensus on whether or not a given television series has successfully met their needs.

2. THE PROBABILITY OF SUCCESSFUL COORDINATION AMONG AGENCIES IN THE PLANNING PROCESS INCREASES WITH THE DEGREE TO WHICH AGENCIES HAVE SIMILAR AUDIENCES

This point is so basic and obvious that it can be easily overlooked. Joint funding and planning of a particular communication project by many agencies would seem to be possible only when the audiences for which participating agencies have responsibility are similar. It seems quite clear that much of AIT success in achieving cooperation is due to the fact that the age groups for each project are the same for every agency.

This is not to say that there are no cultural/ethnic differences. There are. The planning process recognizes these differences, and serious attempts are made to achieve balance across the different possible combinations of ethnic and racial groups, as well as geographical settings (East-West, North-South, United States-Canada, Urban-Rural) in the multiple programs in a series. This finding recognizes that coordinated planning may be more difficult as the disparity between audiences increases.

3. NEEDS DETERMINATION BY USERS INCREASES COORDINATION AND PRODUCT UTILIZATION

There is usually a certain degree of rhetoric among planners of all types about the need to involve clients in the planning process. At AIT this rhetoric has, with one major reservation, been made real.

The reservation is an interesting one. Needs for particular projects are determined by those persons legally responsible for education—school administrators. They are not determined by children or parents (although parent groups can exert pressure on administrators). On the other hand, neither are they determined by experts in universities or federal agencies. The needs determination process at AIT thus parallels, in a sense, the federal structure of education. Administrators are taken to represent and reflect accurately the needs of their primary audience, pupils. The eventual target audience, however, does not directly determine needs, either directly or through research. Decision makers which "control" the audience make needs decisions on their behalf. Participation by these administrators in the identification of needs is the beginning of continuous involvement in project planning, and among other things, gives them long advance notice of the general shape of projects to come.

4.   NEEDS DETERMINATION BY USERS LEADS TO "ACCEPTABLE"
LEVELS OF INNOVATION, INCREASING PROBABILITY
OF PROJECT SUCCESS

AIT staff are emphatic about not being in the business of educational reform. Their projects are not created to change education, at least from outside the formal system. The planning process is so structured as to ensure that projects meet needs as determined by those responsible for the schools. Projects are innovative only to the extent that these administrators are intent upon innovation. AIT is thus a partner in the modest kind of incremental reform which is undertaken by individuals who must make the schools work on a day-to-day basis.

This lesson was learned early in the history of AIT's predecessor organization, NIT, when an ambitious project of high production quality failed to be widely used because its content was too far ahead of current practice in the curriculum area.

5.   BALANCE BETWEEN PARTICIPATION AND CONTROL
IN PLANNING INCREASES PROBABILITY OF SUCCESS

A given consortium project may involve as many as 42 state and provincial agencies. Representatives of these agencies participate in the planning process during conceptualization, design, and production of the communication materials. Their advice and feedback on the project and materials at these various stages of completion is evaluated seriously, and incorporated into the project when feasible.

However, quality cannot be achieved by a committee of this size. Despite general consensus of the shape and content of the project, there is always some degree of disagreement since agencies strive to have the project tailored as closely as possible to local needs. Thus while participation is encouraged, AIT staff retain final decision-making power once a project is begun. This requires staff to be adept at seeking consensus across agencies and to have gained the trust and respect of agency representatives. It also requires that staff have considerable political talent to match their professional and technical expertise.

The result is a style of operation that is both professional and political. AIT cannot afford to give everyone exactly what they want; nor can it afford to ignore advice from participating institutions. Achieving a workable balance between participation and control seems to be a key to the coordination process.

6.   **WELL-ESTABLISHED FEEDBACK MECHANISMS INCREASE TRUST AMONG PARTICIPANTS IN THE PLANNING PROCESS, IN TURN INCREASING PROBABILITY OF SUCCESS**

AIT staff invest a significant amount of their time in communication with various participants in the planning process. The process of forming a consortium, for example, involves extensive correspondence and almost full-time travel by a senior staff member. At least three full meetings of consortium agencies are held during the life of the project. Every four to five years regional meetings are held to establish priorities. Staff members make presentations at conventions of national professional societies in education and broadcasting. In a given year as many as 50 national consultants in various fields come to staff headquarters for planning work, providing another information network.

In short, through a variety of mechanisms, AIT staff manage to stay in constant touch with their clients. That this task is taken seriously is evident from internal policy on incoming mail and telephone calls, all of which are answered immediately and fully. Achieving and maintaining an image of a responsive agency which *listens* is a major informal policy at AIT.

Interviews with clients in state agencies confirm the importance of this informal policy. With few exceptions, respondents volunteered statements indicating that AIT staff makes serious efforts to listen to their concerns, and follows through when feasible. The need for final decision making at AIT, however, is also recognized, even though there is a lingering wish among some clients for somewhat more control of projects.

7. HIGH QUALITY PRODUCTS AT RELATIVELY LOW COST INCREASES PARTICIPATION, WILLINGNESS TO ACCEPT CENTRAL CONTROL, AND THE PROBABILITY OF SUCCESS

Clients uniformly report that the major reason for participation in the consortium process is economic. Education agencies receive a product of considerably higher quality than is possible with local production at bargain prices.

A single example serves to illustrate. The basic membership for a small state in a recent project was US$8,000 plus one-half cent per student, or a total of US$17,100. In addition, the state purchased one set of 15 videotapes at US$1,425, plus costs for teacher guides. The total cost for the materials came to about US$22,000. With open broadcast distribution facilities, the cost per pupil in the appropriate age group averages out at about 50 cents. And since consortium members get unlimited rights to use the materials for seven years, this initial investment is amortized over that period. This is a relatively small investment for materials which cost over one-half million dollars to develop.

This case indicates that the economic benefits of participation in coordinated communication planning, linked with quality considerations, may be a centrally important component in successful action.

8. THE DEGREE TO WHICH A COORDINATING ORGANIZATION HAS A COHERENT AND SHARED ORGANIZATIONAL PHILOSOPHY IS DIRECTLY RELATED TO SUCCESS

One of the more consistent findings in interviews with AIT staff is the degree to which there is shared understanding and commitment to a basic philosophy. There is strong commitment to the goal of the agency, and there are clear understanding and commitment to the process of cooperative planning and development. New staff members are carefully indoctrinated into this philosophy. The result is consistency of response to external inquiries. It also makes it possible for staff to operate

292

with considerable latitude for independent judgment: a common philosophy leads to consistency in effect for individual decision making. This latitude in turn increases the ability of the agency to manage large activities with a small staff and to move quickly with little bureaucratic constraint.

9. "SUCCESS" CRITERIA MAY VARY, BUT WILL BE EFFECTIVE TO THE DEGREE THAT THEY ARE AGREED TO BY PARTICIPANTS IN THE PLANNING PROCESS

At AIT this process is called "matching of expectations." The agency was created with full participation of client agencies to strengthen education through television and other technologies. This goal has been operationalized as the development of high quality (as judged by clients) instructional materials which are widely used (in comparison with other series). AIT projects have won awards for production and education quality and, except for "Sesame Street" and the "Electric Company," three of the six most widely utilized school televsion courses in 1974 were AIT consortium efforts (Katzman, 1975).

In a sense, this is a closed system. When it works well, AIT asks agencies what they want, involves them in planning and production to keep the project on target with the need, then delivers the product with a range of important support materials and services. Verification of fit between the "expectations" of the client agencies and the "expectations" of AIT is built-in at several points in the planning process: (1) when needs are determined; (2) when an agency reviews a project plan (prospectus) and decides to fund; and (3) when agencies review prototype products and evaluation results at meetings during the production process. Final verification (extent of utilization) comes only after these enroute check points.

What is exceptionally interesting about this process is that ultimate kinds of measures of the "value" of a project are not taken. That is, there is no systematic attempt to determine if materials enable students to achieve learning objectives. Formative evaluation focuses on the lesson—both television and print components—measuring attention to the program and on general comprehension of the content. This evaluation is carried out only for materials produced early in the process, and is used for adjustments in the materials. The total series of television and print materials (for all lessons) is not evaluated in full use in the classro

In practical terms, the strength of this approach is that it explicitly recognizes that projects must meet expectations of those who identify the needs—and pay the bills. If expectations are matched, additional projects will be funded. If client agencies were to expand their expectations to include criteria such as learning gain, then AIT would have to add this evaluation component in order to match these expectations.

Communication Findings

10. USE OF THEORY

My view of the communication planning process is that it is essentially an exercise in the application of theory to particular problems within policy and resource constraints. Thus one would want to examine the communication planning process to identify where and how theory is applied.

Such an examination in the study of AIT reveals consistent, planned use of theory. Once needs are identified, a project is conceptualized and designed by a series of consultant committees. Members on these committees are chosen for their recognized standing in the content area to be taught, in educational television and in instructional design. These individuals are expected to bring with them to the planning process a good grasp of theory and research. No "planning research" in the sense of original data collection is done. This is partially due to a relatively strong existing data base, and partly due to time and cost consideration. In any case, planning documents in fact reflect considerable theoretical analysis as the basis for project design.

However, these committees change in composition from project to project. The result is variation in theoretical models applied, often for projects in the same curriculum area.

The study has discerned no relationship between the type and/or quality of theory application and the success of programs. (This may well be because of the nature of the success criterion —see No. 9 above.) Thus it seems premature to frame the "use of theory" issue as a hypothesis at this point. However, the extent to which institutions apply theory in the planning process, and the way in which this is done, seems to be an area for further systematic research.

294

11. AUDIENCE ANALYSIS INCREASES THE QUALITY, AND THEREFORE UTILITY, OF COMMUNICATION PRODUCTS

Recent work on the application of communication for the achievement of particular social goals has stressed the importance of audience analysis as the basis for communication design (Kincaid and Schramm, 1975). These lessons seem to have been well learned at AIT. Early planning for projects invariably draws on secondary analysis of existing data on the age group for whom the project is intended—including data on stages of development, learning patterns, existing knowledge in the curriculum area, and so on. As designs are translated into television programs, scriptwriters and producers work with children of the appropriate age group to develop scenarios and presentation modes; scripts are pretested with the audience to cross-check comprehension, use of language appropriate to the audience, attention, liking, and similar variables. Previously made films are tested similarly.

This serious attention to audience variables appears to be closely linked with success of AIT programs, although in the absence of true experimental comparison of programs with and without audience analysis, firm conclusions are difficult. The issue seems important enough to warrant further serious study, if only because of the strong theoretical rationales for audience analysis that have been advanced.

12. THE DEGREE TO WHICH COMMUNICATION SOFTWARE REFLECTS PLANNED PURPOSES IS DIRECTLY RELATED TO THE DEGREE OF CENTRALIZED CONTROL OF PRODUCTION

The general planning/production model at AIT includes strong central control by AIT staff over the process through which program designs and objectives are translated (by production agencies) into program software. The AIT project director has formal approval rights at several stages in the production process, and funds are budgeted for revisions found necessary either from review by the project director and/or consortium agencies, or from formative evaluation data.

In a recent project, this model was modified, reducing the strength of central control considerably. Although there were other contributing factors, loss of central control resulted in discrepancies between designs and quality expectations on the one hand, and initial products on the other. The project was halted, redesigned, and central control restored. Things now appear to be going more smoothly.

Uniting educational design with the creative energy and talents of producing agencies has been cited as a component in the success of "Sesame Street" (Land, 1972; Polsky, 1974). The need for strong control of the process seems evident in that instance, where production is an in-house activity, as well as with AIT, where production is decentralized.

13. UTILIZATION OF PRODUCTS, AND CLIENT SATISFACTION, ARE HANCED WITH THE INCREASE IN BROAD FOCUS COMMUNICATION ACTIVITIES SUPPORTING EACH PROJECT

The introduction of new instructional programs into American and Canadian schools is a complex task. Acceptance and utilization, given the policy context in education, is not automatic. Teachers must be motivated and trained; administrators and other influentials have to be informed of the program goals and content. And, for many of the curriculum areas in which AIT has worked (health education, affective education for emotional problems of early adolescence), parents must be informed and, when possible, brought into the educative process.

As a result, AIT develops communication and training materials—and strategies—to support classroom materials. The effect is a multimedia, multiaudience communication program when projects are introduced. Students and teachers view television programs and participate in structured classroom discussion and activity as designed in a teacher's guide. Teachers view in-service training programs and participate in workshops designed from prototype materials prepared by AIT. Parents view special programs (usually produced locally) which explain the series. They also have access to parent discussion guides which enable them to talk about program content with their children.

Extensive "packaging" of a total communication strategy —at least at this level of complexity—is one of the features frequently mentioned by clients as a major component of program quality. It sets AIT programming apart in terms of quality from local projects produced on much lower budgets.

Planning for these components of the total package is also done by expert committee, with client participation.

DISCUSSION

One of the most interesting general conclusions that may be drawn from these tentative findings is that the organizational aspects of communication planning are as important to the total process as those aspects more directly related to the communication process, at least under conditions of coordination. It is difficult to imagine AIT being successful if organizational aspects of the planning process were not well done. It is equally difficult to imagine success if the communication design procedures did not result in high quality programming.

The implication of this general conclusion for the study of communication planning is clear: studies must encompass both organizational and communication variables. This in turn implies the need for strong interdisciplinary approaches to the problem. It also tends to confirm the common sense notion advanced at the beginning of this paper that models and theories from many disciplines have applicability to this kind of research. This notion is further confirmed by a cursory check of the organizational findings against two different theories related to organized action. One is the "user-oriented model" as described by Havelock and Mary (1973):

> First, user need is the paramount consideration and the only acceptable value stance for the change agent; second, the diagnosis of need always has to be an integral part of the total process; third, the outside change agent should be non-directive, rarely, if ever, violating the integrity of the user by placing himself in a directive or expert status; fourth, the internal resources, i.e., those resources already existing and easily accessible within the client system itself should be fully utilized; and fifth, self-initiated and self-applied innovation will have the strongest user commitment and the best chances for long term survival.

Even a brief description of the AIT planning process in this paper indicates that the conditions of the user-oriented model are almost totally satisfied.

A second theoretical construct with applicability relates directly to interorganizational coordination. As summarized for application to family planning programs (Beal and Middleton, 1975), this theory includes 20 propositions regarding conditions facilitating coordination between organizations. These are reproduced in the Appendix to this paper.

Again, it seems clear that most of these conditions have been met through the AIT planning process.

To mention these models in this context is not to give them an empirical test, nor to suggest that they are the only models that can help interpret data on communication planning. They are part of this paper only to support the idea that such models can help us understand the communication planning proces

Strategies for Future Research

Hypotheses such as the ones developed in the case study can form the basis for more rigorous data collection and analysis. A number of the hypotheses (1, 4, 6, 8, 9) can be tested through various methods, including role analysis and communication network analysis. Surveys of participants in the planning process could lead to more thorough exploration of other hypotheses (2, 3, 7, 9).

The case study technique can continue to be useful, particularly if the design incorporates comparison of planning processes where evidence of differing levels of success can be found. Comparison of institutions fitting into different cells in the matrix in Figure 1 would be valuable as well. Systems studies, in which different teams of investigators carry out independent analysis of different system components, followed by comparative analysis and a second round of data collection would be helpful, particularly in studying linkages between policy/national levels of planning and institutional levels. Systems studies should incorporate strong economic analysis components, since the flow of resources can have major impact on the planning process.

Last, but not least, the issue of cross-cultural comparative studies must be dealt with. Patterns of organization and planning are presumably affected by communication patterns, among other variables. There is reason to believe that these patterns vary between cultures (Riggs, 1964). Interdisciplinary research planning will be important here, perhaps involving anthropology and cross-cultural psychology.

Much work remains to be done in developing strategies and methodologies. The challenge, however, is clear. As nations, states or provinces, and institutions increasingly view communication systems and projects as integral parts of social and economic development, the need to understand the process through which communication theory is combined with theory and principles of organized action to achieve social goals will increase.

APPENDIX: INTERORGANIZATIONAL COORDINATION PROPOSITIONS*

Proposition 1
The probability of successful coordination will be increased if there is organizational staff knowledge, understanding, and skill relating to interorganizational coordination processes and strategies.

Proposition 2
The probability of successful coordination will be increased when the problem, as well as goals and means for solution of the problem, are clearly defined, understood, and accepted as important by organizations in the organizational set.

Proposition 3
The probability of successful coordination will be increased when it can be shown that there are common, converging, or complementary goals among the organizations who are judged to have potential for coordination.

Proposition 4
The probability of successful coordination is increased when specific proposed coordination activities are set in the context of a "wholistic" framework rather than in a "categorical" framework.

Proposition 5
The probability of successful coordination will be increased when there is strong continued emphasis on goals or objectives that are stated in terms of serving client systems (people), rather than in terms of activities used to achieve goals.

Proposition 6
The probability of successful coordination will be increased when an organization perceives that program goals can be reached more efficiently and effectively by coordinated (interdependent) rather than individual organizational (independent) action.

Proposition 7
The probability of successful coordination is increased when there is a clear analysis and agreement on the kind, amount,

---

*From George Beal and John Middleton. *Communication and Coordination in Family Planning Programs* (Honolulu: East-West Communication Institute, 1975), 163-175.

and quality of the resources needed and available for realistic steps toward the solution of the problem (goal achievement).

Proposition 8

The probability of successful coordination is increased when a realistic and equitable exchange system can be worked out among organizations.

Proposition 9

The probability of successful coordination will be increased if there is formalization and standardization of interorganizational exchanges and agreements.

Proposition 10

The probability of interorganizational coordination will be increased if coordination occurs at all levels of the organization.

Proposition 11

The probability of successful coordination is increased if, in addition to coordination agreements at higher levels, there is a high degree of effective two-way communication vertically within organizations. This communication should specify coordination agreements, activities, resources, and sanctions, and should be reinforced at the various vertical levels by interorganizational coordinating groups.

Proposition 12

The probability of successful interorganizational coordination is increased when the organizations are linked structurally (for example, overlapping leadership, officers, advisory committees, influential members) and/or functionally (for example, past coordination activities, reciprocal obligations, similar programs).

Proposition 13

The probability of successful coordination is increased when it can be shown that the organization has a "unique" resource to contribute to the project, resources are highly valued by the organization, and the organization believes it will receive recognition for the delivery of the resource.

Proposition 14

The probability of successful coordination is increased when there is agreement by important people and groups in the organization that the specified activity or resource asked of an organization is clearly within the domain of that organization.

Proposition 15

The probability of successful interorganizational coordination will be increased when it can be shown that there is the potential for more total resources if there is coordinated activity.

Proposition 16
The probability of successful coordination will be increased when organizations recognize (or can be convinced) that they are mature enough to engage in interorganizational activities (a form of systemic linkage) rather than being entirely concerned with internal programs.

Proposition 17
The probability of successful coordination is increased when coordination is presented and recognized as a viable alternative to competition and conflict.

Proposition 18
The probability of successful coordination will be increased when the opportunity to establish, maintain, or increase the organization's prestige or status (increase support base) by engaging in coordinated activity is demonstrated.

Proposition 19
The probability of successful coordination will be increased when the coordination activity offers an organization which is seeking new areas of activities the opportunity to engage in new and desirable activities.

Proposition 20
The probability of successful coordination will be increased if organizations can be shown that without coordination another organization may take over functions or activities that the organization perceives as its own area of interest, responsibility, or competence.

Works Cited

ASCD: American Society for Supervision and Curriculum Development. 1971. *Freedom, Bureaucracy, & Schooling.* Washington, D.C.: ASCD.

BEAL, G. and MIDDLETON, J. 1975. *Communication and Coordination in Family Planning Programs.* Honolulu: East-West Communication Institute.

BENSON, C.S. 1968. *The Economics of Education.* Second Edition. Boston: Houghton Mifflin Co.

CASE STUDIES OF EDUCATIONAL INNOVATION: IV. STRATEGIES FOR INNOVATION IN EDUCATION. 1973. Paris: Organisation for Economic Co-operation and Development (OECD), Centre for Educational Research and Innovation.

HAVELOCK, R.G. and HAVELOCK, M.C. 1973. *Training for Change Agents.* University of Michigan: Center for Research on Utilization of Scientific Knowledge.

KATZMAN, N. 1975. *Program Decisions in Public Television.* Washington, D.C.: Corporation for Public Broadcasting.

KAUFMAN, R.A. 1972. *Educational Systems Planning.* Englewood Cliffs, New Jersey: Prentice Hall, Inc.

KINCAID, D.L. with SCHRAMM, W. 1975. *Fundamental Human Communication.* Honolulu: East-West Communication Institute.

LAND, H.W. 1972. *The Children's Television Workshop: How and Why It Works.* Jericho, New York: Nassau Board of Cooperative Educational Services.

MIELKE, K.W., JOHNSON, R.C. and COLE, B.G. 1975. *The Federal Role in Funding Children's Television Programming.* Vol. 1: *Final Report.* Bloomington: Indiana University, Institute for Communication Research, Department of Telecommunications. (Pre-publication draft.)

NEW EDUCATIONAL MEDIA IN ACTION: CASE STUDIES FOR PLANNERS— VOL. I. 1967. Paris: Unesco.

POLSKY, R.M. 1974. *Getting to Sesame Street: Origins of the Children's Television Workshop*. New York: Praeger Publishers, Inc.

RIGGS, F. W. 1964. *Administration in Developing Countries*. Boston: Houghton-Mifflin Co.

COMMUNICATION SYSTEMS IN THE IMPLEMENTATION OF AN INTEGRATED RURAL AGRICULTURAL DEVELOPMENT PROGRAM

Rogelio V. Cuyno

This paper describes and examines communication problems in a specific development project. It focuses on the implementation of a pilot action-research project of *integrated rural agricultural development* (IRAD), undertaken by the University of the Philippines at Los Baños (UPLB) and Quezon Province. The nature and structure of this project are extremely complex, with an unusually high communication requirement in its implementation. In this paper, we examine the communication subsystem of IRAD and show how it is contributing to the overall goal of the project.

THE PROJECT IN CAPSULE

The IRAD project grew out of initiatives taken by the University of the Philippines at Los Baños and at the national and provincial levels. During his inaugural address in January 1974, Dr. Abelardo G. Samonte, the first chancellor of the University of the Philippines at Los Baños, proclaimed that he would like to see the institution play a vital role in achieving integrated rural development in the country. He envisioned that a sound approach to development must be holistic, integrated, and focused on people as the beginning and end of development. He defined true development as the "process of actualizing people's potentialities, the release of their creative energies, and realization of their capabilities for the improvement of their quality of life." In his terms, the condition of the people is the final and only true measure of development. He particularly wanted to see this done in the rural sector where about three-fourths of our entire population lives.

Chancellor Samonte argued that the institutional capability of UPLB put it in a unique position to adopt a multidisciplinary approach to development. This strength lay in a substantial pool of agricultural scientists, engineers, statisticians, forest resource managers, as well as communication specialists, humanists, economists, and other social scientists, all of whom are well trained and oriented to the study and solution of major problems besetting Philippine society. This manpower resource was a major impetus for the university's involvement in IRAD.

Outside the university, there were also developments in the direction of integrated rural development. In January 1974, President Ferdinand E. Marcos appointed Secretary Arturo R. Tanco of the Department of Agriculture as chairman of the Cabinet Coordinating Council on Integrated Rural Development Projects. This heightened interest in integrated rural development within the Department of Agriculture was manifested through an initial grant of P700,000 to UPLB to undertake a pilot project in integrated rural development.

Within that year everyone seemed to have been thinking about integrated rural development, including Quezon Province's Governor Anacleto Alcala. On January 22, 1975 he wrote Chancellor Samonte asking for technical assistance in the preparation of a "five-year comprehensive and integrated agricultural development program." This initiative of Quezon province was influential in its eventual choice as the pilot area for IRAD.

On October 15, 1975, Chancellor Samonte and Governor Alcala signed in behalf of their respective institutions a memorandum of agreement on a five-year cooperative action-research project in integrated rural development. Broadly, the agreement stipulated that UPLB and the province of Quezon would set up a project management system on a counterpart arrangement to generate resources and to plan and manage the project in four pilot municipalities.

PURPOSE OF IRAD

The interest of the university in this project as enunciated by Chancellor Samonte is to generate lessons, experiences, analysis, and trained personnel so that policy-makers at the national, regional, and provincial levels can make informed decisions on how to accelerate integrated rural agricultural development. In addition, IRAD provides the university with the opportunity to participate in a socially relevant and timely project and provide learning situations for its faculty and students in integrated rural development.

Objectives

IRAD has two sets of objectives—field action program objectives and research objectives.

ACTION OBJECTIVES

The intended outcomes in the field programs are:

1. A productive farming system and an efficient post production system in order that farm families may obtain higher income and ultimately attain material needs.
2. Strong, viable, and functional local institutions that can spur and sustain the developmental activities in the community.
3. Responsive, effective, and efficient local officials as well as government services in agriculture, health, nutrition, family planning, agricultural extension systems, public works, formal education, etc.
4. An enlightened rural population that is able to adapt to changing circumstances, evaluate options, and seek critical information for decision making.
5. Adequate health, housing, nutritional, and family life conditions for the rural population.

RESEARCH OBJECTIVES

The research outputs expected are:

1. A conceptual definition of integrated rural agricultural development, with key components identified and their interplay analyzed.
2. A methodology for attaining integrated rural agricultural development.
3. Identification of forces/factors that significantly influence the shape, direction, and performance of

integrated rural development and an analysis of their roles.

4. As assessment of the impact of the IRAD inputs on the pilot communities, farm families, individuals, local institutions, and social organizations. (Impacts on the neighbor communities will also be determined.)

Organizational Structure

Two parallel organizational systems were set up to implement the project—one for UPLB and another for Quezon Province (Figure 1). These two organizational systems are functionally linked at all levels from the highest offices, chancellor and governor, down to field operations.

On the part of UPLB, the chancellor initially appointed two project officers—the program leader and the associate program leader who then recruited the appropriate staff. Research teams from all units of the university were formed in the areas of management systems, rural training systems, evaluation, farm production and processing, resource and institutional factors, ecological infrastructures, and family development patterns. Each research area (called project) has several specific studies. The topics covered by the studies include problems of agriculture, management, cooperatives, agri-business, land-use and rural technology. Advising the whole UPLB-IRAD is a consultative group composed of senior members of the faculty and some heads of units.

In each of the four pilot municipalities, two action officers are assigned by the UPLB-IRAD to work hand-in-hand with the local officials and line agency representatives. A field operations officer supervises the work of these action officers.

A training unit has been established to coordinate various nonformal education or training programs for municipal officials, line agency representatives, local leaders, out-of-school youth, and homemakers.

On the part of Quezon province, the governor has overall responsibility for the program. He delegated field monitoring to the provincial development administrator, his action officer for developmental activities in the province. Advising the governor on IRAD matters is a Coordinating Council chaired by the governor himself and composed of heads of all line agencies in the province. A project officer coordinates the field activities for the

FIGURE 1. PROPOSED ORGANIZATIONAL STRUCTURE. QUEZON-UPLB-IRAD PROGRAM.

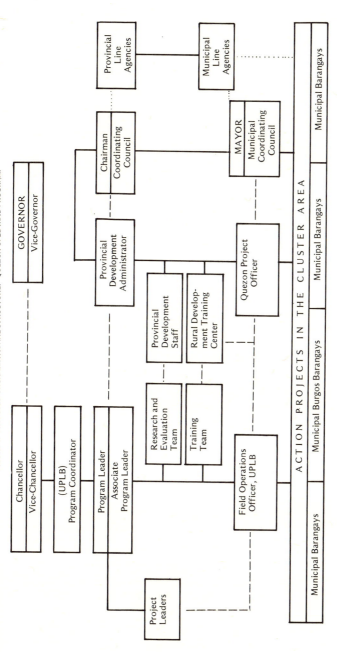

province in the four pilot municipalities. He is the counterpart
of the UPLB field operations officer.

At the municipal level, the mayor (who is the chief
executive officer of this level of government) is responsible for
the program. Assisting him in program planning are the municipal
council (an elected body) and representatives of line agencies.
Line agency representatives take care of implementing the field
program at the *barangay* or village level. They are assisted by
volunteer leaders and elected officials.

A training unit will soon be formed to work with the
UPLB counterpart. At present the project officer is serving as
the training coordinator for the Quezon province side of the
project.

DESCRIPTION OF THE
PROGRAM AND GUIDING CONCEPTS

There is no grand theory guiding the project nor specific
hypotheses that are to be tested. In the absence of solid local
experience and careful and well thought-out research on integrated rural agricultural development, it was deemed wise not to
make assertions or establish preconceived notions about what
ought to be done. There are, however, operational concepts and
structural features which set boundaries for utilizing human,
fiscal, and time resources and to guide thinking.

1. *What is integration?* We have adopted Philipp Coombs'
(1974) operational definition of integration:

> It is the linking of related functions and elements together so that
> their collective impacts and accomplishments will be greater than if
> they acted separately. Integration in this sense is the opposite of
> fragmentation.

Operationally, this calls for an interagency arrangement
for problem identification, program planning, and implementation. Instead of the usual agency-oriented program planning, it
is the community problems that determine what agencies should
be doing. In other words, the problem should integrate the
agencies rather than the agencies delineating the problems.

Moreover, this approach requires the meshing together
of biological, physical, and social technology to analyze and
solve human and community problems.

Finally, this approach recognizes the integration of the world of action and the world of research. Much waste and error can be avoided if field activities are guided by available knowledge on the subject. Furthermore, the feedback information that research can provide can rectify unwanted deviation from set directions. On the other hand, research must have action as its subject of inquiry. The research enterprise as a whole has to address socially meaningful subject matter if it is to contribute to the improvement of human conditions. Thus, the design of this program is action-research. This will enable the researchers to make an input into the "intervention" process and at the same time systematically observe events as they unfold.

2. *Focus on depressed rural sector.* Unlike other pilot projects which are situated in areas where conditions are highly favorable, and therefore have greater chances of success, IRAD has chosen for its pilot area four depressed communities in Quezon province. That these four municipalities have been isolated from previous development efforts is evidenced by almost impassable roads in the monsoon season, poor health services, no electricity, poor domestic water supply, and an inadequate number of government agricultural technicians serving the area.

3. *Systems approach.* As a method or strategy, integrated rural development adopts the viewpoint that true development is a total and unified process. Viewed from this perspective, it is necessary to consider the problem in its totality rather than piecemeal. The systems approach suggests that multifaceted components—economic, social, political, cultural, and physical—have to be treated as complementary and mutually reinforcing rather than competing and mutually exclusive. It further assumes that if one component lags behind in the attainment of the desired end, the whole system cannot be regarded as truly developed, even if the other components have attained growth. For growth without balance and distribution is not development. As Pope Paul VI in his famous Encyclical *Populorum Progressio* says, "no man can be left out . . . and no part of man can be left out."

4. *Entry point.* Development is transformation requiring changes in the social structure and in value patterns of the system over time. Changes, however, cannot be expected to originate from within. More often, the forces existing within the system tend to restrain and fix the system to the status quo rather than

favor change. Therefore, an appropriate entry point has to be carefully chosen to generate disequilibrium and incentive within the system and eventually to bring about its transformation. The entry point has to be through the components that provide the most constraint to the system and where the highest opportunity lies. It has also to be based on the existing strengths and resources of the system. Considering that resources for development are always in short supply, it is advisable to use these limited resources mainly on the component(s) chosen as the entry point(s).

5. *Local participation.* Development, as systems transformation, suggests that it is only due to internal will and self-power that the system will be ever dynamic. External inputs merely prime or catalyze the change process. The mobilization of people and the growth of their self-capability and self-reliance through participation and experience are necessary conditions for development—and ends in themselves.

The project management structure emphasizes that the Quezon province counterpart takes the lead in the planning and the implementation of the various projects. UPLB will only provide advice on technical matters, training of manpower, feedback information, and the needed research to guide action.

6. *Who should be the integrator?* It is inevitable that the question of who should integrate or coordinate the inputs of the various agencies will be an issue. In the past this task of integration or coordination has hinged on the outside bureaucratic system personified by a local representative (who is also an outsider). Considering that the line agencies are on the same level and are therefore co-equals, there are usually problems of a lack of cooperation and interagency jealousy. In the IRAD approach, the local political system (through the elected officials) serves as the integrator or coordinator of developmental planning up to implementation. It is argued that this activity is a management function that has to be exercised by the political system. Not only will this minimize interagency jealousy, it will also strengthen localization of the management capability. Theoretically, this should work because the local political system has a stake and vested interest in the development of the locality.

STATEMENT OF THE COMMUNICATION PROBLEM

The IRAD project has not yet completed its first year of

operation. Most of what has been done thus far consists of taking benchmark information, organizing, planning, orienting new recruits, and reorienting the veterans. We are learning to work together, listening to local people, looking around for what we can do, deciding what we want to do and how to do it, re-channeling and smoothing out personal and professional orientations, and explaining to ourselves and to others what integrated rural agricultural development really is.

All this indeed is a communication problem requiring a communication solution. The novelty of the idea (at least in our part of the world), the complexity of the project's organizational structure (the cooperating parties have inherently different structures, purposes, manpower training and orientation, and power bases), the multidimensional nature of integrated development, the great number of relevant systems that are to be involved, and the interdependence and interrelatedness of these various relevant systems demand from the initiators and change agents a sensitive and responsive communication strategy and skillful communication performance.

The communication problem, as we see it, appears at various levels and varies with levels. Within the academe, the project leaders in the different study areas start with an uncommon notion about action-research. We have taken an evolutionary way of organizing the research component, the action component, and the training-education components. Moreover we have interrelated these components in a more spontaneous way. We have observed overlaps among different study areas which need constant clarification and adjustment. Even the giving of titles to the studies has to be handled sensitively and discretely. A number of scholars do not feel comfortable with this perceived lack of "system."

Then there is the nagging issue of lack of a more definitive conceptualization of integrated rural agricultural development. There were long and animated debates within the consultative group with respect to the question of locating the entry point. What should be the role of the university *vis à vis* the province of Quezon and the line agencies working there? There are also differences in approach. Some would like to see testable hypotheses derived from past lessons in rural development to guide the "intervention" process. Others would like to take a problem-oriented approach to project design without *a priori* notions of what ought to be done.

Role definition of the university field officers is still presently being clarified. Should they work only with and through existing structures? Could they initiate projects by themselves? If they can initiate projects, how do they work with other line agencies and the technical experts from UPLB who are expected to have a say on what ought to be done?

At the provincial level, within the Coordinating Council, concerns were raised on possible overlapping of IRAD with existing coordinating bodies and other integrated development programs.

At the municipal level, agency representatives are anxious about time allocation. How much time would they devote to this more localized, problem-oriented and interagency program and how much time should they spend for programs handed down to them from the central office? Will their efforts and expenses in this program be legitimate in the eyes of their own agencies?

In terms of program planning, how is integrated program planning done? How different is it from previous programs prepared by line agencies? How will the local political system respond to their role as integrator or coordinator?

What about the local people themselves—what problems do they consider as hindering their progress? What would they like IRAD to work on? The people are less concerned about organizational arrangements. What they are concerned about are better roads, electricity, better prices for their commodities, domestic water supply, and a better health delivery system.

COMMUNICATION ACTIVITIES

In our IRAD project we have no overall communication plan to solve the many problems cited above. The title of this paper therefore is a bit presumptuous when it uses the term "communication system." However, in defense of ourselves, we had no prior indications that we were going to encounter these problems, so we had to take on the problems one at a time and we had to react with spontaneity. These problems can be reduced and simplified as follows:

- lack of consensus across levels about a definition of what we are about.
- differences in perception of implications of IRAD on agency programs.
- lack of experience by line agency representatives working as a team.

- lack of a philosophical orientation of development across levels.

To somehow meet these problems we have undertaken certain activities:

1. *Round Table Conference on Integrated Rural Development.* This was a gathering of heads of programs and agencies that are themselves engaged in integrated rural development. Programs or agencies who participated in this conference were the Population Commission, National Nutrition Program, Community Comprehensive Health Program of the University of the Philippines College of Medicine, Development Academy of the Philippines, UP-Searca Social Laboratory Project, Philippine Business for Social Progress, and University Extension Center of the University of the Philippines at Los Banos. The theme of this small conference was "Towards a Common Understanding of Integrated Rural Development." We in IRAD sponsored this conference in order to obtain insights and experiences from those who have tried integrated development. These insights and experiences helped us conceptualize the IRAD program.

2. *Dialogue-workshop with Extension Field Agents.* Selected extension fieldworkers from the Bureau of Agricultural Extension, Bureau of Plant Industry, UP-Searca Social Laboratory, International Institute for Rural Reconstruction, UP-Community Comprehensive Health Program, Philippine Business for Social Progress, Roman Catholic Church Social Action Program, and the Dairy Training and Research Institute participated in this three-day live-in activity. The purpose of this activity was to probe into the problems encountered by the front-line development workers and also to find out about their own thinking of development.

On the part of IRAD this was a chance to evolve a philosophical orientation of development and to pretest it on professionals who are in the front-line and actually working with the rural people. For this activity, IRAD produced a book of readings on development. This book was sent to the participants before the workshop so that they would have a chance to read and reflect on key concepts. During the workshop, small discussion groups were formed and questions based on the articles were prepared for discussion. It was observed that at this level of the agency hierarchy, it was quite difficult to get an intelligent expression of a basic or philosophical orientation of development. But it was rewarding to hear from the participants during the evaluation period that the whole dialogue was refreshing and enlightening for them.

3. *Interagency Orientation on IRAD.* All heads of line agencies in Quezon province participated in an interagency orientation to establish a working relationship between UPLB and Quezon province workers under the IRAD umbrella by establishing a common framework for and orientation toward integrated rural development. The first half of the one-day activity was spent in a seminar during which UPLB speakers, using charts, explained the UPLB tentative formulation of integrated rural development. Also, UPLB and Quezon representatives expressed their expectations of one other in the IRAD venture.

At the open discussion, questions were centered mostly on clarification of interagency cooperation and coordination, financing of IRAD programs and projects, and agency roles and responsibilities in IRAD. The vice-governor, who was the presiding officer of the conference, urged all agencies to support and cooperate in the program.

In the second half of the conference, small groups discussed questions that had been prepared earlier and that dealt with concepts of integration, guiding principles of integration, possible projects that lend themselves to integration, organizing for integrated rural development, and problems of implementation of integrated programs.

The conference closed with some apprehension on the part of the heads of line agencies arising from the fact that there are already existing interagency structures within the province. They were a little uncertain as to how IRAD would relate with these structures.

4. *Municipal Development Council Orientation.* This was a series of seminars in all four pilot municipalities to orient elected municipal officials, representatives of line agencies, and elected village officials regarding the concepts, organization, and possible IRAD projects in the area. Toward the end of the one-day activity, the participants were asked to present problems they wanted attended to. This activity served as a forum for the local officials to voice their problems and complain against the apparent lack of government action on their problems. These problems and complaints were recorded as reference for future community program planning.

5. *Workshop on Community Program Planning.* All line agency fieldworkers in the four pilot municipalities were called to a two-day workshop. The workshop was designed to establish a common orientation toward integrated rural development, to

establish a common procedure and format for preparing a community program plan, and to start to build teamwork and team consciousness. The two key questions were: What is development? What is the rationale and need for interagency cooperation and coordination? These were mulled over on the first day. Selected readings on integrated rural development and extension approach were provided to supplement the presentation. A cooperation game was played in this workshop for the participants to experience a situation where cooperation is needed to complete a team task. This game is played as follows: a team of five players is asked to form a square out of several cut-up pieces of cardboard initially provided to each player. By continuously exchanging these pieces with the other co-members of the group, each player can eventually form a square. The rules are: (1) players may not ask for a piece but can give anyone a piece of cardboard; (2) players are not allowed to communicate to one another in any form; and (3) the game is finished when everyone in the group has completed a square. After the game, we posed a question to the group. "Based on your experience in this exercise, what are the preconditions in order for interagency cooperation to succeed?" The following comments were mentioned by the participants:

- We have to be sensitive to the needs of others
- We have to share our resources with others
- We need to have a common idea or goal of what we are accomplishing
- A leader or catalyzer is needed to rechannel our individual efforts and resources
- We have to give encouragement to someone who is feeling low
- Cooperation is constrained without communication

In this workshop, we presented a slide-tape on integrated development which showed the many facts of development (economic, social, political, cultural, and physical) and which stated the meaning of progress from the viewpoint of a rural person named Mang Tony.

After the showing we asked two questions: First, "What is Mang Tony's meaning of progress (development)?" Invariably, most of the intended key points of the slide-tape were recalled, indicating the promise of this medium for cognitive learning. The second question was, "Do you agree with Mang Tony on his views about progress?" With only a few exceptions and qualifications, the general comments were affirmative.

In the workshop on community program planning, a university professor first made a critique of the existing procedure and format currently used by the agencies. He followed this up with a presentation of a modified program planning model and format. Agency programs are usually prepared independently of one another, following lines suggested by their respective national offices. In the proposed model, the exercise starts with identification by the interagency team of community problems, constraints, resources, and opportunities. Following problem identification, the workshop group proceeded to identify a package of solutions and activities, interagency participation, preparation of the budget, and organizational arrangement or management system to use in implementing the interagency program. We call the whole exercise coordination by joint planning.

6. *Planning Workshop to Prepare Framework Plan for Rural Learning Center.* One principal assistance that UPLB provides to Quezon province under the IRAD umbrella is the establishment of a learning center for the rural people of Quezon. It is formally called Quezon Rural Development Training Center (QRDTC). The center seeks to continuously provide the rural people of Quezon with learning opportunities in agriculture and other related activities. Its rationale rests on the assumption that education at the grass roots is a necessary condition for rural transformation because it brings into the system the inputs of technological information, knowledge of new opportunities, new skills, new perspectives, and new commitments. The center, as proposed in the framework plan, will be directly under the office of the Governor and managed by a full-time staff. Some trainers, however, will be on an on-call basis from line agencies within the province and from UPLB. An Interagency Program Planning Committee will help the center's director in drawing up an annual program. A team of specialists from UPLB and line agencies will design the various training programs.

The framework plan for the center was prepared in a workshop by an interagency task group chaired by a UPLB representative.

7. *Project Leaders' Seminars.* For greater integration and coordination within UPLB, the different project leaders report to one another on their project plans. This seminar is done as often as necessary.

8. *Consultative Group Mini-seminars.* Chaired by the chancellor, the consultative group advises the UPLB-IRAD staff

on basic issues, such as the conceptualization of the whole project, identification of research areas, and relationship with cooperating agencies. It also reviews the progress of the work in the field. Position papers and documents written by IRAD staff are distributed before every meeting of this group.

SUMMARY OF THE
IRAD COMMUNICATION ACTIVITIES

In summary, it can be noted that the purpose of the communication activities in the initial implementation of IRAD is mainly to establish a common framework and orientation among the many organizational systems and personalities involved within the university level, the provincial level, and the municipal level. This includes obtaining common understanding of key concepts of development, particularly integrated rural development and interagency cooperation and coordination. At the interorganizational relations level, we sought out the communication objective of establishing a positive working relationship and trying to gain acceptance of UPLB's presence in the area.

For the IRAD staff from UPLB, this initial phase was a period of listening, explaining, and trying to feel the pulse of the task environment.

The communication approach used to attain the above objectives was mostly interpersonal, using dialogues, group discussions, planned presentations, and packaged messages in the form of print materials and slide-tapes. These activities were conducted mostly in a group setting, involving interagency or interunit participation, and always requiring work sessions.

Works Cited

COOMBS, P.H. with AHMED, M. 1974. *Attacking Rural Poverty: How Non-Formal Education Can Help.* Baltimore: Johns Hopkins University Press.

LANGUAGE, NATIONHOOD, AND COMMUNICATION PLANNING: THE CASE OF A MULTILINGUAL SOCIETY

Eddie C.Y. Kuo

INTRODUCTION

Making one of the earliest theoretical expositions of the role of communication in national development, Karl W. Deutsch (1953,1966) suggests that language and literacy are important elements in social communication and mobilization, which are in turn basic measures of national development. He shows persuasively that communication is essential to the formation of a people, a community, and a nationality and that the degree of linguistic assimilation is indicative of communicative ability, which determines the level of national assimilation or differentiation.

From Deutsch's conceptualization, it becomes clear that, in multilingual societies, both language planning and communication planning are essential to national development and that the two are closely and inescapably related.

A review of current literature, however, reveals that there has been little systematic analysis treating language as a variable in communication planning. One possible explanation is that language as the built-in "medium" in all verbal communications—interpersonal or through mass media—is often taken for granted. Most discussions on communication planning therefore tend to "by-pass" the language issue; and the communication planners and researchers are typically concerned only with the problems of training, budgeting, production, development of infrastructure, etc. Yet for those with practical experiences in a multilingual society, the language issue is in fact omnipresent at almost every stage of communication planning. In many cases, the language factor simply cannot be "taken for granted." Judging from the fact that linguistic diversity and language group identity are elements closely associated with nation-building and national development in multilingual states, as we shall see in the later discussion, it is suggested that language should be treated as an important variable in communication planning in multilingual states and that communication planning scholars should look into the problem carefully and systematically.

LANGUAGE DIVERSITY AND NATION-BUILDING

For most developing countries in Asia and Africa, the task of nation-building is constantly confronted with problems of multi-ethnicity and language diversity. The presence of competing ethnic/language groups in these new states generally means that the establishment of a new nationhood requires the cultivation of a new national identity. The emerging national identity can be achieved either through an expansion and elevation of an indigenous ethnic identity imposed upon other "less" indigenous and usually minority ethnic groups, or through the development of a new supra-ethnic identity treating various ethnic groups as of equal standing. In either case, it is expected that the emergence of a new national identity in the new states is not likely to be natural or spontaneous. Some planning efforts from the part of the ruling elite are consequently required. Both communication planning and language planning can and should play important roles here. While the significant role played by communication in development has been extensively explored (Lerner, 1958; Pye, 1963; Schramm, 1964; Lerner and Schramm, 1967; and Frey, 1973) and thus is better known to communication scholars, the position of the language variable in the communicative system in relation to nation-building deserves further discussion.

According to Deutsch (1966), linguistic and cultural assimilation in multi-ethnic states is a slow process that may involve decades and generations. As a contrast, growth in economy, technology, and societal structure such as transportation and marketing systems can be very rapid. Deutsch sees a great danger in this differential growth pattern in national development. He states:

Much of this economic or technological development may force people into new and inescapable contacts with each other as workers, customers, and neighbors—contacts far narrower, perhaps, than the range of human relations that can be communicated within one culture; but contacts far wider than the relations which can be communicated in the absence of a common culture to outsiders. Linguistically and culturally, then, members of each group are outsiders for the other. Yet technological and economic processes are forcing them together, into acute recognition of their differences and their common, mutual experience of strangeness, and more conspicuous differentiation and conflict may result (1966, pp. 125-126).

Apparently, Deutsch is pessimistic that mere contacts at the societal level without meaningful social communication may lead to tension and conflict. By implication, however, careful communication planning, taking into consideration the language situation of the society, should be able to help in reducing tension and conflict and in improving communicative integration and social cohesiveness.

Herbert C. Kelman analyzes the problem from a socio-psychological point of view. He points out that sentimental attachments within respective ethnic/language groups in a multilingual society pose a potential barrier to participation in the national system and to the development of a national identity. Less pessimistic than Deutsch, he believes that so long as the existing socio-political structure is efficient enough to help the individual to achieve his own ends or the ends of his ethnic community, the resultant instrumental attachments may eventually lead to sentimental attachments to the new state and then to the emergence of a new national identity. In such case, we have a type of nation-building "in which the primary push is from state to nation" (Kelman, 1971, p. 27).

Accordingly, in such new states, Kelman argues, language policies ought to be based entirely on functional considerations:

That is, in selecting languages for various purposes . . . central authorities ought to be concerned primarily with two issues: (1) how to establish and facilitate patterns of communication . . . that would enable its socioeconomic institutions to function most effectively and equitably in meeting the needs and interests of the population; and (2) how to assure that different groups within the society . . . have equal access to the system and opportunities to participate in it. Out of these processes, a national language, evoking sentimental attachments, may gradually emerge (1971, p. 40).

What Kelman terms a transition from state to nation, Joshua A. Fishman calls "state-into-nationality" processes, involving a transformation from "politico-operational integration," comparable to Kelman's sentimental attachment. He also

emphasizes that the state-to-nationality processes and national-
ity-to-state processes reflect "the two kinds of integration bonds
upon which all nations depend and which constantly reinforce
each other" (Fishman, 1972a, p. 231).

> Just as the state-to-nationality nations stress(ed) their common
> sociocultural bonds, particularly in times of stress, so did (and do)
> the nationality-into-state nations stress politico-operational insti-
> tutions as soon as they gain(ed) independence and face(d) the func-
> tional problems of modern nationhood (*ibid.*).

Viewing language policy as a crucial issue in the new
states, Fishman (1972b) further distinguishes three types of
multilingual societies, each with a set of language decisions perceived to be most appropriate for nation-building under the
given social conditions. Fishman's typology proves to be very
useful in understanding and explaining the language policy
adopted by a given state at a given stage of development. We
will draw extensively from Fishman in the later discussion of the
Singapore case.

From the above discussion, it should be obvious that the
crucial problem faced by most new multi-ethnic states is the
potential conflict between loyalty to one's speech community
and loyalty to the wider national community. The essential
question is how can the two be reconciled rapidly and smoothly
to facilitate the process of nation-building. The determination
and implementation of the language policy is therefore often
given priority in the new states. While, as many communication
scholars have shown, careful planning in communication operation can assist in this process of nation-building, such planning
invariably must take into consideration the given language
policy. Again here we see the connection between the language
issue and communication planning.

LANGUAGE AND NATION-BUILDING
IN SINGAPORE

As an independent state, Singapore is small in size and
short in history, yet heterogeneous in ethnic and linguistic composition. The present population of Singapore, totaling over
2.2 million people, is composed of approximately 76 percent
Chinese, 15 percent Malays, 7 percent Indians,[1] and less than 2
percent others, including Eurasians, Europeans, etc.

(Arumainathan, 1973). Linguistically, each of the three major ethnic communities is composed of a number of dialect speech groups. A recent study (Kuo, 1976) shows that there are five major languages (Malay, English, Mandarin, Tamil, and Hokkien) and three minor languages (Teochew, Cantonese, and Hainanese) in Singapore today. With each of the three major ethnic communities sentimentally associated with its "ethnic mother language"[2] and cultural tradition, linguistically, Singapore represents a prototype of what Fishman (1972b, p. 203) designates as a "multimodal nation . . . characterized by a conflicting or competing multiplicity of . . . Great Traditions,"and what Dan Kwart A. Rustow describes as a pattern involving "a variety of unrelated languages each with its own literary tradition" (1968, p. 102).

As a compromise among the three major, and potentially competitive, ethnic communities, the leaders of Singapore decided at the time of independence in 1965 that there would be four official languages in the new Republic. Malay, (Mandarin) Chinese, and Tamil were selected to represent the three ethnic-cultural traditions in Singapore; and English was selected because of its international status and Singapore's colonial background. Of the four, Malay was designated the national language, reflecting both the historial and geographical position of the island-state and performing a role that is more ceremonial than functional.[3] The official language policy of Singapore can best be described as multilingualism or linguistic pluralism. The competence levels in various major languages among the three ethnic groups in Singapore are shown in Table 1.[4]

The policy of multilingualism in Singapore prescribes that all four official languages should be treated as equal in principal. This policy is most clearly manifested in Singapore's educational system of four language streams of schools and in its communication policy of multilingual programs in mass media communication, as we shall discuss later. Few would argue seriously that all the four official languages are treated precisely equal in actual practice in Singapore, and it is known that some are more equal than others (Kuo, in press). What is significant about the policy of multilingualism in Singapore is that the amount of formal recognition is sufficient enough to rule out any substantial inter-ethnic conflict based on the language issue.

Being more equal than the others, the English language as a non-native language has evolved to occupy a dominant status in Singapore, functioning as a unifying working language for

TABLE 1. COMPETENCE IN OFFICIAL LANGUAGE IN SINGAPORE, BY ETHNICITY

ETHNICITY	OFFICIAL LANGUAGE			
	MALAY	CHINESE	TAMIL	ENGLISH
CHINESE				
Literacy (%)[a]	1.0	46.0	d	31.2
Comprehension (%)[b]	50.9	76.3	0.3	53.6
MALAYS				
Literacy (%)[a]	70.2	d	d	33.0
Comprehension (%)[b]	100.0	0.5	1.0	61.5
INDIANS				
Literacy (%)[a]	10.1	0.1	38.8	48.0
Comprehension (%)[b]	98.1	d	89.5	70.5
TOTAL[c]				
Literacy (%)[a]	11.4	35.6	2.8	33.7
Comprehension (%)[b]	61.3	59.4	6.7	56.6

a   Referring to population aged 10 and over; 1970 census data.
b   Referring to population aged 15 and over who can understand a given spoken language; 1972 SRS sample study. See Note 4.
c   Including "Other" minority ethnic groups
d   Less than 0.1%

Sources: Literacy data based on Arumainathan (1973). Comprehension data based on Survey Research Singapore (1972).

politico-operational integration at the national level. Administratively, it is the language of government bureaucracy. Legally, it is the language for the authoritative texts of all legislation and the judgments of courts of record. Besides, English in Singapore is commercially the language of the international trade and socially the most prestigious. The situation fits strikingly well with what Fishman describes as "Type C decisions," typical in a multimodal nation, whereby,

> In order to avoid giving any party an advantage—and in order to avoid constant rivalry for greater national prominence among the various contenders—a foreign language of Wider Communication is frequently selected de jure or utilized de facto as (co-) official or as working language at the national level (sometimes in conjunction with an indigenous national language which may actually be little employed by those who are ostensibly its guardians) (Fishman, 1972b, p. 204).

In order to understand the role of language in relation to nation-building in Singapore and to apply the paradigms of

Kelman and Fishman, it is therefore important to single out English as a non-native dominant language[5] in contrast to the other official languages that are "more indigenous" and thus sub-national. In Singapore, English is promoted as the language of modernity, progress, technology, and economic development, and as a means to achieve politico-operational integration and to develop instrumental attachments to the supra-ethnic national system among the ethnically heterogeneous population. As a contrast, the ethnic mother languages are retained under the policy of multilingualism to maintain socio-cultural integration at the ethnic-speech community level, as well as for the sake of sentimental attachments.

The immediate motivations behind the double-barrelled language policy can be found at both the collective and the individual levels.

At the collective level, English is accepted as instrumental to Singapore's national development—to attract foreign capital, to promote international trade, and to absorb technical know-how. There is nevertheless the concern that English, being a Western language, is associated with the "decadent Western values" of sex, drugs, violence, hippy-ism, and materialism. Such undesirable "Western values," it is believed, are to be counter-balanced by the learning of one's ethnic mother language and the traditional virtues believed to be attached to it.

At the individual level, it is similarly found that English is instrumental to career development and social mobility. The choice of English education is associated with economic considerations and occupational opportunities. As a contrast, those parents who send their children to vernacular schools are thought to be strong in sentimental attachments to the ethnic culture and are more concerned with moral training and character building (Murray, 1971).

A persistent state of multilingualism, however, does not solve the problem of the potential conflict between the primordial ethnic identity and the wider national identity. The dilemma is hopefully to be solved by making English the dominant working language in Singapore.

The fact that English is utilized as the working language in the politico-bureaucratic and socio-economic systems serves two important functions in Singapore. In the short run, the use of English, a non-native language, means that all ethnic groups have relatively equal access to the national system and equal opportunities to gain social mobility. The danger of ethnic conflict and tension can thus be extensively reduced. (Language stream of education—English versus non-English—is a factor that may result into differential mobility and thus is potentially more divisive. But the danger here is less since the division in the education stream cuts across ethnic lines.)

In the long run, it is hoped that through the utilitarian values of English at both the collective and the individual levels, instrumental attachments will eventually strengthen legitimacy of the state and contribute to further sentimental attachments and thus facilitate the emergence of a supra-ethnic national identity.

MULTILINGUALISM AND COMMUNICATION PLANNING

Many communication scholars have pointed out that communication serves important functions in mobilizing the population to participate in the national system. In a multilingual society, however, the mobilization-participation process is often more complicated than what the above statement implies. This is so because the presence of various functionally-specific languages may create a disjunction in this seemingly simple process of mobilization-participation. In the case of Singapore, as we have shown in the last section, the language of participation is English. The situation is quite different when we focus on the mobilization process,[6] which is closely related to the operation and planning of communication.

The mobilizing effort is often initiated from the "top," represented by the political elite, to the "bottom" through various communication channels. The objectives of such communication can either be to inform, to educate, to persuade, or simply to entertain. The ultimate goal of development support communication, however, is to mobilize human resources and mass support for national development. In order to effectively appeal to the mass in a multilingual society, it is generally advisable that such mobilization messages be conveyed in a language that is sentimentally attached to the target audience involved. In other words, communication in ethnic mother languages should be effectively used especially in the cases of persuasion, information, and education. The total communicative network should therefore adopt the policy of multilingualism, to carry messages in as many languages as economically feasible in order to reach and to mobilize large segments of population.

The case of Radio Television Singapore (RTS) will be discussed to illustrate the policy of multilingualism in communication planning in Singapore.

RTS is a government-owned, government-operated organization, functioning under the Broadcasting Department within the Ministry of Culture. Protected by the Radio and Television Act of 1963, which gives the Government of Singapore the exclusive privilege of establishing any broadcasting station, RTS is also entrusted "with the responsibility of interpreting the long-term objectives and policies of the Government, and particularly in maintaining a sense of national identity" (Ministry of Culture, 1973). The mission of nation-building is thus clearly prescribed.

It is significant that the maxim of RTS is "From Many Cultures, One Voice," which reflects the multicultural and multilingual nature of its programs and its audience. *Radio Singapore* broadcasts four separate language channels[7] on both the medium-and short-wave bands. Languages used in broadcasting are English, Malay, Tamil, Mandarin, and six other Chinese dialects. Each channel goes on the air for about 16 to 19 hours daily between 5:00 a.m. and midnight. The relatively equal allocation of transmission hours in four language groups, ranging between 20 percent to 30 percent of total transmission, is shown in Table 2.

Television Singapore operates on two channels with a total of more than 100 weekly transmission hours. Again all four official languages and some Chinese dialects are transmitted. In the case of television broadcasting, mainly because of differential availability of various language programs, the allocation of hours among various languages is much more uneven, with English taking more than half and Tamil less than one-tenth of the total transmission hours. (See Table 2.) The situation however is to some extent improved by the subtitling service—that is, Chinese programs with English or Malay subtitles, and English with Malay, Chinese, or Tamil subtitles.

Radio and television broadcasting in Singapore is development-conscious and emphasizes much on information and education programs. Table 3 shows that these types of programs take up an average of about 34 percent of the total radio transmission hours and 26 percent of the total television transmission hours. It is especially interesting to note that the percentages of information and education program hours within various

TABLE 2. LANGUAGE AND RTS BROADCASTING IN SINGAPORE, 1975

	LANGUAGE OF PROGRAM				TOTAL
	MALAY	CHINESE*	TAMIL	ENGLISH	
RADIO SINGAPORE					
Total Hours Per Week	126	147	105	126	504
% of Total	25.0	29.2	20.8	25.0	100.0
TELEVISION SINGAPORE					
Total Minutes Per Week	685	1,560	560	3,435	6,240
% of Total	11.0	25.0	9.0	55.0	100.0

*Including Mandarin and six other Chinese dialects.

Source: Based on Parliament Debate Report, Notice Paper No. 80 of 1975; also reported in *Straits Times,* Singapore, 12 November 1975.

TABLE 3. PERCENTAGE OF INFORMATION AND EDUCATION PROGRAMS[a] IN SINGAPORE BY LANGUAGE, 1975

	MALAY	CHINESE[b]	TAMIL	ENGLISH	TOTAL
RADIO SINGAPORE	33.3	38.8	36.2	27.8	34.1
TELEVISION SINGAPORE	39.4	27.2	42.9	24.9	29.0

[a] As defined and calculated by Ministry of Culture, Singapore.
[b] Including Mandarin and six other Chinese dialects.

Source: Same as Table 2.

language transmissions are higher in the three ethnic languages than in English. Especially in the cases of Tamil and Malay television programs, the relatively shorter periods of transmission are slightly compensated by higher proportions of information and education programs. It is 42.9 percent in Tamil programs, 39.4 percent in Malay, but 27.2 percent in Chinese and 24.9 percent in English. (See Table 3.) It seems that Tamil and Malay language audience can be expected to turn to other language channels, notably English, for entertainment. But ethnic language programs of informative and educational nature are maintained to make sure that the messages are received by members of various ethnic communities.

Programs on "current affairs," specially designed for nation-building purposes, are produced by a Central Production Unit under RTS. According to a Ministry of Culture publication, programs produced by the Central Production Unit,

> give the rationale for Government action, explain the aims of Government policy, and suggest to the audience a particular way or choice. Broad and national in scope, these programmes are aimed at stimulating interest in the political, economic and social developments of our society as well as those of other countries (Ministry of Culture, 1973).

One such program is "In Parliament Today," which broadcasts parliament proceedings when the parliament is in session. Other "current affairs" programs that are development-oriented and nation-building-conscious include "Opinion" (a panel discussion television program on current issues), "Inquiry" (a radio feature on current issues such as pollution and family planning), "Singapore Impression," "Daily Digest," and so forth.

Without empirical data based on audience studies, we are not in a position to evaluate the success of RTS's development-oriented communication efforts. We could however point out the relevance of multilingual programs by comparing the ethnic background of the audience with the language of programs they listen to. Table 4 shows that about 36 percent of the population aged 15 and over in Singapore claimed they listen to *Radio Singapore* regularly. Proportion-wise, Indians (63.3 percent) and Malays (52.8 percent) have more exposure to this medium than the Chinese (30.3 percent). It is clearly shown that audience from each of the three ethnic communities listen predominantly to programs broadcast in their own ethnic language; many exclusively so. The only language programs shared by audiences from all three communities are, as expected, programs

TABLE 4. PERCENTAGE OF POPULATION AGED 15
AND OVER WHO LISTENED TO *RADIO SINGAPORE*
"YESTERDAY," BY ETHNICITY AND LANGUAGE
OF PROGRAM, 1972

| ETHNICITY | LANGUAGE OF PROGRAM HEARD | | | | |
	MALAY	CHINESE[a]	TAMIL	ENGLISH	ANY
CHINESE	b	24.7	b	6.4	30.3
MALAYS	50.0	b	5.0	2.2	52.8
INDIANS	8.2	1.0	57.1	7.1	63.3
TOTAL[c]	6.9	19.3	4.8	6.7	35.8

[a] Including Mandarin and six other Chinese dialects.
[b] Less than 0.1%
[c] Including "Other" ethnic groups

Source: Computed from *Survey Research Singapore,* 1972, Vols. 1 and 2,
Tables 23B.

in English. The choice of language programs by the audience
therefore further justifies the multilingual policy of RTS broadcasting[8] at the present stage of nation-building in Singapore.

In this connection, it should be pointed out that the
policy of multilingualism in media communications in Singapore
is implemented not without problems and difficulties. It is
obvious that the sharing of budget and broadcasting hours means
a smaller piece of pie for programs in each of the four languages involved. The quality of broadcasting is therefore understandably
lower than if all resources are channeled to fewer languages. The
quality problem is further complicated by the difficulty in re-
cruiting and training qualified personnel for the production of
programs in various languages, especially non-English ones. The
difficulty is likely to become even greater as the better-educated
population in Singapore is becoming more predominantly English-
educated. Here again we find the relevance of the language
factor in communication planning in the multilingual society.

CONCLUDING REMARKS

This paper is much less than a comprehensive country report on communication planning and policy in Singapore, since we deal only with a rather narrow aspect of communication planning in this island-state. At the same time, however, this is intended to be more than just a case study. The Singapore case is presented here as an illustration of the significance of the language issue in relation to communication planning and policy in many new nations.

As has been pointed out earlier, language is clearly and inescapably a crucial factor in communication planning that deserves careful research and systematic theorization. Analytically, the research issue involves the following variables:

1. The language situation in a multilingual society is a contextual variable that communication planners must take into consideration in planning and policy-making.

2. The language policy, if there is one, is an independent variable that has direct bearing upon communication planners in their decision making.

3. Nation-building and national development are dependent variables, or goals to be achieved through communication planning.

4. Communication planning and policy comes in between as an intervening variable, or a means to achieve the goal of nation-building.

The above scheme is suggested to facilitate systematic research. It is hoped that further analysis on the relationships among language policy, communication planning, and national development will be carried out in various multilingual nations. This, I believe, promises to be a problem area with potential of developing into a middle-range theory.

Notes

1. In Singapore, the category of Indians includes Indians, Pakistanis, and Sri Lankans.

2. We use the term "ethnic mother language" or "ethnic mother tongue" to refer to the language that has been officially and socially associated with one of the three major ethnic communities in Singapore. The ethnic mother language of the Chinese is Mandarin Chinese; that of the Malays in Malay; and that of the Indians, Tamil. These three are supposed to "represent" the three communities respectively, despite the fact that they are not necessarily the mother tongues of members of these communities.

3. In Singapore, the National Anthem is sung and military commands are given in the Malay language. A pidginized form of Malay, Bazaar Malay, is however used as a *lingua franca* among people from different ethnic backgrounds in the market place and other more "traditional" domains (Kuo, 1976).

4. Data on language competence are based on a Survey Research Singapore survey. Survey Research Singapore is a private market research group. The 1972 survey was carried out among a representative cross-sectional sample of the population aged 15 and over in Singapore, using the multi-stage random sampling procedure. A total of 4,603 were interviewed between July 1971 and June 1972. I am grateful to Survey Research Singapore for permission to use some statistics from *SRM Media Index 1972* in the current study.

5. For a detailed discussion of the status of English in Singapore, see Kuo, 1976, in press.

6. Riaz Hassan has pointed out that a "striking aspect of the development process" in Singapore is "the mobilization of resources for development without mass participation" (1975, p. 94). Two factors, immigration and urbanism, are suggested to explain this process of mobilization without participation. From a socio-linguistic point of view, I suspect that the language factor is also contributory to the phenomenon. The fact that, in Singapore, the language of mobilization is an ethnic language

and that the language of participation is English may have resulted in a certain amount of alienation.

The situation is likely to be aggravated since the population is becoming further mobilized to participate and to expect more. As is pointed out by Balder Raj Nayar, " . . . the social mobilization of differentiated cultural groups, not posessing a common language but nonetheless highly relevant politically, makes both political management and nation-building enormously difficult. This is so because the capacity to communicate . . . between elite and mass is at the heart of the modern political process and the cohesion of nations" (1969, p. 5). One solution is to further promote the language of participation, English in the case of Singapore, among the mass.

7. The Tamil Language channel is shared by some Chinese language programs.

8. We do not have data on television viewers to substantiate the generalization in the case of television broadcasting. The basic arguments should remain the same.

334

Works Cited

ARUMAINATHAN, P. 1973. *Report on the Census of Population, 1970, Singapore.* Vol. 1. Singapore: Department of Statistics.

DEUTSCH, K.W. 1953. *Nationalism and Social Communication.* Cambridge: MIT Press.
_____ . 1966. *Nationalism and Social Communication.* Second Edition. Cambridge: MIT Press.

FISHMAN, J.A. 1972a. "The Impact of Nationalism on Language Planning." In J.A. Fishman, *Language in Sociocultural Change.* Stanford: Stanford University Press, 224-243.
_____ . 1972b. "National Languages and Languages of Wider Communication in the Developing Nations." In J.A. Fishman, *Language in Sociocultural Change.* Stanford: Stanford University Press, 191-223.
FREY, F.W. 1973. "Communication and Development." In I. Pool, W. Schramm, et al., (eds.), *Handbook of Communication.* Chicago: Rand McNally, 337-461.

HASSAN, R. 1975. "A Note on the Developmental Process in Singapore," *Journal of Southeast Asian Studies,* 6, 87-94.

KELMAN,H.C. 1971."Language as an Aid and Barrier to Involvement in the National System." In J. Rubin and B.H. Jernudd (eds.), *Can Language be Planned?* Honolulu: The University Press of Hawaii, 21-51.
KUO, E.C.Y. 1976. "A Sociolinguistic Profile." In R. Hassan (ed.), *Singapore: Society in Transition.* Kuala Lumpur: Oxford University Press, 134-148.
_____ . In press. "The Status of English in Singapore: A Sociolinguistic Analysis." In William Crewe (ed.), *English in Singapore.* Singapore: Eastern Universities Press.

LERNER, D. 1958. *The Passing of Traditional Society.* Glencoe, Illinois: The Free Press.
LERNER, D. and SCHRAMM, W., eds. 1967. *Communication and Change in the Developing Countries.* Honolulu: East-West Center Press.

MINISTRY OF CULTURE. 1973. *RTS: From Many Cultures One Voice.* Singapore: Ministry of Culture Publication.

MURRAY, D. 1971. "Multilanguage Education and Bilingualism: The Formation of Social Brokers in Singapore." Ph.D. dissertation, Stanford University.

NAYAR, B.R. 1969. *National Communication and Language Policy in India.* New York: Praeger.

PYE, L.W., ed. 1963. *Communications and Political Development.* Princeton, New Jersey: Princeton University Press.

RUSTOW, D.A. 1968. "Language, Modernization and Nationhood: An Attempt at Typology." In J.A. Fishman, C.A. Ferguson, and J. Das Gupta (eds.), *Language Problems of Developing Nations.* New York: Wiley, 87-106.

SCHRAMM, W. 1964. *Mass Media and National Development.* Stanford: Stanford University Press.

SURVEY RESEARCH SINGAPORE. 1972. *SRM Media Index, 1972, General Report for Singapore.* Vols. 1 and 2. Singapore: Survey Research Singapore.

CONSTRAINTS ON THE
COMMUNICATION PLANNING PROCESS

Alan Hancock

INTRODUCTION

This paper is a case analysis of factors that can constrain the process of communication planning and thereby affect outcomes. It is based upon the experience of a Pre-Investment Study of Educational Mass Media in Thailand, carried out by Unesco between December 1973 and June 1974.

The thesis proposed is that the operational constraints imposed upon communication planning, including both political and procedural aspects are quite as influential as the effectiveness of a planning design. This has been argued frequently enough with regard to project implementation, but it is the author's contention that such constraints are equally felt during an initial planning or pre-investment phase.

The Thailand study must, however, be considered as a special case of communication planning. It was, first of all, concerned with planning for educational mass media: hence it operated at a sectoral level. Second, it was mounted under technical assistance arrangements; the study was financed by a Funds-in-Trust agreement with the Government of the Netherlands. Third, it was carried out by a multidisciplinary, multicultural team, working throughout in a group setting. Each of these factors had its impact, as will be seen below, upon both the conduct and outcomes of the study.

ORIGINS OF THE STUDY

The Thai Pre-Investment Study had its origin in discussions between the Ministry of Education and the World Bank, as part of negotiations for a major educational loan (in connection with the country's Third Development Plan). Educational radio had existed in Thailand for over twenty years, under the control of the Ministry of Education; and for more than ten years local and experimental national educational television transmissions had also been maintained. But these were relatively restricted in scope, and their educational impact was slight.

The main object of the study was, therefore, to produce a framework, and elaborate a project, for the development of educational mass media in Thailand; the resulting media system was to help improve educational quality and opportunity at both in-school and out-of-school levels. The outcome of the study was visualized as a complete project plan, with the full range of logistical and financial data likely to be required by whatever agency finally accepted the project (nominally the World Bank). The plan would necessarily include a detailed account of the project's objectives, its justification (including an economic justification), its organizational and institutional framework, some detail of program and materials production, and phased proposals for staffing and training, utilization, evaluation, and research.

Such requirements are, of course, common to all projects; the special interest of this particular study was its context, and the means by which the end result was to be achieved.

The study was to be undertaken, first of all, as part of a radical program of educational expansion for Thailand, being prepared by the Ministry of Education and covering both formal and nonformal educational sectors. It had, therefore, to be associated with other educational planning initiatives and to be consistent with their proposals (some of them were also the subject of Bank negotiation).

Second, it was to be derived from as objective an evaluation as possible of the existing educational media system and was to build upon what was already in place, insofar as this was considered effective.

Third, the process of project design should reflect maximum involvement of the Thai Government, in particular the Ministry of Education. It should follow a model of analysis and re-analysis: in other words, a pattern of cooperative decision making by which, once system objectives were established, various alternatives which might meet these objectives should be formulated, discussed at all relevant government levels, and preferred solutions identified, in a step-by-step sequence.

DESIGN OF THE STUDY

In this section, only a general account of project design will be given as a guiding framework, since the main focus of the paper is on the experience of implementation.

Detailed plans for the study were first developed by a Pre-Feasibility Survey in August 1973; the Unesco team at this time consisted of a communication media specialist, an educational planner, an educational technologist, and an engineer.

The planning approach recommended by the team was broken down into three phases, sequenced as follows:

Phase One

A. A data base would be established which would give all necessary information for the planning team, both to evaluate the present system and to plan for a new one.
B. The objectives of the educational and social system in relation to media use were to be precisely determined.
C. The relevance of the present media system with regard to these objectives was to be determined.
D. After reconciling (B) and (C), a new set of educational media objectives was to be determined.
E. A matrix of media possibilities for meeting or assisting with these objectives was to be devised, and each variant costed and evaluated.
F. The Thai Government was to be asked to compare the alternatives proposed and to decide upon preferred strategies.

Phase Two

G. Those strategies selected were to be investigated in

greater detail, and their cost and potential analyzed more elaborately.

H. A second evaluation by the Thai Government should then lead to a single preferred strategy.

Phase Three

I. Finally, this chosen strategy should be planned in considerable detail to meet the logistical, financial, and organizational requirements of both the Thai Government and other interested sponsors.

The team considered that, ideally, something like a 12 month span would be needed to complete this work, but it was known from the outset that less time would most probably be available. Consequently, some of the tasks of the first phase were begun during the Pre-Feasibility Survey itself: in particular the collection of a data base and a first evaluation of existing media facilities. The team also developed a costing matrix, covering a variety of system possibilities, which became the basis of a good deal of scenario construction and decision making. In outline, this matrix is produced in Figure 1: relating various combinations of basic mass media, (*radio, television,* and *support media*), ranging from centralized to localized forms, to the key processes of *production, distribution/transmission,* and *reception/ utilization,* across a variety of potential audiences. The matrix itself was primarily a costing tool, but the accompanying commentary considered the educational and social impact of different permutations; taken together, therefore, these gave a guide to alternative systems. Various media strategies could be produced by tracing paths through the matrix, each fixed according to different system objectives, to logistical demands, and to cost.

It is evident that the matrix did not try to be exhaustive about system possibilities; first discussions with the Thai authorities were enough to delimit its range. For example, a purely regional or local system was not considered at all; some central units were already in existence, and would inevitably be continued. A good deal of attention also had to be paid to the existing media pattern within the country, which was characterized at the time by numerous small radio and television stations, and a poorly developed national network, with a strong commitment to commercial programming. On the other hand, one of the issues to be taken up, prompted by the education authorities, was that of electronic versus physical distribution of materials—

	PRODUCTION	DISTRIBUTION	RECEPTION
RADIO	Centralized Production Only	Various permutations (FM and AM) for Independent Educational Network	Radio Receivers Only
	Reduced Central Production with Medium-sized Regional Centers	New Shared AM Network	Cassette Recorders Only
		New Shared FM Network	
	Centralized Production with Smaller Regional Centers	Use of Existing Radio Network as Available	Receiver/Cassette Combination
		Physical Distribution of Audio Cassettes	
TELEVISION	Centralized Production Only	New VHF Network (ETV)	Receivers Only
		New UHF Network (ETV)	
	Reduced Central Production with Medium-sized Regional Centers	New Shared National VHF Network	
		New Shared National UHF Network	Receivers and Video Cassette Recorders
	Centralized Production with Smaller Regional Centers	Use of Existing TV Network as Available	
		Physical Distribution of Video Cassettes	
OTHER MEDIA	Centralized Production Only	Physical Distribution from Center	16 mm Projection
	Reduced Central Production with Medium-sized Regional Centers	Central and Regional Physical Distribution	8 mm and Loop Projection
	Centralized Production with Smaller Regional Centers	Central, Regional, and Local Physical Distribution	Other A/V Media (including print)

for which cost comparisons were needed. It should also be emphasized that the study was concerned only with *mass* media forms; it was not to project small format technologies or traditional audiovisual aids, except where these might reinforce the mass media strand.

Finally the Pre-Feasibility Survey outlined the consultancy needs of the main study to follow, based on a six to nine-month time frame.

For continuity, a small core group of four specialists was visualized for the bulk of the period; this included experts in media systems planning, educational planning, media utilization, and broadcast engineering.

Other consultants were to be appointed for shorter periods, on an ad hoc basis, and in theory every consultant would also have a full-time Thai counterpart, with some experience in his particular specialism. The final range of specialisms within the project was composed of: educational media systems planning; educational and economic planning; curriculum reform; media utilization; rural sociology; media evaluation and research; educational radio production; educational television production; rural broadcasting; audiovisual, print, and support media; community media; development communication; distance education; broadcasting transmission systems; broadcasting production systems; media administration; architecture and design; systems analysis.

IMPLEMENTATION

In practice the events leading up to and succeeding the Pre-Investment Study followed the time frame below; the study itself (compressed by political disturbances in Thailand) finally occupied only seven months.

Original negotiations with Pre-Investment Study with World Bank	March 1973
Informal discussions with Unesco	March/April 1973
Pre-Feasibility Survey	July 1973

Main Pre-Investment Study— First Phase: Production of Interim Report	December 1973/ January 1974
Consideration of alternative strategies in Interim Report by Thai authorities	February/March 1974
Main Pre-Investment Study— Second Phase	April/May 1974
Completion and publication of Final Report	June/July 1974
Submission to Thai authorities	July 1974
Appraisal by World Bank team	September 1974

The First Phase

By the time the main study began, a number of basic decisions had already been taken by the Thai Government. It was, for example, already decided that broadcast terrestrial distribution would be proposed, not satellite broadcast or the physical distribution of tapes. Similarly, a mix of central and regional production centers was foreseen. And, very importantly, arguments put forward by the Pre-Feasibility Team in favor of an independent educational radio transmission network—to offset the random nature of commercial broadcasting in Thailand—had been accepted. Finally, requests by the team for financial parameters had led to a ceiling of US$20 million being imposed for the total system.

These decisions were given concrete form in the shape of certain media strategies, which the Thai authorities considered promising enough to be followed up in detail by the Pre-Investment Team.

During the first phase, therefore, three major activities were carried out. First, all available research relating to educational media in Thailand was identified. In addition, information on the current range of media and reception equipment in the schools—and the extent of their utilization—was collected through a specially designed questionnaire survey.

Second, the characteristics of various types of media and their applicability to the Thai situation were studied. From this

process—combined with an analysis of educational problems—
objectives of the media system for both in- and out-of-school
audiences were derived.

Third, on the basis of this work, the alternative strategies considered viable by the government were analyzed, costed,
and evaluated.

Although the three strands are reported sequentially,
since only two months were available, they had in practice to be
conflated, with as much interaction between them as could be
secured through personal dialogue among team members. This
interaction showed that, if anything, the reduction of media
strategies at such an early stage had been precipitate; although it
had been done to mitigate the pressures of team working and of
time, in practice it tended to confuse the issue by coming down
too firmly, too soon, in favor of particular media combinations,
at a time when overall objectives were still diffuse. More rigorous discussion showed that the so-called media strategies were
made up of many sub-strategies. It was, therefore, decided to
place these strands once again in a media matrix, with the same
axes as before.

The team commented upon the matrix in relation to its
educational findings and also indicated, as earlier, a preferred
"critical path," leaving final decisions open to the Thai authorities.

The Second Phase

During February and March the Ministry of Education
studied the proposals and accepted the strategy preferred by the
team, with some relatively minor alterations. The project had,
by this time, been refined to a point where its main components
were seen as:

- an independent radio network for education, consisting of central production resources and a subsidiary
  regional network, serving the interests of both in- and
  out-of-school education, including development communication;
- a limited educational television resource, based on
  facilities outside the education sector and phased
  according to national television development plans—
  again catering for both in- and out-of-school needs;
- experimental work with local and community media;

- supplementary print and audiovisual materials;
- prototyping and evaluation means. The main impetus of the system was toward the qualitative improvement of education and toward social development.

Throughout April and May, the team was able to concentrate its attention on the preparation of a detailed report covering a main project and associated subprojects. The reason for dividing up projects in this way was an assumption that, while the main media system would probably be financed by a single donor, other donors might well be prepared to contribute to particular areas and still accept the logic of an integrated system as described in the report.

Whatever could not be included within the report itself (even though it ran to five volumes) was retained in a background dossier. The final report thus had two main functions: first to act as a project request document, to be presented to foreign aid donors; and second, to serve as a handbook for implementation.

The report was made available to the Thai Government in July 1975 and formed the basis of discussions with the World Bank in September.

CONSTRAINTS UPON THE STUDY

The constraints experienced during the study can be divided into three categories: (1) those which were realized from the outset, but were felt to be unavoidable or were accepted as being negotiable; (2) those which were realized as the study proceeded and which were, to a greater or lesser extent, counteracted; and (3) those limitations which were realized in retrospect.

1. Constraints Realized from the Outset

The principal constraint which had to be accepted was that of time; it was this factor which led the Pre-Feasibility Survey Team to undertake far more in the way of preparatory work than it had anticipated. For the same reason, the identification of consultants was begun even before the survey had been finally negotiated, and background data needed for the study was stockpiled in advance. A questionnaire was also devised and sent out to schools, asking for information about reception equipment and its utilization, but this had to be done hastily and the questionnaire was not piloted in advance.

In view of the fact that the project is still not implemented as of 1977 something further should be said on the nature of the time constraint. It may well be asked: why was timing so important, if in the end the decision to proceed was deferred indefinitely? The main point at issue was the confirmed schedule of *overall* negotiations with the World Bank, involving not only the media project, but also other educational projects—and indeed projects outside the educational sector, connected with the country's Third Development Plan. It was felt by the Thai Ministry of Education and Unesco planners that the commitment of other sectors of government and of the Bank to a Pre-Investment Study, and even more so to a follow-up investment project, was precarious enough for its success to be totally neutralized by a delay in completion. The choice therefore appeared to be one of proceeding with the study on limited time-scales, or not proceeding at all.

2. Constraints Realized during the
Conduct of the Study

PHASING

Not unexpectedly, therefore, the first constraint highlighted during the course of the study was the realization that, whatever had been done to mitigate the pressures of time, this was not enough. The study had opted for a model of phased development, requiring regular consultations with the Thai Government, a model which had (once it was begun) to be continued, otherwise the whole scheme would be invalid. The situation was not helped by political difficulties which delayed the project's beginning. There appeared to be no complete solution to the time problem, beyond increasing individual workloads far beyond desirable levels, and on occasions taking some short cuts, for example, delimiting the detail with which alternative strategies were concerned, or reducing the "breath pauses" scheduled for the Thai Government to take stock, with the consequent disadvantages of steering the government in the direction of a particular strategy earlier, and more positively, than would have been ideal.

In the event, the "breath pauses" suffered most. Two such periods were included in the design, but these were reduced by the Pre-Feasibility Study to a single interval which actually occupied two months, coming after the production of the Interim Report. It is doubtful, even so, whether this reduction of scope was enough. The most difficult period of the entire study was that immediately prior to the production of the Interim Report, when a vast amount of data had been collected, but could not be adequately analyzed until the work on educational objectives had been completed. At this time many team members were anxious, because they could not see the shape of the final product or even the route by which it could be reached. The production of the Interim Report therefore represented a major hurdle after which matters eased, although perhaps as an over-reaction to its pressures, more specific recommendations on final media choices were offered to the Thai authorities than would have been ideal.

CONSULTANTS AND TEAM WORKING

It had been realized during the first planning stages that there would be difficulty in hiring specialized consultants, particularly as these were needed for short periods ranging from one to six months.

In practice the difficulties proved even worse than expected. There is no readily available international data bank of suitable specialists, and a good deal clearly depended upon the team leader's own experience and upon his personal grapevine. The final composition of the team had far too great a preponderance of European specialists. This was not by intent, but through both a lack of familiarity with specialists from other regions and the related fact that often five or six alternative choices were necessary.

Consultants from developing countries were few; in many fields, they apparently do not exist at the present time, since the disciplines are too new, or too rarefied, for them to have been trained and to have secured experience. Indeed, in some areas, for example, economists specializing in communication media, there are few available specialists in any country, and some element of learning on the job has to be accepted.

One factor which was not seriously predicted (for short missions of this kind) was that of culture shock. Two consultants left the project after only a few days, apparently unable to cope with the culture and with the nature of the study. More predictable, however, was a degree of insularity in the team's working,

which led consultants to group together as a small sub-culture
in both working and leisure hours.

It can be argued that such a degree of insularity is not
only inevitable, but has its advantages. Consultants cannot be
on call for twenty-four hours a day, and they have both a need,
and a right, to relax in the fashion of their own culture. Moreover, this is a two-sided situation; compromises have to be made
by local counterparts as well as by consultants. Some cultures,
such as the Thai culture, are private, with a dislike of public
statement or public intimacy. And decision making may be
associated with the extended family, with blood lines, with status, with religious practice, as well as with career considerations.
It could easily be offensive, as well as ill-judged, to attempt to
break into this pattern over a relatively short period. On
balance, more could be done to mitigate the effects of insularity
by providing shared working accomodation for consultants and
counterparts, and by selection procedures which emphasize cultural adaptability, but the argument should not be overplayed.

The position of counterparts was, however, critical. It
had originally been planned that every consultant would have a
full-time Thai counterpart and it was hoped that this would both
reduce the alienation of external experts and increase the Thai
involvement. Unfortunately, this did not happen. Only one or
two officials from the Ministry of Education were seconded full-
time to the project, and these had necessarily to cope with all
team members, especially in areas where other ministries were
involved, when even part-time Thai personnel were not always
available.

Such a situation was very damaging as it restricted the
involvement of the host country in a study which was premised
upon maximum involvement. Involvement is something that is
demanded at all levels: of decision making, of working specialisms, of administration. It is not merely a question of motivation or commitment; unless there is a continuous sharing at the
early planning stage, the rationale behind decisions which inevitably include elements of compromise will be forgotten, and the
process of implementation will be made far more difficult.

The limitations placed upon involvement therefore produced difficulties of many kinds. While reports or summaries of
reports were always considered at a senior level, there was only
limited understanding of their contents at more junior levels, and
an opportunity was lost for a form of in-service training which

could have had benefits far beyond the reduction of team insularity. This situation might have been prevented, had it been possible under technical assistance procedures to *pay* counterpart personnel, but the standard assumption is that counterpart contributions are the recipient government's responsibility.

Some other difficulties affected both consultants and counterparts were generally anticipated by the team leader and deputy team leader, and by those with prior experience of developing country studies involving large teams. Personality difficulties were bound to occur, some of them arising from the tensions which always arise within a miscellaneous group, but others stemming from professional insecurity. In large teams some consultants are bound to be better, or more relevantly qualified, than others, and this study was no exception. Working in a team setting requires a number of skills beyond specialist experience, the most important of which are the ability to accept group working and corporate decisions and the flexibility to work outside a particular specialism in order to make up for inevitable gaps in group experience. Such difficulties can only be resolved on the spot.

It is likely that many of these difficulties were exacerbated by the selection procedures adopted by international organizations. Consultants can rarely be interviewed; they have to be contracted on the basis of paper qualifications, supplemented by personal reports if available. Political considerations of nationality and of overall team balance also come into play, sometimes as importantly as professional experience.

However, these standard difficulties were compounded in the case of the Thai study. As a result of the phased decision-making model, in some cases different consultants *within the same specialism* had to be recruited for Phases One and Two of the study since the same expert was not always available for both periods. Naturally enough, the second specialist was not always in agreement with what had been planned by his predecessor, and at times this predictable reaction intensified into a desire to "reinvent the wheel."

Another difficulty caused by the timing of consultants largely affected the first period of the study. It was properly a difficulty of systems analysis, although it was not understood as such when it first emerged. The difficulty was caused by the fact that the objectives of the Thai educational system were not in themselves particularly clear, and in order to work out suitable media strategies, the whole planning base of education had first to be explored, analyzed, and codified. It was revealed for example that, although there had been a number of changes in the country's Development Plan and in its educational development goals, these were not reflected in the curriculum, which had often remained static even when goals and targets had been radically modified. This state of affairs was quickly apparent to the educators on the team and was hardly surprising, but it produced a feeling of limitation and inadequacy in some of the media speicalists, who were not able to proceed with their work until the problem of objectives had been satisfactorily resolved. For a few weeks the problem was not acute, because an evaluation was being made of the technical and human capacity of the existing media services, but this review could not go on indefinitely; thereafter, from a producer's point of view or from that of an enginner it was difficult to understand why the planning process could not proceed more rapidly. Media professionals knew only too well the inflexibility of timing being imposed on the project, and realized that they were called upon to develop, within a period of a few months, complete plans for a large-scale media system. Given such imperative deadlines they resisted very strongly the idea that they should wait for objectives to be confirmed, alternatives to be considered, and strategies to be evaluated before entering into detailed technical planning; indeed, in some cases they resisted the concept of presenting alternatives altogether since they felt that, from their own experience, they could stipulate what the preferred strategy should be.

3. Constraints Realized in Retrospect

SEQUENCING OF ACTIVITIES

It was clear in retrospect that activities should have been even more carefully separated out, and the author would now suggest that at the time of establishing educational objectives and media strategies, only educational planners and educational technologists should have been present. These people have a common understanding of the nature of educational problems, which other practitioners do not necessarily share. It would probably have been better, even given the reduced time scales, to have confined the first phase of the study to specialists in educational media systems, educational planning and economics, media utilization, evaluation and research, rural sociology, and communication media in adult and non-formal education, and to defer the arrival of producers and technicians to a second phase. In this way a first stage of the project could have established educational media objectives; a second stage would have worked out alternative media strategies; and a third phase would then have elaborated the final project design.

Against this, it may be argued that the pressure from engineers, producers, and technicians to come up with specifics was a necessary, and productive force, because without it the urgency of defining objectives would not have been acknowledged. The impetus of those who are used to meeting deadlines, and who know the consequences of not doing so, is often salutary; and it has been noted before that the planning stage of media systems (with a sophisticated network of programs, buildings, facilities, and organizational structures to accommodate) can reveal inadequacies and inconsistencies which were previously obscured. But in this particular case, the pressures were too diverse and contradictory to be anything but confusing. Moreover, the pressure from an engineer or producer is not primarily to declare the objectives of a system; it is rather a specific plea of "Let me get on with designing a building" or "What programs do you want me to produce?" If this situation is not delicately handled, any suggestion that there may be more than one way to achieve an obejctive may easily be construed as a criticism of professional competence.

A more precise sequencing, and division of labor, of the kind now proposed would also have had advantages for team working, since it would have reduced to a minimum the tensions arising from group activities. It would equally have given team members more time and leisure to associate themselves more personally with Thai counterparts, to search them out if necessary, to work with them professionally, and to immerse themselves in the country's educational and cultural situation through a process of in-service training (surely the best way, since it is based upon interaction rather than detached analysis).

TEAM COMPOSITION

A further drawback which was not immediately apparent was caused by the limited spread of nationalities reflected in the team—partly by the paucity of Asian consultants, but also by the emphasis upon European tradition. There are two traditions in educational media, the European and the American, and creative planning for new media systems should ideally blend these two traditions more fully than was possible in the event. The European tradition is strong on programming and media performance; the American is stronger in utilization, teacher involvement, and on research-based operations. A wider spread of representatives of both backgrounds should have produced a better synthesis, and if this could have included more Asian experts—who themselves mirror the two main strands of American and European influence—the result should have been better still.

TRAINING AND PROMOTION

It was also apparent that some opportunities were lost for training and missionary work. The study would have been an ideal milieu for internships for Asian consultants, if this could have been arranged financially. Furthermore, if more opportunities for promotion had been created, for example, group lectures and presentations of the thoughts of the mission to representative Thai agencies, more innovative approaches might finally have been included than was the case.

DATA BASE

Like most studies, the survey suffered from a lack of hard information and it was unfortunate that more specific compilations of data (certainly a better use of questionnaire surveys) could not have been organized. The questionnaire survey which was undertaken occupied a great deal of time and energy, but still missed many opportunities. Had an evaluator with statistical competence been included at a very early stage, for example, at the time of the Pre-Feasibility Survey, he might have had the chance to devise better survey formats, which could both produce data for the study and anticipate later demands.

PRESENTATION

Ideally, there is a buffer period at the end of a project before a summary report is completed: a time when the considerable amount of data which has been collected can be sifted, and gaps filled, before final writing and editing begins. In the case of the Thai study, this was not possible, and report writing was actually proceeding (to meet printing and submission deadlines) as the last planning stages took place.

There is always a paradox in the presentation of a complex report—with its close reasoning and extended references, coming after months of specialist study—if this document is also to serve as a basis for decision making. The complete report is needed for project implementation and for professional inspection at the agency level; but decision makers cannot be expected to cope with such detail. Alternative versions are needed; and fortunately from the outset a summary volume of the report was proposed, which could be used for senior decision makers with restricted time and in many cases limited interest, if the field of educational media was outside their sphere of responsibility. However, similar arrangements should have been made for preparatory and interim documents, which were perhaps even more important, since these were the basis of critical mid-project decisions. In addition, more should have been done in the way of simplification and translation into Thai. These factors were realized but the necessary logistical support was unfortunately not available.

INVOLVEMENT OF FINANCING AGENCY

A final constraint did not become fully apparent until quite late: this was the lack of involvement of the prospective financing agency (in this case, the World Bank). Ironically, a large study involving 23 consultants was followed by a month-long Bank review mission, consisting of only five members, some of whom were unfamiliar with the political situation of Thailand, did not have time to digest the report properly, and were even in some cases unfamiliar with Bank policies and procedures since several external consultants were employed. The appraisal mission disagreed with a number of elements in the report which had been the subject of protracted negotiations with the Thai authorities, and the government declined in January 1975 to accept the mission's judgments. Probably this confrontation could have been avoided had Bank representatives worked throughout with the main Pre-Investment Study Team. As a result of these disagreements, negotiations for the actual project were unduly protracted; and ironically projects that had received far less attention and study have been accepted in the meantime with relatively few queries. Partly, this must be attributed to the mixed financing arrangements, whereby the Pre-Investment Study was financed by one agency (the Netherlands), while follow-up was expected from another; this was against the advice of the executing agency, but accepted for reasons of political expediency.

SOME BASIC PRINCIPLES

The principles advanced below follow logically from the earlier analysis, but it should be useful to draw them together. At the same time, it should be emphasized that they are recommendations based upon a single, albeit complex, experience; they are subjective; and while they are intended to be realistic, there is no guarantee that they can all be accommodated in future planning exercises, any more than was possible in the Thai study. A constraint is a limitation upon a theoretical design; too much insistence upon removing constraints may also remove the possibility of acting at all. The critical decision to be taken is on a minimum level of acceptability, below which no satisfactory results can be assured in the way of planning.

This being said, a sufficient number of viable general principles emerge from the Thai study to be worth emphasizing. They are listed below under headings of "Policy Principles" and "Operational Principles" to separate out political from pure planning components. Principles of *policy* are the most difficult to accommodate; they often require structural changes in the organization and behavior of governments and international agencies which, if conceivable at all, must take a good deal of time to prepare, and which are likely for some years to come to be subject to compromise. *Operational* principles are easier to accommodate, though they are advanced here as tentative recommendations: in most cases, they need further investigation and validation.

Policy Principles

1. The first requirement is adequate time. While it is accepted that deadlines are often imposed externally, taking little account of theoretical planning models, the scale and complexity of each study must be related, systematically and realistically, to the time available. Compromises will in most cases

have to be accepted, but a willingness to reduce time scales must be matched either by a rational increase in resources, or by a restriction of planning demands.

2. The second requirement is one of sensitive phasing. The work proposed has to be broken down rationally into its sequential components, and necessary interactions have to be allowed for. In the main, this is not a mechanistic process; the habits, biases, procedures, and preconceptions of decision makers at many levels have to be assessed; and while systems analysis is invaluable as a tool for preplanning, it must be seen as a guide, or as an instrument, not as an immutable process.

3. A third requirement is therefore one of flexibility. The design of the study must allow both for slippage and for changes of direction, in response to unforeseen events and emergencies.

4. The final result, and impact, of a planning study is determined by the people involved, not by the sophistication of its design. Identification and selection of consultants are critical in this process.

5. A full participation of country counterpart officers, specialists, and institutions must be secured during the study.

6. The involvement of the counterpart government or agency in decision-making processes at all stages must also be insisted upon; this is more than a nominal insistence, but has to be built solidly into the planning design.

7. Finally, the involvement of the financing agency for the study (and/or of the financing agency for the eventual project foreseen) should be demanded.

Operational Principles

8. The role of consultants must be established at the earliest possible stage. In some cases, they will be working primarily as advisers, monitoring the basic work and decisions of counterparts; in other cases, they may be serving virtually as technical consultants, contracted to perform a particular task. Irrespective of the pros and cons of each approach, an understanding by each consultant of his personal role is important.

9. Patterns of team working should be carefully studied and adjusted to suit the particular composition of each group. There are no invariable rules to govern the choice of, say, open-plan working, the frequency of team meetings, the degree to which

direction needed from the team leader is accepted or is resisted. Yet it is important to establish such patterns early in the planning study on the basis of a sensitive response to the team's corporate identity.

10. The principal members of any comprehensive planning exercise should be full-time throughout.

11. As representative a group of consultants as possible should be obtained for a planning team, and this mix should reflect both cultural traditions in the industrialized world and the developing world.

12. The abilities to be demanded of consultants are generally as follows:*

- the ability to work in a team, to respond flexibly to arguments advanced by other team members, to abide by corporate team decisions;
- adaptability to unknown cultural situations and ability to relate to local people at all levels;
- the ability to work beyond a narrow professional discipline and to relate academic and professional experience, practically, to new environments and unfamiliar problems;
- specialist experience and qualifications;
- planning skills, and the ability to organize work programs effectively;
- prior experience in a developing country.

This is not to say that professional competence or prior experience in the developing world is unimportant; rather it is to emphasize that empathy and adaptability are the most essential ingredients in a personality mix.

13. The appointment of a team leader is crucial; apart from wide-ranging professional competence, he must be able to act as a sympathetic leader, experienced in group dynamics.

14. Evaluation disciplines—and evaluators—should be considered an indispensable part of any planning study and be included from the outset.

15. Links with related initiatives, fields, projects, etc. should be carefully considered from the outset, and adequate representation secured to reflect their perspective.

---

*These are placed subjectively in order of importance.

16. It should not be assumed that information which is required from fields outside the immediate communication discipline will necessarily be well ordered or well thought-through. In particular, it cannot be assumed that educational or development objectives will have been properly analyzed and coherently stated; nor can it be assumed that economic and statistical data will be available, or will have been collated in a satisfactory form.

17. The ability and willingness of decision makers to review material and to follow closely argued presentations must be realistically assessed.

18. In the design of any planning study, attention should be paid to promotional and public relations needs. It is important for team members to take time to explain their conclusions, and the processes by which they were reached, to decision makers.

19. The value of communication planning studies as in-service training programs and experiences for counterparts should not be forgotten.

20. Finally, planning surveys need to be monitored and evaluated throughout, in as systematic a way as possible: partly to help record the processes of decision making and to log changes from original planning scenarios, but also to help improve the construction of future planning designs.

CONCLUSIONS

Although the principles argued in this paper have been general, and mostly pragmatic, they should still have some wider implications for education and training, applied research, and in particular, the kinds of technology transfer that are characteristically effected through technical assistance.

Education and Training

Communication planning is admittedly a new field, with few precedents on which to draw, so that even rule-of-thumb experience is often ruled out. But the argument of novelty can be over-stated. Some of the difficulties outlined above are characteristic of development planning exercises in many fields. The agreement to mount a planning mission is often arrived at late; and while, no doubt, studies should be structured according to the time available, in practice this can mean that comprehensive surveys will never take place, unless and until an adequate run-up of time is guaranteed by those responsible for financing.

The situation in communication planning will presumably improve as the discipline becomes better researched and better tools are available. But in the end, the education of decision makers seems the critical factor, and this implies that a part of any study should be the education of key people in the real time benefits of adequate preparation.

A special focus, therefore, should be on the long-term education of planners and politicians in communication fields, and on long-term advocacy of a rational treatment for the communication sector. It is this kind of platform which is envisaged by the Unesco program on communication policies and planning, including both the series of intergovernmental meetings on communication policies and more technical communication planning workshops handled at a regional level.

It may seem, in this case, that there is relatively little to be done in the way of specific training programs. Certainly, at times, an insistence upon training for communication planners seems to beg a number of questions: Training for whom? In what? And why? There is some danger in holding seminars and workshops too early in the emergence of a discipline, because they run the risk of involving the same people repeatedly in the same discussion, so deferring genuine research and development. Similarly, there is a risk in training prematurely, if the substance and the methodology of that training are inadequately known or explored. The main need at present is for more experience of communication planning, more opportunities to find out the snags and to build up a substantive analytical base. In the meantime, training programs should be created only for very specific audiences, distinguishing carefully between different levels of ability and empathy in this new field, and they should be phased with some economy. There is a danger in over-selling, if the product is not yet consumer-tested, or is still in short supply.

Applied Research

In research, the most urgent need is for applied studies: of technology transfer, of technical assistance procedures, of planning processes and constraints, and of the group dynamics of team operations. A similar priority should be given to the development of resources for communication planning. It is quite true that superior analytical tools are needed: both new tools, in areas such as the economics of communication and the adaptation of tools from other disciplines—for example, educational and economic planning or educational technology—to the communication scene. But equally, more reference dossiers are needed on relevant agencies, institutions, consultants, and better annotated bibliographies of the field. There is still no genuine communication planning network to provide the kind of insight on media planning problems which exists, usually informally, in other spheres.

A promising area for field study is that of operational phasing, which has to reconcile issues of systems working with human factors of team composition. For example, in the case of the Thai study, would the final objective have been better served by a smaller team of consultants, operating more homogenously over a longer period, but without the varied specialisms which were actually available?

A larger team of specialists is easier to find; it embraces a fuller range of technical disciplines; it has more capacity to deal with wastage (in the sense that one or two less competent consultants will have fewer adverse results overall). At the same time, because of the relative shortness of each consultant's work, it makes for less continuity, less team involvement, and less understanding of the whole systems design.

Part of the difficulty is the issue of complexity. It has been agrued that the Thailand study was too complex in design, and it is true that, for some short-term members and for some casual Thai participants, the intricacy of the planning, and the permutations of choice, represented a major hurdle. It must be accepted that more in the way of explanation and education should have been attempted. But can communication planning ever avoid being complex, when, apart from being a new discipline, it is trying to reconcile so many variables, including social and political as well as economic and technical forces? Moreover, is not a complex design often necessary in order to secure flexibility of planning and to avoid premature decisions, preconceptions, unfounded assumptions? Complexity becomes troublesome when aids to understanding are missing. And in such circumstances it may well be argued that only a long-standing acquaintance with the circumstances of the planning design, and the issues affecting its modification and adaptation, will allow consultants to enjoy a coherent role.

Another important area is the difficult case of decision making. Unfortunately this aspect of the Thai study could not be monitored very closely. While there were ample data on team interactions, the processes by which the Thai authorities reached concensus on preferred strategies were not recorded in the same way and can only be inferred from hindsight. On balance, however, it did appear that these decisions were taken with far too little real understanding of the issues raised. While a good deal was attempted in the way of commentary and briefing, it could have been improved by more frequent, better illustrated digests of work in progress. It could have been helped most of all by more regular meetings between both parties. The difficulty lay, predictably, in securing adequate time from busy people.

A parallel need in decision making is research into the means by which projects are ultimately financed. This paper is not concerned with the final outcome of the scheme, but reference has been made to the impasse that was reached between the Thai authorities and the World Bank appraisal mission. Only now, in 1977, has enough time passed for these discussions to be revised. It is clear that far more care from both sides should have gone into the financing review: an unusual volume of preparatory work was largely wasted because of the urgency of financing deadlines and the consequent lack of opportunity for real negotiation.

Technical Assistance and Technology Transfer

The Thai study was carried out under a technical assistance umbrella, and many of its experiences are primarily relevant to this field. Some of them are quite basic: for example, the selection of consultants.

Certainly far more is needed in the way of cooperative working between communication agencies (which are not too numerous in the world) and in the compilation of reference banks with reliable information on the qualities of experts. But improved selection is a requirement for the procedures of *all* agencies, international, bilateral, and private, and it seems to be a matter for advocacy as much as research. We know well enough that it is wasteful to hire consultants purely on the basis of paper qualifications, as well as to appoint them at the last minute. Yet this kind of difficulty seems to be endemic in technical assistance recruitment. Parallel difficulties occur with project design, which is by now committed to systems procedures. The simple techniques of networking that have been used have been borrowed from technical disciplines, where processes can be estimated more exactly because they are often mechanistic. But in communication planning, the elements of slippage are less calculable. Patterns of decision making are less well-known; and even when they are understood, they are rarely declared or published. If they are arbitrary, or politically based, this cannot easily be admitted. Yet they must somehow be implicitly allowed for in systems design.

To do so would, of course, demand a greater flexibility on the part of donors and executing agencies than has previously been allowed. Conditions are still imposed, whereby project plans and documents are constructed to satisfy theoretical principles, or to be internally faultless. This sometimes requires a basic planning framework to assume that its outcome is known even before it is begun. Open-endedness is apparently untidy. Thus agencies and funding procedures alike insist upon a description of consultancies in advance, or even a precise estimate of report length and format, knowing full well that the situation is unreal.

An issue on which executing agencies and donors could be more easily emphatic is the wholehearted involvement of counterparts. All too often, a recipient government agrees nominally to release full-time counterpart personnel, yet often these are only part-time and are expected to continue with normal functions. A determined stand could surely eliminate this obstacle. Sadly donor and executing agents are often at odds. There is frequently a tension between the funder (who feels that his money justifies him in being autocratic) and the executor (who resents his lack of control over finance), that inhibits any common philosophy. If involvement is to be more than a political platform, it must imply the continuous association of all parties, from the planning stage onwards, including donor, host country, and executing agency.

These problems are frequently exposed by action research; researchers and practitioners alike know where the weaknesses lie. But the traditional pattern of doing things is so well established, inertia so great, and the researchers' own influence and authority so limited, that the mistakes persist. Each new planning team is faced with the same choice: whether to proceed imperfectly, in the hope that remedial action can somehow be forced later, or to abandon the exercise from the outset. Mostly, each new mission decides to go ahead, in the hope that, over a period of time, the worst practices will disappear through attrition. Hopefully, they are right.

Far more complex issues, however, arise when we consider the rationale of the technical assistance formula.

It is often argued that this amounts to a classic imposition of one planning system—its people, techniques, values—upon another: One which is likely to fail because it is bound, to a considerable degree, to ignore, depart from or discard the *real* political, cultural, and value context of the environment in which it is working. However much the design employed is one of participation, shared and uncommitted analysis, there will be pressures, precedents, and other requirements from agencies and sponsors which will work against this design. The latter will be looking for closely reasoned arguments, internally consistent presentations, but the context of implementation will remain diffuse and inconsistent, with decisions often based upon intuitive judgments by policy-makers, attuned to a milieu which they know from experience.

Nevertheless, the technical assistance formula—certainly in the communication field—is likely to persist. The commitment to pre-investment studies in the communication sphere is not such that they can yet be financed from within, and the planning disciplines required must often come from more than one culture. The need, therefore, is still to refine the technical assistance framework further, to make it more flexible and responsible, to educate agencies, minors and cooperating governments better in the implications of their attitudes, and to make the models of participation less crude.

We cannot claim that the donors, especially the international agencies, are insensitive to such problems. United Nations Development Programme (UNDP) in particular, is trying to evolve a "New Dimensions" policy, and a new concept in Technical Cooperation between Developing Countries (TCDC). At times, however, it seems that this is being considered primarily at a political level and that the basic needs in technology transfer—ensuring real involvement, forcing honest appraisals of problems and objectives, genuinely matching technologies to local conditions—are being overlooked in a drive to recruit the maximum number of Third World experts, almost on a head-counting basis. As a long-term, even as a short-term, goal, this is both necessary and laudable, but it has to be interpreted in a spirit of genuine learning and discovery.

The communication field, moreover, has special difficulties to face. While the nature of technology transfer is increasingly studied in relation to more traditional industrial systems, communication is only now being approached in the same way, and new problems are encountered because in communication a number of systems—industrial, information, commodity—overlap. The fact that communication outputs are programs, messages, and information rather than goods or products obviously complicates the formation of relevant analogies and models.

Once again, as with communication planning methods, we are at the threshold of investigation. And once again, we are short of hard data: especially well-monitored field experiences from which to derive or test hypotheses. It is far too early to insist, in blanket terms, on formulae which exclude the expertise of the developed world altogether. Many consultancies are in fields which are technologically complex and demanding, little is known or researched, and specialists are rare in any society. Schemes such as the associate consultant scheme, developed within Unesco's communication sector (which allows Third World junior consultants to accompany planning teams to gain experience, with a view to their being recruited later for independent missions) seem to be on the most rational lines. Even more significant, perhaps, are a number of studies of communication development programs, based on field experience as much as on theoretical analysis. In such contexts, students from both worlds have a great deal of mutual territory to explore.